The Wonder of Christmas

Chicken Soup for the Soul: The Wonder of Christmas
101 Stories about the Joy of the Season
Amy Newmark

Published by Chicken Soup for the Soul, LLC www.chickensoup.com
Copyright ©2018 by Chicken Soup for the Soul, LLC. All Rights Reserved.

The publisher gratefully acknowledges the many publishers and individuals who granted Chicken Soup for the Soul permission to reprint the cited material.

Front cover photo of Christmas tree in background courtesy of iStockphoto.com/HASLOO (©HASLOO)
Front cover artwork of Christmas tree in Christmas bulb courtesy of iStockphoto.com/ Wavebreakmedia (©Wavebreakmedia)
Front cover artwork of Christmas bulb and ribbon courtesy of iStockphoto.com/SilverV (©SilverV)
Back cover photo courtesy of iStockphoto.com/Sasha_Suzi (©Sasha_Suzi)
Interior photos: young girl with Santa hat courtesy of iStockphoto.com/eli_asenova (©eli_ asenova), Reindeer Sled courtesy of iStockphoto.com/RomanBabakin (©RomanBabakin), young couple courtesy of iStockphoto.com/svetikd (©svetikd), Snowman courtesy of iStockphoto. com/Choreograph (©Choreograph), Gingerbread House courtesy of iStockphoto.com/Sasha_ Suzi (©Sasha_Suzi)
Photo of Amy Newmark courtesy of Susan Morrow at SwickPix

Cover and Interior by Daniel Zaccari

Distributed to the booktrade by Simon & Schuster. SAN: 200-2442

Publisher's Cataloging-In-Publication Data
(Prepared by The Donohue Group, Inc.)

Names: Newmark, Amy, compiler.
Title: Chicken soup for the soul : the wonder of Christmas : 101 stories about the joy of the season / [compiled by] Amy Newmark.
Other Titles: Wonder of Christmas : 101 stories about the joy of the season
Description: [Cos Cob, Connecticut] : Chicken Soup for the Soul, LLC, [2018]
Identifiers: ISBN 9781611599824 | ISBN 9781611592825 (ebook)
Subjects: LCSH: Christmas--Literary collections. | Christmas--Anecdotes. | Holidays--Literary collections. | Holidays--Anecdotes. | Joy--Literary collections. | Joy--Anecdotes. | LCGFT: Anecdotes.
Classification: LCC GT4985 .C454 2018 (print) | LCC GT4985 (ebook) | DDC 394.2663/02--dc23

Library of Congress Control Number 2018951878

PRINTED IN THE UNITED STATES OF AMERICA
on acid∞free paper

25 24 23 22 21 20 19 18   01 02 03 04 05 06 07 08 09 10 11

The
Wonder of
Christmas

101 Stories
about the
Joy of the Season

Amy Newmark

Chicken Soup for the Soul, LLC
Cos Cob, CT

Changing your world one story at a time®
www.chickensoup.com

Table of Contents

❶

~Christmas Miracles~

1. Christmas Miracle, *Cindy Hval* 2
2. A Light in Darkness, *Rozanne Hill* 5
3. St. Nick's Deli, *Michael J. Schlagle* 8
4. Three Christmas Miracles, *Connie Nice* 10
5. To Sandy, Love Mom, *Candace Thompson* 13
6. My Name Is Sara, *AJ Sandra Principe* 16
7. Christmas Lilly, *Julia M. Toto* 19
8. Murl's Miraculous Nativity, *Donna Lorrig* 23
9. The Voice, *Patricia Merewether* 29
10. Meant to Be, *Geno Sloan* 31

❷

~Giving Thanks~

11. Crazy Always Finds a Way, *Mark A. Howe* 34
12. The Thanksgiving Boyfriend, *Charlotte A. Lanham* 37
13. The Blessing, *Sharon Landeen* 40
14. A Circle of Kindness, *Dawn Murrell* 42
15. A Walk Around the Block, *Shery Hall* 44
16. Divorced Person's Thanksgiving, *Roz Warren* 47
17. My Miracle on 34th Street, *Valerie Archual* 50
18. Turkey Baby, *Amanda Girolamo* 53
19. Closed Doors, Open Heart, *Brian Wettlaufer* 57
20. Operation Food Package, *Joyce Newman Scott* 60

③

~O Christmas Tree~

21. A Tree from Heaven, *Ela Oakland*.. 65
22. A Living Memory of Christmas, *Jon Peirce*........................... 69
23. Benjamin, *Eriqa "Q" Hermen*... 72
24. 'Twas a Night Before Christmas, *Mandy Lawrence*............... 75
25. The Trashy Turquoise Tree, *Sergio Del Bianco* 78
26. My Elf Extraordinaire, *Alice Muschany* 81
27. The Missing Ornament, *Jessica Harrington* 84
28. Operation Christmas Tree Removal, *Grace Rice*................... 87
29. The Christmas Tree Resistance, *Mary C. M. Phillips* 91
30. First Married Christmas, *Jeffree Wyn Itrich*......................... 94

④

~Making Traditions~

31. Two Trees, *Briana Almengor* 99
32. Mom Knows Best, *Allison Andrews* 102
33. Tangerines and Walnuts, *John M. Scanlan*......................... 105
34. Ryan's Gift, *Amy Catlin Wozniak*..................................... 108
35. Hats and Moustaches Christmas, *Laurie Decker* 112
36. Turkey Red, Turkey Blue, *Jenny Pavlovic* 114
37. Christmas Stockings, *Catherine (Cat) Moise*...................... 118
38. Hanukkah Lights, *D. Dina Friedman* 121
39. All's Fair… *Sara Matson*... 125
40. Random Yule Action Now, *Amy Catlin Wozniak*................. 129

⑤

~Christmas Kindness~

41. A Musical Gift, *Lori Carpenter Jagow* 133
42. The Shenanigator, *Patricia Merewether* 136
43. Snow Angels, *Shirley Redcay*.. 138
44. Potato Prayer, *Andi Lehman*.. 140

45. Twelve Days of Christmas, *Kate E. Anderson* 143
46. A New York City Christmas, *Maureen FitzGerald O'Brien* ... 146
47. The Christmas Witch, *David Hull* 149
48. Space Mountain at Midnight, *JL Kennedy* 152
49. Neighborly Miracles, *M. Ellison* 155
50. The Norway Spruce, *Jill Burns* 157

❻

~The Perfect Gift~

51. The Countdown before the Countdown, *Diane Stark* 161
52. The Best Christmas Present I Ever Bought,
    Margaret Jan Feike 165
53. The Pillow, *Christine Shultz* 168
54. The Last Gift, *Traci Clayton* 170
55. Paperback Christmas, *Jessica Snell* 173
56. Unpacking Christmas, *Kathy Eliscu* 176
57. I'll Be Home for Christmas, *Debby Kate Stahl Ramsey* 180
58. A Perfect Exchange, *Linda Gabris* 183
59. The Writing Desk, *Jaime Schreiner* 186
60. The Best Christmas Ever, *Alanna Parke Kvale* 188

❼

~Holiday Hiccups~

61. Hands Up, *Steffanie Brooks-Aguilar* 193
62. On Our Way to Bethlehem, *Darin Cook* 196
63. Busted, *Erika Hoffman* 199
64. Christmas Upside Down, *Rhonda Dragomir* 201
65. Glam-ma's Red Christmas Suit, *Francine L. Billingslea* 204
66. All Around the Table, *Edith Hope Fine* 207
67. Almost Perfect, *Heather Rodin* 210
68. Dad's Christmas Rant, *Michael Fulton* 214
69. Locked Out, *Rita Warren DeFoe* 216

70. Holiday Perfection, *Jeanie Jacobson* 219
71. Three Bags Full, *Linda Sabourin* 222

❽

~There's Nothing Like Family~

72. The Other Wife, *Loreen Martin Broderick* 227
73. My Obsession, *Connie Kaseweter Pullen* 231
74. The Labels, *JoAnne Bennett* 234
75. Thanksgiving with the Family, *Kira Popescu* 236
76. Ashley's Angel, *Arlene Janet Ledbetter* 239
77. Thanksgivings with Grandpa, *Whitney Woody* 242
78. Home for the Holidays, *C.L. Nehmer* 246
79. The Joy in Giving, *Connie Kaseweter Pullen* 249
80. Quiet Christmases, *Dana E. Williams* 252
81. Christmas in July, *Tricia Koeller* 254

❾

~Four-Legged Festivities~

82. A Bull Terrier at Christmas, *Sally Dixon* 259
83. Cat Warning System, *Kristi Adams* 263
84. Our Amazing Christmas Gift, *Kathie Leier* 267
85. A Late-Evening Snack, *Rita Durrett* 269
86. Foiled Again, *Alexis Sherwin* 272
87. Attitude of Gratitude, *Mason K. Brown* 274
88. Pawing the Tree, *Shari Marshall* 276
89. Solved, *Nemma Wollenfang* 278
90. Misty's Thanksgiving, *Nicole Ann Rook McAlister* 280

91. An Unforgettable Christmas Card, *Laurie Adams* 284
92. Christmas Canter, *Rosemary L. Rigsby* 286
93. More Precious than Gold, *Dana Lamb-Schaubroeck* 289
94. Christmas Above the Arctic Circle, *Victoria Terrinoni* 292
95. A Special Delivery, *Mildred L. Farrior* 295
96. A Christmas Like No Other, *Sheryl Maxey* 297
97. Full House, *Jennifer "JennyMac" McCarthy* 299
98. The Accident, *Iona Dupill* 306
99. Open Last, *Cory Rasmussen* 309
100. Lessons in Living, *Julie Ottaway Schmit* 311
101. All Those Years, *Betty White Coleman* 313

Meet Our Contributors 315
Meet Amy Newmark 331
About Toys for Tots 333
Thank You 335
About Chicken Soup for the Soul 336

Chapter 1

Christmas Miracles

Christmas Miracle

Don't believe in miracles — depend on them.
~Laurence J. Peter

now falls as I write, and the white-shrouded world reminds me of another December, eighteen years ago, when I received a much-needed reminder of the miracle of Christmas.

Our fourth son had arrived three months earlier. Sam was born with a congenital diaphragmatic hernia (CDH). A hole had formed in his diaphragm during gestation, allowing his stomach and intestines to move into his chest cavity, crowding his heart and lungs. In Sam's case, this prevented his left lung from developing.

When he was three days old, he underwent surgery to repair the hole in his diaphragm. After a three-week stay in the neonatal intensive care unit at Sacred Heart, we brought him home. He needed no medication or supplemental oxygen, nursed enthusiastically, and had none of the dreaded complications or additional health problems common with CDH.

He also had only one lung.

He did have bits of tissue where his left lung would have grown, and doctors told us that lungs continue to grow into a child's early teens. Even if that didn't happen for Sam, we were assured it's possible to live with one lung.

But I worried.

Night after night, I sat vigil on the floor next to his cradle, watching his chest rise and fall, counting his respiration rate, often dozing off with my hand on his chest.

Exhausted, I did my best to care for his three older brothers — ages ten, eight and five. When December dawned, I decorated and baked in a fog of fatigue.

We reached a milestone on December twenty-third — Sam's final post-op visit. Snow fell heavily as I packaged a plate of Christmas cookies for the surgeon's office.

Each visit began with a series of chest X-rays, and I'd grown adept at deciphering the shadowy shapes in my son's chest cavity.

Dr. Holland moved his stethoscope over Sam's chest, listening intently while my baby grabbed his hair and blew spit bubbles. Scratching his head, Dr. Holland stood, and then once again bent over Sam, listening, and then listening some more.

Then he tickled Sam's three chins and turned to scrutinize the latest X-rays while I wrestled the baby back into his winter layers and waited for the surgeon to speak.

But he didn't say a word. Instead, he let out a low whistle, peering at the images. Running his fingers through his hair, he whistled again, and then said, "Cindy, I'd like you to take a look at these."

And my heart sank.

This was it — the moment I'd dreaded since the hours following Sam's diagnosis. The moment when I'd learn the nightmare hadn't ended. The other shoe had dropped, and I didn't know if I could bear it.

Seeing my stricken face, Dr. Holland beckoned me closer.

"What's that?" he asked, pointing to the image.

"That's Sam's right lung," I answered.

He nodded and pointed to the other side of the image.

"And what's that?"

"That's Sam's left lung," I replied dutifully.

Silence. Apparently, lack of sleep was making me hallucinate.

"Except he doesn't have a left lung," I mumbled.

"He didn't," Dr. Holland agreed. "But he does now."

He traced the outline with his finger. "A fully functioning left lung."

And the surgeon beamed.

I clutched Sam and sank down into a chair, tears falling and dampening his downy blond head like melting snowflakes.

"I don't understand. Is this a miracle?"

Still smiling, Dr. Holland shrugged. "We don't like to use that word, but I've honestly never seen anything like this before."

Dazed, I left his office, trying to process the news.

That night as usual, I sat at Sam's cradle feeling his lungs (*lungs!*) expand, watching my hand on his chest rise and fall. The clock ticked its way to Christmas Eve, and I finally climbed into bed where, for the first time since Sam's birth, I slept — truly slept.

Today, at some point, my six-foot-one-inch baby boy will bend down and wrap his arms around me. I'll lay my head on his chest and feel it rise and fall, grateful for the reminder.

Christmas has always been about miracles.

— Cindy Hval —

2

A Light in Darkness

What we have once enjoyed deeply we can never lose.
All that we love deeply becomes a part of us.
~Helen Keller

I had begun to dread it shortly after my husband died in a boating accident — the first Christmas without him. He loved Christmas and everything about it — the lights, the decorations, the music.... And after our daughter was born, he especially loved spoiling her and sharing her excitement. How was I supposed to enjoy Christmas when all it would do is remind me that he wasn't here to share it?

As the months went by, Christmas went from a vague dread to a very real pain. On ordinary days, I could convince myself that Derek was just off fishing or with friends. But on special days — days he wouldn't have missed for the world — his absence loomed large. I had made it through our little girl's third birthday, only two months after the accident, by having it at Chuck E. Cheese's, where all the details were taken care of. Easter, Halloween and my own birthday went by in a blur as I went through the motions and tried to ignore the dark, empty space where he should have been. None of these days was easy, but each was only a stepping stone to the holiday Derek loved most.

My daughter was only three that Christmas, so there was no skipping it, as much as I wanted to just hide until it was over. I braced myself to find a way to get through. Christmas at our house had always begun right after Halloween, when I'd have to convince Derek that it was too early to put up Christmas decorations. Instead, we'd plan what we wanted to put up and what gifts and decorations we wanted to buy, and then, finally, on the day after Thanksgiving, he could pull out the Christmas boxes and go wild.

Now, I dreaded pulling out those boxes. I just couldn't imagine Christmas without him, so I decided to find a way to keep him a part of our Christmas. I bought a gift "for Derek" to put under the tree — something he would have wanted but that we could use as a family. Then I ordered a memorial ornament that we could hang on the tree every year. Including him did seem to help, as did concentrating on making the holiday special for my little girl, which kept my mind on other things for a short time. It wasn't always easy — I allowed myself time to feel sorry for myself and miss him — but for the most part, I was doing well. Until it came time to put up the tree.

So much about tree decorating brought him to mind — the ornaments we bought together, the angel topper he picked out, disagreements over the red bows I loved so much and he hated. And my favorite part... sitting together on the couch admiring our work with only the tree lights on. As I set about the task with a heavy heart, I felt the weight of his loss. We always strung the lights on the tree so that each strand went from the top to the bottom. We used three stands — one that stayed lit and two that blinked. That way, when the two strands blinked, there was never a totally dark section on the tree. Dutifully, I put up the three strands and plugged them in. One of the strands didn't light. I'd forgotten to test them! I couldn't believe it... It felt like a huge failure, like I just couldn't do this without him. The weight of my grief consumed me, and it seemed to represent not just this moment, but how inadequate I felt to do any of this alone. Suddenly, the years of life without him stretched endlessly before me, and I felt hopeless.

As I sat feeling overwhelmed by it all, I noticed something. I couldn't tell that a string of lights on the tree was out. The two working strings shone brightly, leaving the dark strand in the shadows. I couldn't tell anything was missing. The two strands were doing the job, despite the third strand being out. It seemed like a metaphor for our family. I couldn't see the dark strand, but it was there — just as much there as the two lit strands. And all at once I felt like the three of us would always be a family, even if only two of us still shined. It was a sign that, although I couldn't see him any longer, my husband would always be a part of my life and our daughter's. I left that dark strand there, and when I missed my husband, I would look at the tree and remember that, like that dark strand of lights, he was still there — in my heart, in my memories, and in our daughter.

It has been fifteen years since we lost Derek, but I've never forgotten the lesson of that one string of lights. I still believe that it was no accident. I rarely tell this story — it seems a bit ridiculous to read so much into a single strand of burned-out Christmas lights — but that moment was a turning point for me. It reminded me that God allows pain, but never fails to stay with us during the course of it. Not only can He send signs, but He can send them in something as innocuous as a string of lights, if only we are open to see them.

— Rozanne Hill —

St. Nick's Deli

There are two ways of spreading light: to be the candle
or the mirror that reflects it.
~Edith Wharton

On Christmas Eve, when most people set aside a plate of cookies for Santa Claus, we have a different tradition. We make him a nice bologna-and-cheese sandwich. For our boys, it means they get to leave something special for old St. Nick. For my wife and me, it is a tradition that dates back to our first Christmas together and reminds us that the true spirit of the holidays is found in the simplest of miracles.

It all started on Christmas Eve 1982. Sharon and I had recently moved to Colorado and were spending our first holiday away from family and friends. We were living in an old motel outside of Denver.

Snow started falling lightly on Christmas Eve morning. The prospect of a white Christmas brightened our spirits. We went to the Cinderella City mall for some last-minute shopping. When we emerged with our packages, we were greeted by a raging blizzard. Luckily, we were able to catch the final bus home. It was snowing so furiously that the driver had to stop every block to clear off the windshield. Darkness had fallen by the time we reached our motel.

Once inside, we realized that we had forgotten to get food for our Christmas dinner. Once again, we bundled up and ventured into the stormy night, hoping to find a store not closed for the holiday or by the snowstorm.

Outside, the night was an incredible fury of snowflakes and howling wind, obliterating all but the faint glow of street lamps and Christmas decorations. The roads were deserted except for the cars buried in the mounting snowdrifts. Chilled to the bone by the bitter wind, we had all but given up hope when we rounded a corner to see a deli shop owner turning off his lights and closing up the store. When we drew closer, we realized he was dressed in a Santa suit, beard and all! As we approached, he called out "Merry Christmas!" and explained he was off to surprise his grandkids.

We explained our plight, but he shook his head and told us that the storm had completely emptied the shelves. Then he thought for a moment, invited us inside, and led us to a back room where he had a small fridge. Inside were two big hunks of bologna and cheese, which he placed in a sack, along with a loaf of bread, a bag of pistachio nuts, and a bottle of ginger ale. We laughed when he quipped, "Santa's favorite snack," and patted his big, round belly.

He accepted only our heartfelt thanks and gave us each a warm hug. Once outside, he reached into his pocket, handing us each a candy cane. With a hearty laugh, he wished us "Merry Christmas" once again and disappeared into the night.

That night, as we feasted on bologna, cheese and pistachio nuts, we marveled at the Christmas gift the kind store owner had bestowed upon us, for when we walked back into the night and he had faded into the storm, we realized we had never gotten his name. It was when we turned around to see the name of the deli that we realized we had experienced a touch of Christmas magic. The name of the deli was Nick's Place. To this day, our family shares this story around the Christmas tree to remind each other that it is indeed the wonder-filled moments that bring treasured meaning to the miracle that is Christmas.

— Michael J. Schlagle —

Three Christmas Miracles

Where there is great love, there are always miracles.
~Willa Cather

I gazed into David's eyes as he squeezed my hand and mouthed the words, "It will be okay. I love you."

How? How could it be okay? Nurses and doctors swirled around us as I attempted to understand how the events of the day could have brought us here. In the frantic scramble to save my husband, bags of blood and drugs pumped their life-sustaining fluids through what looked like miles of tubes connected to his still body. I gave him a gentle kiss on his forehead as they wheeled him away and watched him disappear through the double doors for emergency surgery.

The surgeon said that even if he survived the night, I should not expect him to walk again. In a daze, I stumbled into the hospital chapel and dropped to my knees to pray for a miracle.

Six months earlier, we had stood together in our little Mennonite church, surrounded by friends and family as we exchanged our marriage vows. Many told us we were too young to get married, but young love often overrules common sense. So, at nineteen and twenty-one, we promised to love one another in sickness and health, not having any idea of how soon that vow would be challenged.

December 23, 1977. With only two days left until Christmas, David had spent the day taking full advantage of his dad's woodshop to build frames filled with wedding pictures as our holiday gift to family. Money was tight, and those handcrafted reminders of our recent "happy day" would be all we could offer our loved ones on Christmas morning.

At home, I finished up chores and waited for David to come. My family had chosen to celebrate Christmas a few days early on my dad's birthday—a double celebration before my sister's family took off for the holidays. A big dinner followed by gifts was what I expected for the evening, but as the clock ticked away the minutes, I paced back and forth in our little rental house. I was excited to spend time with my family, but anxious that David was so late. Where was he?

Finally, I gave in and dialed the phone number for my in-laws' home. It rang and rang. *Dave must be in the shop and can't hear it,* I thought. A few minutes later, I dialed again. After a few rings, a strange man's voice answered.

"May I speak to David, please?" I asked, wondering who this man was.

"No!" was the reply. *Click.* He hung up.

My hands were shaking as I dialed the number for the third time. The unknown man answered again.

"I must speak to David. I am his wife." The words were strong, but inside I was weak and scared.

After what seemed like forever, the man's response made my heart stop. "You must go to the emergency room at once! There has been an accident."

I don't remember how I ended up in the car with my dad. I must have called him to come and get me. I must have told the emergency-room clerk my name. They must have led me to David's side. But what I remember was that gurney taking him away and the hard chapel floor as I knelt to plead with God to spare his life.

As family and friends arrived at the hospital, the story emerged gradually. A younger brother with emotional, drug-fueled anger. An older brother trying to set an example of how to walk the straight road—or else. A loaded rifle. A hard metal bullet. A moment and a choice that ended with my husband on the shop floor, blood spilling out his side. A tearful final exchange between brothers that resulted in words of forgiveness. An ambulance with medics rushing to stabilize the lifeless man. Police taking notes and shaking their heads as they led the brother away. A mother lying in a hospital bed, sedated and oblivious to the events of the evening, having suffered an emotional breakdown earlier that week from the stress of dealing with a cherished child under the spell of drugs. A tearful father unable to process what had just happened — his hands wringing, his heart breaking. A dying man, lying on the cold, hard concrete, surrounded by blood and encircled in white light. A peaceful voice whispering, "It's not your time."

We waited six long, agonizing hours. We were so tired as we slumped in the stiff waiting-room chairs, but no one slept. We just sat with dazed faces and blank stares. The surgeon finally returned. The bullet had torn a path side-to-side through David's mid-section, hitting the spine and grazing the spinal cord, shattering a rib, and blowing out a kidney along the way. He had severe blood loss and paralysis in his lower extremities. But he was alive. *Thank you, God!* We would handle the rest later. He was alive! That's what mattered.

It was now Christmas Eve. Just as the wise men brought three gifts to honor the birth of the Christ child, so God blessed us with three Christmas miracles that year. First was the miracle of forgiveness between David and his brother. Immediate. Powerful. Unexplainable and unconditional. The second was the miracle of life that baffled even the surgeon as David not only survived, but walked out of the hospital ten days later despite the severity of his injuries. The last was the miracle of giving, as our little church family blessed us with a monetary gift on Christmas morning to help ease the burden of hospital expenses.

It has now been forty years, but every year at Christmas, as we decorate the tree and wrap the presents together, I reflect back to that moment when the best gift was not wrapped in paper and bows. It was wrapped in the miracle of forgiveness, the joy of life and the power of love.

— Connie Nice —

To Sandy, Love Mom

Christmas magic is silent. You don't hear it —
you feel it, you know it, you believe it.
~Kevin Alan Miline

I sat at the dining room table, carefully sorting through the plastic bin full of cheery Christmas bags and festive tissue paper. Any bag that had a slight wrinkle or tear went into the donation pile for my son's upcoming Holiday Gift Shop at school. Local vendors would fill our elementary school's gymnasium the next day, offering discounted gifts for more than 900 students to buy for their loved ones. My kindergarten son was thrilled to participate and was already making his shopping list: Mommy and Daddy, baby sister, grandparents.

I had decided to donate used gift bags, tissue paper, and wrapping paper to the Holiday Gift Shop's wrapping station as a way to clear out clutter and do a good deed at the same time. My donation pile was growing bigger by the minute. Suddenly, I came across a large gift bag decorated with gaudy teapot houses and gold teddy bears. Various flowers adorned the border and peeked out among the bears and teapot houses. Despite its ugliness, I paused and felt the familiar tug of grief constrict my heart. My grandma had given my dad a gift in this bag for Christmas years ago. It still had the tag attached that read, "To Sandy, Love Mom."

I touched the silly bag and thought about how long I had kept it. Why was I holding onto it? My grandma had passed away five years earlier. I had plenty of things from her, including wonderful memories and keepsakes. So why hold onto this ugly bag? That clinched it for me. I tore off the tag and added the bag to the donation pile. Grandma would want it put to good use rather than stuffed in a tote never to be used again.

The next day, my son and I dropped everything off at school. The huge gymnasium had been transformed into a winter wonderland lined with vendor tables decorated with cheerful Santas and glittery snowflakes. The Holiday Gift Shop leader enthusiastically received our donations.

"Thank you so much! We always need gift bags and wrapping paper for the kids' gifts. It makes it so much more special for them." I walked away feeling merry, but my heart still pinched a little at the thought of giving away my grandma's gift bag.

I made sure my son had everything he needed for the Holiday Gift Shop. He had his checklist of names, money, and a fifth-grade helper who would help him choose gifts and count his money. After school, I picked up my son and saw he was carrying a huge bag filled with smaller gift bags and gaily wrapped presents. He couldn't wait to show me his treasures.

As I looked through his bag, I saw a large gift bag decorated with gaudy teapot houses and gold teddy bears. Various flowers adorned the border and peeked out among the bears and teapot houses. My breath caught in my chest. I pointed to the ugly bag and said, "Whose gift is in that bag?" My son beamed with pride and said, "That's Papaw's gift!" Tears welled in my eyes as I started laughing, shaking my head at the coincidence. My grandma's gift bag had come full circle, once again containing a gift for my dad, my son's Papaw.

I know my grandma was there with her great-grandson that day at the Holiday Gift Shop while he carefully chose a special gift for his Papaw, her Sandy. And I know she made sure my dad's gift went into the most special bag of all. After my son gave his gift to my dad, I told the story, and we all laughed and cried together. Now the bag is safely displayed in my dad's workshop, never to be given away again.

The ugly teapot houses and gold teddy bears are here to stay, but this time with a special story that was created together by my grandma and her great-grandson.

— Candace Thompson —

My Name Is Sara

One person can make a difference,
and everyone should try.
~John F. Kennedy

I t is Christmas Eve, and I am wearing a safety harness so my team can attach me to the fifth-floor balcony. My job is to convince a young girl not to jump.

"Hi, my name is Alex."

She appears not to hear. *If she is as cold as I think she is, her sense of perception is going to be off. She might slip.*

I want to get her attention before we both freeze. It is the type of cold where your lips start stammering and you can't get them to stop.

"What's your name?" No response. "Oh, I almost forgot, look what I have in my pocket."

I hand her a new pair of gloves and a hat. Not really a girlie colour, but warm. I usually purchase several sets at dollar stores just in case. She has no socks, a thin summer coat and very thin pants. All are worn but clean.

She looks at the hat and gloves... just looks. Then she reaches out ever so slowly and says, "Thank you."

It's a start.

She tucks her hair under the hat and says, "Sara. My name is Sara." Her name is like a whisper, like she doesn't matter.

"Thanks, Sara." Now we can have a conversation.

"Am I in trouble for being here?" she asks.

"No, but we all want you to be safe."

"I don't want to be safe," she says, still not making eye contact. "I'm too tired of trying."

I ask what she was trying to do.

"I work, buy my own food and clothes, and look after my mom when she can't get up. My parents don't know I exist except when they take my money and I'm left with nothing. Girls at school make fun of me because I don't have the right clothes or lunch. I'm doing my best, but I have no one to help me."

In my earpiece, I am getting information that Sara's parents have been located. They are passed out at the kitchen table, and the only room in the home that is clean is Sara's.

"I should have been thrown away when I was born. No one wanted me."

I've heard this before, but my heart will never accept the treatment some children have to endure. Sara is fourteen and exhausted from trying to pretend her life is normal. She has never had a family dinner, clean clothes, lunchbox notes, homemade cookies or Christmas treats. She had never experienced any of it.

She says it again. "I'm a throwaway. No one ever wanted me. No one has ever said, 'Good work,' or 'Great job.' I don't want to be here anymore."

"I have a small problem with that, Sara. If you don't want to be here anymore, would you like to give me the kitten you have in your coat so it doesn't get hurt?"

She looks at me like I have just done a magic trick. She leans forward and whispers, "How did you know?"

"Well, she has been wiggling for a while. Can I see her?"

She takes out the kitten, and I see that she is wrapped in Sara's very thin mittens.

I say, "Sara, you are looking after a kitten!"

"She was thrown away, too." Now comes the anger and crying.

"She was in a Dumpster, hungry and cold. I took her and pretended it was my Christmas gift. But I can't even feed myself. How am I going to look after little Sammy?"

It is definitely a time for Christmas magic and miracles. Sara decides not to jump, and she and Sammy are placed in a foster home together. Sammy waits for Sara every day after school on her favourite chair.

Three years later, I see Sara again. I am invited to her high-school graduation. Sara's valedictorian speech is spectacular. Her foster mom and I could not be prouder. Sara gives me a huge bag of cookies she made herself and says, "My name is Sara, and I want to thank you."

— AJ Sandra Principe —

Christmas Lilly

Compassion brings us to a stop, and for a moment
we rise above ourselves.
~Mason Cooley

Everyone has heard the saying that life is what happens while we're making other plans. In our case, it proved to be true. My daughter crawled out of bed one cold December morning, kissed her husband, confirmed their future reservations for New Year's Eve with friends, and went to work like any other day. By sundown, she'd made a decision that would change all of our lives… forever.

I remember the phone call well. With Christmas only a week away, she'd been busier than usual at work, a treatment center for troubled teens. So I was surprised when she called me in the middle of the afternoon from Walmart.

"Mom, I have to make the decision tonight," she said.

"Tonight?" I tried to hide my concern. She'd often hinted that I worried too much, but then my dear daughter had never been a mother.

Recently, however, she'd been mentoring a young, single mother who was now asking my daughter to keep her baby over Christmas. Until now, I'd been completely supportive, but this latest development baffled me. "Isn't this a bit… risky?" I asked.

"Risky? Seriously, Mom, you should come to work with me one day. On second thought, bad idea."

She'd never been afraid of a challenge, that's for sure. But this?

This felt different.

"I think I can handle a baby for a couple of weeks."

"Of course. You're great with kids." That wasn't what concerned me. "But what if someone all pumped up on drugs or something comes banging on your door?"

"Well, fortunately, I have a relationship with both DHS and the police if trouble comes knocking. Don't worry. It's only until a spot opens up for her and the baby at the unwed mothers' home."

"I still don't understand why her older brother is willing to let her stay with him, but not her baby. Do you think she's giving you the whole story, honey? And are you sure she's been accepted into…"

"Slow down," my daughter interjected. "I spoke with both her brother and the program director. The brother is sharp. His place is tiny. Honestly, they probably have a better shot at reconciliation without a baby around."

"And the program?"

"Both baby and mother are guaranteed residency at the end of the month. It's an excellent facility. If anyone can help her succeed, they can. Everything will be fine."

Fine, she'd said. An optimist by nature, my daughter had also become a realist as a result of her profession. She knew the risks. I had to trust her. And God knows I wanted that baby to be safe and warm while the young mother tried to work things out with the only family member willing to help.

Still, I couldn't help but be concerned for my own daughter. The mother had run with a pretty rough crowd. And what if she didn't follow through? Suppose she took off — then what?

"What does your gut tell you, honey?" I asked finally.

"I believe she loves her baby the best way she knows how. I also believe she can learn the skills to become a responsible parent if she wants to."

I admired my daughter's courage and compassion and was proud of her, in spite of my concerns.

"Sounds like your decision has already been made. What does your husband think about having a little one around for Christmas?"

"I'm not sure." She hesitated. "We haven't had time to talk yet."

Had I just heard my daughter correctly? For the second time in fifteen minutes, I was speechless.

"Mom? You there?" she asked. I could almost feel her eyes rolling. "It's not like I'm keeping anything from him. Someone has to do something, and apparently that someone is me."

My daughter and her husband had always talked about having children, but so far their only family walked on four furry feet — two dogs and a cat. I thought my beloved son-in-law would be okay with his wife bringing home a child for a day or two, but two weeks?

"Mom, this is happening so fast. I texted him earlier with as much info as I knew at the time. I told him we needed to discuss something really important, and I asked that he please not say 'no.'" Her voice choked. "At least, not tonight."

I wanted to reach through the phone and hold her — my brave, sweet, and fiercely independent girl. She'd always been respectful of her husband's opinions, even when they differed. I heard the dilemma in her voice.

"I understand, honey. Dad and I are behind you both."

"Thanks, Mom."

I thought our conversation had come to a close, but there was more.

"Mom? I have to tell you something else. I guess I have made a decision, as much as is up to me anyway, but not just for the reasons we've discussed. Something happened today. Here, of all places." I could hear the emotion in her voice. "For the first time in my life, I stood in a shoe department completely bewildered."

That was something. My daughter loved shoes, and shopping for them had always been cathartic for her. I almost chuckled.

"I held these two little boxes of shoes but had no idea what to buy. Mary Janes? Sneakers? High-tops? So many selections. Even more confusing was the range of sizes. All I know is that her little toes nearly ruptured the pair she has now," she continued. "And the price tag, wow! With Christmas coming, our budget has already been stretched. I seriously began to question if I was doing the right thing. I started thinking, *What if?* And then I heard a voice say, *What if you are buying shoes for your daughter?* Mom, the voice wasn't audible, but the words were clear as day. And, suddenly, so was my decision." She sobbed. "I knew exactly what I was supposed to do."

Tears spilled from my eyes. I took a deep breath and straightened my shoulders. How could I have ever let fear and doubt question my daughter's willingness to be the hands and feet of Jesus? Especially at Christmas. "Lord, please forgive my unbelief," I prayed.

I, too, knew what my daughter and son-in-law would be doing that cold December night. They'd be making room at the inn… for Lilly. And now, my precious granddaughter Lilly is five, and Christmas is her favorite time of year. In fact, she starts planning for it in October, asking me when I'm coming to visit. Somehow, I think she remembers….

—Julia M. Toto—

Murl's Miraculous Nativity

What matters most is how well you
walk through the fire.
~Charles Bukowski

The first Christmas spent with my future in-laws, I noticed a unique and spectacular nativity set on the mantel above their fireplace. When asked about it, my future mother-in-law told how she had handcrafted it in a ceramics class. It was beautiful, and I could tell that it held special meaning for her. When I inquired more about it, she responded with a short explanation. "Working on that set gave me hours of time to pray through some challenging situations in my life."

Later, I learned that she and a good friend had taken the ceramics class together. Instead of picking a simple "first attempt" type of project, Murl had chosen the large thirteen-piece nativity, which she decided to finish in a complex, multilayered glaze design that created a stunning modern-art effect. It was truly eye-catching.

Over the years, various Christmas tree and stocking styles came and went from my in-laws' Advent décor, but that nativity set remained the standard feature. The holiday decorating was not complete until the entire set, including the floating angel that was secured above the display on a strategically placed nail, was in its place on the mantel. The individual pieces were large enough to fill the five-foot-long mantel, and they were always arranged in the same order. Mary and Joseph, looking lovingly at the baby Jesus lying in the manger, were placed in the center. The wise men and camels were set on one side of the Holy Family, while the shepherd, sheep, cow, and donkey were on the other.

As the years went on, I knew that each time Murl looked at that nativity, she saw more than an artistic portrayal of a beloved story; she saw her answered prayers.

On June 11, 2013, nearly 500 families lost their homes in the Black Forest Fire. Our little cabin in the woods and the retirement home of my in-laws on the lot next door were included in that loss.

Fortunately, we were able to get computers and photo albums out ahead of the fire, but Ray and Murl had evacuated without grabbing more than essentials—imagining they would be returning home shortly. We were especially glad to have had those computers with the photo files, which we had used to create a slide show several years back when we had celebrated their fiftieth wedding anniversary. As a result, we were able to replace some of their wedding and family photos, and we set them around their bedroom and living space at the rental house just a few weeks after the fire.

We invited just a few close friends over to celebrate Ray and Murl's fifty-seventh anniversary with us while we figured out how we should move forward after such a devastating loss. Some of those who joined us that evening had also lost their homes in the fire. It had been several days since we had been allowed to return to the burn zone to attempt to retrieve any surviving items. The fire had burned fastest and hottest through the area where we lived, and there wasn't much left in the ash heaps where our homes had been. The children used wood and wire-mesh frames constructed by local Boy Scout troops to sift through the debris. Each day, they brought back what they found. A portion of a singed page to a beloved children's storybook, the contemporary-art-looking shape of melted aluminum that had been a hub cap, and a ceramic teapot were some of their treasured finds.

Ceramic and fired-clay items were the most recognizable articles in the box in the garage where they stored their collection. A few of the pieces they had found were in an alcove at the entryway and were noticed by one of the other fire "survivors" who came by to celebrate Ray and Murl's anniversary with us that day.

"Look at the baby Jesus from your nativity set!" my friend Susan exclaimed, turning over the blackened figurine in her fingers. "Our nephew found the lamb of our Precious Moments nativity set in the rubble, too. Isn't it just like a breath of hope to have found those tiny pieces?"

Murl walked into the room just then and piped up enthusiastically, "Well, you will never believe what the grandchildren found in the rubble at our house — all thirteen pieces of my nativity! I don't know how none of the pieces broke, since it was in the attic above the garage when the house burned down. How do you think that happened?"

No one had an answer for how every piece of the large nativity set could possibly have survived all that when so little else was recognizable. Each piece was easily identifiable and laid out on a shelf in the garage, looking like dirty, unfired ceramic pieces. The beautiful glaze was gone, but the entire set was complete.

Murl smiled over the soot-stained pieces and said, "I have no idea what I'll do with them, but I'm glad to have them."

The coming year was filled with dealing with insurance and construction issues, and the nativity and other rescued items went out of mind. When Christmas came, the treasured nativity was not on the mantel for the first time in over thirty years. Although it seemed like a small thing in the midst of everything we were dealing with, I made a mental note to remember to look for a ceramics shop that could restore the set before the following Christmas.

A year after the fire my in-laws moved into their new home on the old lot. At first, there was a lot of joy and excitement as new furniture and furnishings were being picked out. However, shortly after the move, Murl began to decline. Her chronic back issues seemed to intensify, and then she was hospitalized several times while they tried to figure out how to treat her symptoms. Over Thanksgiving, she took a turn for the worse. After an extended hospital stay, she moved into rehab. We took turns staying with her, and she seemed to be losing the will to live.

Out of the blue, I remembered the nativity set and decided to set out in earnest to find a ceramics shop. I called Paint & Fire Pottery, which I found online, and explained the situation.

"Bring in the set, and I'll have a look at it," said Brenda, one of the shop owners. "I cannot make any promises as I've never had such a request before, but I'll see what we can do."

I brought in the set that evening; Brenda examined each piece carefully.

"Well," she said thoughtfully, "they are actually in a lot better condition than I had expected. If you are willing to allow us to attempt to clean them up, re-glaze and fire them again, I'll give it a go. No guarantees, of course. We just can't tell how delicate the ceramic may be after all it's been through. And there is a slight crack on the back of the Joseph figure. It may break down all together, but there is also a possibility that the new glaze will act like a glue once it's fired again."

"How much will it cost?" I asked.

"I'll do it for $100," came her reply.

That seemed like a bargain to me, and I left all the pieces there and gave them my phone number.

A few days later, I received a call from the ceramics shop.

"I've invited a friend to help me with the restoration project, and we've been brushing and scrubbing all these pieces. They look like new, and we are ready for you to pick out a glaze."

I was excited to head back to the shop and stunned to see how the figures had been transformed — solid white and looking as crisp as the ready-to-go figurines on the shelves. I couldn't believe these were the same black and singed items I had brought in. The hairline crack in the back of Joseph, my mother-in-law's carefully etched M-U-R-L, and year she had inscribed at the bottom of some of the larger pieces were proof that they were one and the same.

The shop owner had never heard of the multi-layered glaze I described, so I chose a speckled brown glaze that I hoped would give a similar effect. She told me that it would take another week for the project to be completed, and I was getting excited about the prospect of my mother-in-law having her treasured nativity by Christmas.

When I went to pick up the set, I couldn't have been more delighted! It looked brand-new, and even the delicate Joseph had survived the restoration process.

Knowing that two people had worked so hard on the whole project, I asked, "How much do I owe you? I know it must have taken more time than you originally anticipated."

"We'd really like to donate our services to this project," the shop owner stated. "It was a pleasure to work on that beautiful set, and we think this is a wonderful thing you are doing for your mother-in-law."

Tears were in all our eyes, but I insisted that they at least accept the originally quoted $100.

"I think this will be a perfect Christmas gift for her this year," I said. "Thank you so much for all you did to make it happen."

Once each piece was carefully packed in bubble wrap, I hurried to Murl's room at the rehabilitation center. I noticed a box of white Christmas lights in the back of the car and decided that they would add a perfect touch to the surprise.

Entering her room quietly, since the lights were dimmed, I made my way to her bed and saw that she was asleep. I unwrapped every piece and arranged them in the familiar pattern on the counter next to her bed, interlacing the string of lights around the bases of the figures so they would be illuminated with a soft glow. Just as I plugged in the twinkle strand, Murl began to stir.

"That is so beautiful," she whispered. "Where did you find that nativity set?"

"It's *your* nativity set," I explained. "I found a ceramics shop that was able to restore it."

Tears welled up in her eyes, and a few trickled down her cheeks. "My nativity? Restored? It looks the same—but different, too."

She was a little groggy, but I could tell she was cognizant and understood what I was saying.

"Yes," I replied. "The same set."

I shared with her all about the cleaning, how I couldn't find the same glaze, and how the ladies had worked so hard to clean and brush each figure down to the raw greenware. She listened intently.

"It's like a Christmas miracle," she said softly. "It came through the fire different, but still beautiful."

"Just like you," I said.

She looked at me intently and said, "Beauty for ashes..."

The joy of the restored nativity set notably lifted her spirits. She told each doctor, nurse, and attendant about it over the rest of her stay at the rehab. She was released to go home shortly after the New Year, and I carefully packed up the nativity and took it home. For the past three years, it has been displayed on the new mantel above the fireplace in the familiar pattern, and a nail for the angel is permanently wedged between stones in the fireplace in the perfect spot for it to hang over the display for the holidays.

Murl still has her ups and downs, but I will never forget how the nativity she created in prayerful need brought her encouragement and hope so many years later, just when she needed them most.

— Donna Lorrig —

The Voice

Angels represent God's personal care
for each one of us.
~Andrew Greeley

Five days before Christmas, I sat in my living room making paper angel ornaments to tie on the gifts for family members. In the past, I'd made paper snowmen, Santas, and Christmas trees. But for some reason, this year I decided to make angels.

I had not been feeling well for a few weeks, but this evening I felt good and was enjoying myself. My husband was working late, and I was listening to Christmas carols and watching the fake video fireplace that crackled on the TV.

Then I heard a voice so clear and real that I looked around the room. The voice said, "Don't be afraid."

Afraid? What would I be afraid of? I put the angel aside and went into the kitchen for a drink of water. The voice was soft, feminine and insistent: "Don't be afraid." What on earth?

The next day, I awoke with a pain just below my right shoulder blade. As the day progressed, it got worse. I took aspirin, used a heating pad and then took a hot bath, but nothing helped. I managed to cook dinner, but couldn't eat. The pain became excruciating, and I finally asked my husband to take me to the emergency room.

When the doctor came into the exam room, he looked worried. He asked how long my eyes had been yellow. I told him I hadn't noticed. After a couple of scans and tests, he told me that my gall bladder had "exploded," and small gallstones were clogging my liver ducts. I needed emergency surgery!

I protested, since the injection of pain medication now had me feeling much better. I couldn't have surgery now! Christmas was a few days away. I had a turkey to cook, and a dozen relatives were celebrating at our house!

He told me that my condition was very serious. Without surgery, I might not be around to cook any future Christmas dinners. I started to feel frightened, but then I remembered the voice, so sweet, clear and insistent: "Don't be afraid." That was my very own Christmas angel, with a message of comfort when I needed it most. I wasn't afraid after all.

— Patricia Merewether —

Meant to Be

Kindness is igniting a light in someone else for no
reason other than to watch them enjoy the glow.
~Author Unknown

My husband Sherman and I lived in central Mexico for several years while his construction company worked on a project for General Motors. We enjoyed our stay there and spent our free time exploring the country's historic sites and places where the locals vacationed instead of Americanized resorts and beaches. We were especially fond of the mountainous city of Guanajuato, with its colorful and unique adobe homes built on steep hillsides. Eventually, we purchased a large painting of that beautiful city to display in our living room after retirement. Following years of travel and adventure, we moved back to our home, a small town on the North Dakota prairie.

Fifteen years later, my husband died of a massive heart attack. Several months later, I put an ad in our local paper offering to give away our six-foot Christmas tree, complete with lights. Since my husband was gone, the Christmas spirit was not the same for me. I didn't want to decorate the large one that we had enjoyed as a couple for so many years, and I had purchased a very small tree instead.

One Sunday the phone rang and a woman with a very pronounced Latino accent asked about the tree. She and her husband worked for a rancher almost sixty miles away, but decided they would drive to town for the tree. I agreed to save it for them, and they arrived an hour and a half later. They walked in the front door and immediately zeroed in on the large painting above my couch.

"Is that Guanajuato?" the man asked excitedly. "That is our home!" He explained that when they are not working for the rancher in the United States, they lived very close to that city in Mexico.

I told him we had lived in Mexico for a couple of years and explained about the project. He was very familiar with it.

"Oh, I know the factory. It is very large and covers the valley below Guanajuato!" They were so pleased to talk about the area, and I told them about all the construction projects we had done through the years, and how much we had enjoyed living in Mexico.

The couple had small children, and this was the first time they would not be in Mexico for Christmas. He said they had looked in the local store, but the large trees were all too expensive. I was so happy to give them our tree, and I added some extra strings of lights and a large bag of ornaments. As they left, I said, "Feliz Navidad."

The spirit of Christmas was back in my heart. My husband would have been so pleased that the tree would now be shining for this family. I like to think that he nudged me toward placing the ad for the tree. Why else would a couple, so far from their country, find such a coincidental meeting on the prairies of North Dakota?

— Geno Sloan —

Chapter 2
Giving Thanks

11

Crazy Always Finds a Way

*Within our family there was no such thing as a person
who did not matter. Second cousins
thrice removed mattered.*
~Shirley Abbott

Mom had always told her four kids to make sure no friend spent a holiday alone. So one year, at our pre-holiday meeting over the dining room table, we excitedly added up the number of "lonely" guests. We'd invited more than eighty strangers to Mom's Thanksgiving! Mom started crying, envisioning the Mount Everest of potatoes she'd need to peel.

We jumped in to help. We were going to make this happen together, as a family, and relieve Mom of as much responsibility as she wanted to relinquish. So, item by item, we asked Mom what she wanted to avoid. First? Washing dishes all day. The china and silver remained in storage, and the paper and plastic headed home from the store. Then we eliminated all in-house pots and pans; aluminum lined the kitchen counters along with our garage-sale serving spoons. If a few utensils got tossed with the trash, so what?

We talked Dad into cooking a pair of turkeys in the smoker, and my brother said he would roast two more in his fraternity-house kitchen.

If our guests asked if they could bring something, we'd assign them an item. My friends and my little brothers' guests would bring side dishes, and the middle siblings would ask for desserts. And everyone should bring food picnic-style so there would be no heartbreak if dishes got lost.

We all pitched in for a pre-holiday housecleaning, led by my brother and sister. They were used to a standard for tidiness I could never meet, and quite frankly I've never let a messy house get in the way of a good time. When we were kids, my mother referred to my brother and me as Felix and Oscar. But I can do what I'm told!

Of course, Mom couldn't let Thanksgiving pass without whipping up a few of her favorite recipes. We kids told her, "Do what you want. If you change your mind, no one will ever know the difference."

On Game Day — I mean, Thanksgiving Day — we made iced tea and lemonade in five-gallon batches. We swore we wouldn't dump them on each other after our big victory. I was in the restaurant business at the time, so I got some industrial-sized garbage bags and borrowed trash cans. My brother borrowed chairs and tables from his frat, and we covered them with disposable tablecloths.

We stationed serving lines in three locations in the house, including the garage. We made a pact that we wouldn't *ask* guests for labor, but we wouldn't turn it down either.

When our guests began to arrive, some asked if they could help. *Phew!* We worked those friends of ours into friends of Mom and Dad in no time at all. I suspect few houses experienced the genuine laughter and good cheer the Howe house did that Thanksgiving. It seemed like everyone was making new friends, and there wasn't anywhere else they wanted to be on a fall Thursday afternoon.

Hours after the last guest left, my family plopped down at the table and swore we'd never, ever do that again.

The next year, we invited only sixty.

Occasionally, I'll hear from old friends who were with us that Thanksgiving, even after all these years. They still think we were crazy to try anything like that, but my family and I have found that crazies adapt and overcome — with big hearts and welcoming smiles… and paper plates.

— Mark A. Howe —

The Thanksgiving Boyfriend

Gratitude can transform common days into
thanksgivings, turn routine jobs into joy, and
change ordinary opportunities into blessings.
~William Arthur Ward

After my daddy died young at fifty-four, holidays just weren't the same. We walked through one celebration after another, experiencing the emptiness because Daddy wasn't there. We mourned, thinking no one could ever take his place.

But for me, one memorable Thanksgiving dinner changed all that.

A phone call in early November brought both good news and bad. The good news was that my mother was coming for Thanksgiving. The bad news was that she was bringing her new boyfriend with her.

I hung up the phone and sat on the edge of the bed, staring out the bedroom window. How could she be dating someone so soon? And why was she bringing him here? I pulled down the shade and cried. I missed Daddy more than ever.

Within a week, however, I was shifting gears… shuffling through magazines and cookbooks, and coordinating linens and china for the Thanksgiving table. A magazine featuring Cornish hens on the cover was my inspiration. I had never cooked a turkey so I didn't quite trust myself. Surely the small hens would be easier to prepare.

Mama and her boyfriend, Haskell, arrived from out-of-state as scheduled. As soon as we heard their car in the driveway, I popped the pan of stuffed Cornish hens into a pre-heated oven, double-checking the recipe that called for a one-hour cooking time.

Then, adjusting my attitude until it read "nice and friendly," I ran to greet them at the front door.

As per the cookbook, dinner was served in exactly one hour. My poor feathered friends on the cover of the magazine were absolutely no match for the stunning specimens I removed from my own little oven that day in Indiana. One whole hen per person, proudly displayed in the center of each plate, made an overwhelming presentation.

We held hands around the table — me, my husband, my mother and the boyfriend — bowing our heads to thank God for His protection, His provision, and His plans for our lives.

It was Haskell who first made the discovery. While the rest of us were busy passing around sweet potatoes and cranberry sauce, Haskell decided to go ahead and take the plunge into his spectacularly golden Cornish hen. With the tip of his knife, he made a small incision through the orange glaze and deep into the breast. As he did so, a combination of blood and grease spurted out onto the tablecloth. Another jab and more blood started filling the bottom of his plate, sadly revealing an undercooked, barely thawed, and bleeding bird. I was seriously embarrassed, so I tried my hen. But it was the same, and unfortunately, I was too inexperienced to know what to do next.

Haskell quickly came to the rescue. Insisting my mother and husband leave the kitchen, he helped me start over. I covered up the dishes on the table while he repositioned the hens in the pan of drippings. He worked confidently, and I observed that his hands were big… just like my daddy's. He shrewdly shaped a tent of aluminum foil and securely covered the pan. He rechecked the cookbook and made an alteration in the temperature. And while we waited for the hens to thoroughly finish cooking, he patted me on the shoulder and reassured me.

An hour later, we sat down to dinner… again. Jokingly, we uttered a second quick prayer, thanking God this time for the well-cooked hens. As we continued on through the meal, I couldn't help thinking how much Haskell reminded me of my daddy. And I clearly remember thinking that Daddy would have liked him had he been there with us at the table.

Haskell eventually took my daddy's place. And to this day, he has no idea how much he actually taught me on that holiday. It was more than a lesson in how to prepare a Cornish hen. It was a timely exercise in how to prepare one's heart for the feast of good things God often has in store for us. For me, one memorable Thanksgiving dinner changed all that.

— Charlotte A. Lanham —

13

The Blessing

When one has a grateful heart, life is so beautiful.
~Roy T. Bennett, The Light in the Heart

"I'll do it!" volunteered my four-year-old grandson, Cody. He bounced up and down on his chair. "I know it! I learned it at school!"

The aroma of roasted turkey, cranberry relish, sweet potatoes, green-bean casserole, and fresh bread wafted through the air. We eagerly anticipated the wonderful meal as we quieted and bowed our heads at the Thanksgiving table.

I felt confident that Cody would remember the blessing he'd learned at his church preschool. I smiled and nodded at him. He took a big breath and began:

Come, Lord Jesus,
Be our guest,
Let these gifts,
To us be blessed.

Cody opened one eye and peeked at the bowed heads. I could tell he felt the power of being center stage. He was the man in charge. While he still had the spotlight, he quickly added:

Fuzzy Wuzzy was a bear,
Fuzzy Wuzzy had no hair,
Fuzzy Wuzzy wasn't fuzzy,
Was he?

Cody smiled proudly and added, *Amen.*

— Sharon Landeen —

14

A Circle of Kindness

In helping others, we shall help ourselves,
for whatever good we give out completes
the circle and comes back to us.
~Flora Edwards

Back in the 1990s, my mom and I drove back and forth to Bowling Green, Kentucky, where I went to college at Western Kentucky University. She was a struggling single mom, but she took the time to bring me clean laundry, food and even money while I was a struggling college student.

One November, two weeks before Thanksgiving, my mom was traveling through Kentucky when her 1989 Nissan Maxima had transmission trouble. She said she was pressing down on the gas, but nothing happened. The engine would rev, and the car would just idle. My mom pulled over on the shoulder of the interstate, and a pickup truck carrying chickens to a farm in Bonnieville pulled up behind her. The man in the truck waited behind her and yelled for her not to open her driver's side door until it was safe to get out.

Now, an older African-American woman like my mom, who grew up in Louisiana, did not know if everyone in Kentucky was friendly. It's a fact of life that some people might not be open to outsiders, especially people who are different. The man in the chicken truck told her to leave her car on the interstate, and then he convinced her to get in the truck with him. He drove my mom down some twisting roads and hills in the chicken truck and invited her into his home. I still chuckle thinking of my sweet, overly dressed mother, who was probably a little scared, riding in the truck with a chicken farmer and a dozen clucking chickens.

The farmer's wife saw my mom, and she did not ask who she was or any other questions. She simply said, "Hi! What do you want to drink — Coke or tea?"

My mom played with their six kids while the chicken farmer and his friends went back to the interstate and fixed my mom's transmission. She was so surprised by the whole situation that she didn't get their names. Nor does she know why these strangers took the time to help her get to safety, introduce her to the farmer's beautiful family with such hospitality, and then get her back on the road for free.

Two weeks later, my mom wanted to pay back the family from Bonnieville for what they did for her. She decided to send a check for $550 and a letter in an envelope thanking them for fixing her car. She addressed it to "The Chicken Farmer, Bonnieville, Kentucky," and by some weird chance the mail carrier got it to the right place. The family then got her address off the check and wrote her back with an amazing story.

My mom called me and said, "Dawn, Dawn, guess what? They got the money, and it was just what they needed! God blessed both of us with that money!"

It turns out that the money she sent them was the exact amount they needed to keep their chicken farm from being foreclosed. They took the money she sent them, paid their mortgage and bought a Thanksgiving dinner with the rest.

I will never forget how their actions truly illustrated the meaning of Thanksgiving. Because these kind strangers gave to my mother, she was able to give back to them. The gifts they gave each other that year turned a random act of kindness into an act of faith in humanity.

— Dawn Murrell —

15

A Walk Around the Block

Miracles come in moments. Be ready and willing.
~Dr. Wayne Dyer

My eyes clicked open to a still dark room. As the mom of three young children, I was used to rising early, but this was ridiculous. The bedside clock glowed 5:30 a.m. It was Thanksgiving Day. I groaned internally so I wouldn't wake my husband. He would have to drive us several hours to get to our family celebration.

The year was 1996, and though we had lived in our home for a few years, I had not ventured out into the neighborhood often. It came as a surprise to me then when I suddenly found myself getting out of bed, dressing, putting on tennis shoes and heading out for a predawn walk around my block.

I must have been halfway around the large circular block before I really woke up. I thought to myself, *What in the world am I doing? I could be sleeping for another precious hour!* But when I rounded the last curve and neared my home, instead of going in and climbing back under the warm covers, I walked past my house and continued around the block again. I could not explain why. This happened again, and then again.

The sky began to lighten to a wintry gray, and it promised to be a frigid day. I continued to walk.

Then, on my fourth lap around the neighborhood, I suddenly

smelled the very strong odor of natural gas. I could not tell exactly where it was coming from, but the house I suspected appeared to be vacant, so I went home. Since this was before cell phones, I called the gas company. I gave them the address I thought was correct, and they assured me they would go out and check it right away.

By this time, my family was waking up, and the next hour was a whirlwind of getting three small children ready and packing the car for our trip. I told my husband what had happened, and he could not believe I had gone for the walk; it was so out of my normal routine.

As we drove out of our neighborhood, I looked up at the street signs. Our circle has some cul-de-sacs and name changes, and as we pulled onto the highway, I began to feel certain I had given the gas company the wrong address! I was distraught, and when we arrived at my grandparents' house hours later, I tried to call the gas company and correct my mistake. There was no answer.

I tried not to worry and just enjoy the day with family, but the thought would not leave the back of my mind. I was worried all day. When we got home late that evening, I made my husband circle the neighborhood until I located the house I thought had the gas leak. Sure enough, I had given the gas company the wrong street name and house number! I felt sick.

When we walked into our house, I saw that the answering machine message light was blinking red. We got the kids to bed, and I went to play the messages. A man's voice I did not recognize began to speak.

"I am calling from the gas company," he said. "We went out to the address you gave us this morning, and…"

I expected to hear there was nothing wrong, but he continued, "… we discovered the main gas line had ruptured. The family was asleep inside, but we were able to get them all out safely and repair the line. The family asked me to call and thank you for reporting it. You very likely saved all of their lives."

I felt the hair on my arms stand up. The wrong address had been the right address after all. To this day, I cannot completely explain what happened that Thanksgiving morning, but I do know that I cannot take the credit for it. I just felt thankful that God put my feet on the road around my block that morning, and that He put the address in my head to give to the gas company.

There has not been a Thanksgiving since that year when I do not wake up and think of that family and feel gratitude. The memory has carried me through some difficult times of my own. When I feel hopeless or alone, when it is dark before the dawn, I remember that God is always watching over us, in ways we do not know or understand.

—Sherry Hall—

16

Divorced Person's Thanksgiving

A good friend is like a four-leaf clover;
hard to find and lucky to have.
~Irish Proverb

M y ex got custody of Thanksgiving in the divorce. Our son would be spending Thanksgiving with his father in New Hampshire, meaning that I'd be alone.

My friend Mark was in the same boat. On Thanksgiving, his daughters would be with his ex.

"Let's spend Thanksgiving together," I suggested.

We dubbed it "Divorced Person's Thanksgiving." It sure wasn't traditional. It wasn't a large family group, just the two of us. And it wasn't a feast. Both of us are light eaters and mediocre cooks. The last thing we wanted was to spend the day in the kitchen. We did want to acknowledge the holiday, but neither of us liked turkey enough to want to actually cook one. However, Mark makes delicious chili, so we decided to go with turkey chili.

It turned out to be a lovely day. I read out loud to Mark as he cooked. The chili was outstanding. We relaxed in front of the fire with our books, and then walked to the library where I work to empty the book drop. A stroll home was followed by coffee and pumpkin pie.

We did our best to distract ourselves from the fact that our kids weren't there, but I missed my son.

That was fourteen years ago. Mark and I have spent almost every Thanksgiving since then together. The turkey chili, over time, has morphed into vegetarian chili, and then vegan chili. And Mark and I, over time, have gone from being good friends to being more. Otherwise, our holiday hasn't changed. We continue to enjoy a quiet meal, followed by an afternoon relaxing by the fire.

And emptying the library book drop has become as much a part of Thanksgiving as pumpkin pie. Now that my son is all grown up, happily married and living in California, I have a Thanksgiving phone call from him (and my daughter-in-law) to look forward to.

Two years ago, because Mark was temporarily living in West Virginia, I realized that I'd be on my own for Thanksgiving. My sister's hospitable in-laws would undoubtedly have welcomed me to their table. But did I really want to spend hours on the road to get to Long Island and spend the day in a large group, even a large group of people I love?

I'd come to relish my quiet, relaxing-at-home Thanksgiving.

Besides, someone had to stay home to take care of Captain, the Yorkiepoo.

I decided that I'd get myself a fabulous turkey sandwich from the deli and pumpkin pie from my favorite bakery. I'd get a turkey sandwich for Captain, too. He'd be very thankful to sink his tiny teeth into some delicious holiday poultry.

Although I felt good about my decision, as Thanksgiving approached, I realized that even though Captain can be excellent company, I was really going to miss Mark. Thanksgiving isn't just another Thursday. And while Divorced Person's Thanksgiving isn't the way most folks would choose to observe this holiday, if I didn't spend the day with Mark, it just wouldn't be Thanksgiving.

I phoned him. "I know it's a really long drive, and you weren't planning on coming in for Thanksgiving," I said, "but I'm really going to miss you."

"I'll be there," he promised.

Once again, we enjoyed chili, pumpkin pie, and each other's company. (And Captain enjoyed his turkey sandwich.) Our celebration may not be traditional, but my feelings of gratitude for this wonderful day surely are.

— Roz Warren —

17

My Miracle
on 34th Street

*Probably some of the best things that have ever
happened to you in life happened because you
said yes to something. Otherwise, things just
sort of stay the same.*
~Danny Wallace, Yes Man

The summer of 2010 marked two years since I had lost my mom. With my dad falling ill earlier that spring, I had my hands full juggling doctors' appointments, trying to run his business, and attempting to keep things "normal" for my two children, who were on their way to different summer camps.

My daughter chose cheer camp. She had been a competition dancer for years, but with her senior year approaching, she decided to participate on her high school's cheerleading team. During camp, she was one of a select group of girls chosen as "All American Cheerleader." While this was certainly a big accomplishment at camp, the excitement fizzled out when she returned home, as my dad took a turn for the worse and passed away in early August.

A month later, I received a call from one of the other cheer moms asking if my daughter was going to participate in the Macy's Thanksgiving Day Parade. Evidently, being named All American Cheerleader qualified her for that.

I had no clue! I had been so preoccupied with losing my dad that I hadn't even researched any of the "perks" of the title, nor had my daughter.

The Macy's Thanksgiving Day Parade! It had always been on my bucket list. I had always warned my parents that we would miss Thanksgiving one year and go to New York City to see the parade instead. But we never did it. It was too much outside my comfort zone, plus I didn't really want to forego a Thanksgiving with my parents.

Now we were on our own, so I called the "All American" hotline for details.

"Is your daughter a dancer or a cheerleader?"

"Well, both I guess..." I clarified that she received the "title" as a cheerleader.

The coordinator asked about her dance experience. She explained that this year the dancers were to perform the opening number on live television to kick off the parade.

"Do you think she would rather dance?"

Well, that was a no-brainer! My daughter's greatest love was dance!

I would talk to my husband and daughter and call her back the next day, which was ironically the deadline — not a lot of time to make our decision.

Unbelievable! Not only would we get to see the Macy's Parade, but we would get to watch our daughter perform in it! But then the coordinator explained that only one parent was invited to accompany the performer.

So, my daughter and I would have to travel to New York City by ourselves. This was not something I was accustomed to. I always had my husband with me on big adventures.

Driving was out of the question, and flying, well, I had not flown since I was a child. My daughter had never flown.

My husband encouraged me to go despite my fears and my naturally cautious attitude. Our daughter would soon be leaving for college. This could be our "last hurrah" together. When would she — when would *we* — ever have a chance like this again?

I prayed a lot and slept on it.

The next morning, I told my daughter we were going. There was no backing out now.

And then, despite my fears, the plane didn't crash, get hijacked or combust in midair. We arrived in one piece.

The week flew by, filled with intense dance practices intermingled with lots of sightseeing. Our alarm went off promptly at 3:30 a.m. on November 25, 2010. We did hair and make-up and met the dance team in the hotel lobby. There was a slight change to the schedule. Instead of being released after the opening number was performed, the dancers would board the subway and assemble again near Central Park to escort none other than the most prominent individual in the parade — the one and only Santa Claus! Wow, the girls were going to be featured twice!

The girls headed off, and despite the cold, I opted out of watching the parade on TV in the lobby with the other moms. Instead, I took the subway, found my way down 7th Avenue, stopped for a hot chocolate, and scoped out a spot in front of a bank where I sat for hours waiting to see the most famous parade in the world.

It was spectacular. Definitely "bucket-list worthy"!

As the end of the parade approached and the dancers led Santa's sleigh into my view, a light and steady snowfall began to dust the streets of New York.

My first Thanksgiving without my mom or dad ended up being one of the most blessed moments I have ever experienced. I have no doubt that somewhere far above the streets of New York, hidden deep in those white snow clouds, God placed two front-row seats that day.

So, yes, it was a parade that taught me that life is about living. And more often than not, it's worth stepping outside your comfort zone to follow your dreams.

— Valerie Archual —

18

Turkey Baby

*Not what we say about our blessings, but how we use
them, is the true measure of our Thanksgiving.*
~W. T. Purkiser

"I'll have one General Tso's chicken combo platter with fried rice and a pork eggroll, extra duck sauce and a root beer. But can you please make sure it's decaffeinated?"

"Okay, anything else, honey?" my husband questioned sarcastically. "Could you possibly fit more food into that pregnant belly of yours?"

I was three days from my due date, and I was so done. But the next day was Thanksgiving, and I had baking to do. I certainly had no time to cook dinner tonight.

Unapologetically, I giggled. "Well, yeah. And don't think for a second you are touching my eggroll after that comment! Love you, bye!" Smiling, I hit "End" on my cell phone. The smile widened as I thought about our new little bundle arriving any day.

I also thought about how much my husband adored Thanksgiving, how much he loved me, and how he could pretend my Chinese food order annoyed him, but he really, truly cherished every second of it.

November 22nd—my mom's birthday and Thanksgiving Eve—was one of the happiest days I'd had. I loved preparing for Thanksgiving. Our family does the same things every year. We eat Cream of Wheat topped with gobs of vanilla ice cream for breakfast while watching the Macy's Thanksgiving Day Parade, *Miracle on 34th Street* and *A Christmas*

Story. By the time we are done, the fantastically large dinner is ready. We fight over the last piece of my mom's sage sausage stuffing and eat until we are sick. The holiday usually ends with an evening of more eating — turkey sandwiches and rippled chips — along with Ravens football and then a food coma that lasts through Saturday.

My ankles throbbed as I assembled chocolate bourbon pecan pies. My chubby fingers were sweaty in my latex gloves. The gloves were necessary to protect my skin from the pecans. I'd been allergic to tree nuts my entire life, but there I stood baking those nut pies. I powered through all these little annoyances, especially the shooting pains that had coursed through my lower back since work ended. Nothing could ruin this. I was very happy.

With pecan pies in the oven and pumpkin pies cooling on the counter, I heard my husband's keys in the front door. Perfect timing! The baby and I were starving. The food rounded the corner before he did. He extended the greasy brown bag my way, bowed, and then spun around to reveal bonus ice cream behind his back. We were pre-gaming for tomorrow, stretching out the old tummy for the big show.

Full of fried foods, we went to bed. The house smelled of our neatly wrapped pies that waited in the fridge for their twenty-minute morning ride over the highway and through the suburbs to my parents' house.

Falling into bed and onto my full-length body pillow, my back screamed. Exhaustion would likely win against hundreds of good movies on cable tonight. My husband's snoring began the minute his head hit the pillow, but I couldn't sleep.

Then, my contractions started.

Fourteen minutes apart.

I called my doctor's emergency line.

"When they are ten minutes apart, call back," I was told. "And relax."

Relax? How could someone relax feeling like this?

My husband slept through it all. Even though never officially diagnosed, I am certain he has narcolepsy. I timed my contractions alone.

By 5:00 a.m. on Turkey Day, I had already called my doctor four more times. She was likely so sick of hearing from me that she sent me to the hospital just to shut me up. I was ready for my husband to zoom us down to the hospital, which is, incidentally, on the way to Mom's house. He didn't zoom anywhere. He did the opposite. He was the reverse of every clichéd movie scene's depiction of the nervous expectant father. No rushing around, no forgetting to zip his fly, no tripping or passing out. Instead, he was cool as a breeze. He delicately placed the pies in the trunk, stopped at 7-Eleven to get a coffee and a paper, and even dropped off the pies at my mom's.

I was furious, but too full of pain and anguish, and too lacking in energy after a completely sleepless night, to say anything.

His chill attitude faded when my mom saw my pain. She gave him a scalding look, scolded him, and insisted that he drive as safely as possible to the hospital. She and my sister would meet us at the Women's Pavilion.

My hero was back. He complied, and we were admitted by 7:00 a.m.

Greeted by our nurse, I was wheeled in for examination, but all I wanted was the epidural. However, we had to wait for the doctor's arrival and a few more checklist items. After a few scares and humbling moments, including a plunge in heart rate and fainting from the epidural, all was right with the world.

"We may have a Turkey Baby!" my mother said, as she plunged through the double doors with my little sister. They wanted to hang out in the room, but I insisted that they go home and make Thanksgiving for the rest of the family.

"Make sure you save us a plate!" my husband yelled down the hall after them as they reluctantly went home. A turkey dinner and a house full of people waited for her, but my mother wanted to see our expressions as we met our Thanksgiving miracle.

The day passed, accompanied by background music from my iPod. We talked about the what-ifs and can't-waits until the time for pushing came. My husband was so adorable, nervously rubbing my legs no matter how many times I told him to stop. Our nurse stayed past her shift because we were the first couple she'd delivered that didn't know their baby's sex, and she wanted to know!

My husband dialed the phone as I held our beautiful new child. Tears of joy filled our eyes. I heard Mom answer on speakerphone with an audience of twenty-two of my favorite people listening intently. "We're all here and waiting," she said.

My husband responded, "At 7:23 p.m. on November twenty-third, Dennis Michael Rosier was born."

I heard them all cheering. And less than twenty minutes later, half of the party moved from my parents' house to my hospital room, with foil-wrapped plates for us to enjoy the next day. The nurses even made the baby a decorated turkey onesie.

It was an extraordinary Thanksgiving, and I remain grateful for it every day.

—Amanda Girolamo—

Closed Doors, Open Heart

*Wherever there is a human being, there is an
opportunity for a kindness.*
~Seneca

W e were going to stay home for Christmas 2016, but a
late-November phone call from my older sister changed
our plans and prompted a trip to my hometown of
Kitchener, Ontario. Due to work schedules, my wife
and I drove on Christmas Eve, leaving Milwaukee before dawn to get
us there by late afternoon. If possible, we'd connect with family that
night. If not, we'd meet for Christmas Day brunch at my nephew's
house.

Upon arrival that night, I called my sister, but I got her voicemail.
When I tried again, Diane answered in a whisper and said she was in
church and would call us back. We waited about an hour, and then
decided to venture out to find Christmas Eve dinner on our own.

Driving along deserted streets, I was soon reminded that, unlike
at home in the States, almost everything closes on Christmas Eve in
Canada. Nothing was open — not even a Tim Hortons!

Finally, we found a hole-in-the-wall Chinese restaurant where
we enjoyed wonton soup and plates of chicken, vegetables and rice. I
chuckled at the thought we were re-living the scene of young Ralphie
Parker and his family in the movie, *The Christmas Story,* settling for

Chinese food instead of a traditional turkey dinner.

Feeling blessed, and convinced our adventure made for a memorable Christmas tale, we had no idea a much more meaningful Christmas supper story awaited us.

Christmas morning, we joined the family gathering at my nephew's house. The place soon filled, and for the rest of the day we were awash in a sea of love, catching up with familiar relatives, meeting new ones and enjoying a sumptuous brunch. We played gift-swap and watched as the children played Jenga with the tipsy-pile of presents under the tree, and then tore them open with shrieks of Christmas glee. Too soon, though, evening came, and we had to say our goodbyes.

As we prepared to leave, it dawned on Kris and me that we were faced, again, with finding supper. We didn't want to repeat the previous night's search, so we asked for recommendations, and my sister said she knew of some restaurants that were open. She decided to join us and, not wanting to cook a second meal, my nephew and his family came along, too. Off our three-car caravan went in search of Christmas Day supper.

We found nothing but closed restaurants. After several fails, my nephew's family headed home, and my sister joined Kris and me as we continued searching. The later it got, the more skeptical I became. But driving along Westmount Road, Kris saw lights in the distance! It was Mel's Diner, a strip-mall burger shop that my sister liked.

Parking, I noticed a curious lack of cars. But before I could say anything, Kris and Diane were headed inside. Entering, I noticed a small, handwritten sign taped to the door they'd passed. It said, "Closed for private event." When I caught up to tell them the disappointing news, the host was asking for tickets. We said we didn't have any, and he replied that we needed tickets to eat. Noticing several open tables, I asked if an exception could be made for us and offered to buy tickets. That's when he told us Mel's Diner was hosting Christmas Day dinner for the poor and homeless, and tickets were available only at area shelters and churches.

I told him we were out-of-town visitors and relayed the story of our Christmas Eve search for supper. We only wanted a place to share

Christmas Day dinner with my older sister, I implored. He apologized, but still refused.

We turned to leave when a man called out, "It's okay, it's Christmas. Everyone is welcome at Mel's Diner tonight." He escorted us to a window booth, and soon a stream of volunteer kids captivated our hearts and filled our table with a complete Christmas feast. We had chicken rather than turkey, but otherwise it was all there: mashed potatoes, gravy, dressing, yams, cranberries, rolls with real butter, apple pie and ice cream for dessert, and endless cups of hot coffee.

As we ate and looked past our reflections at the snowy scene outside, we couldn't believe our good fortune and agreed that God had truly blessed us by directing us to Mel's Diner to witness the true spirit of Christmas. Our escort stopped to check on us and introduced himself as the twin brother of the restaurant's owner. We relayed our story and profusely thanked him for such unexpected kindness.

Sated with food and Christmas cheer, we thanked the volunteers on our way out and stopped at the main counter to speak with a man who looked like our escort, yet just different enough that I wasn't sure. Instead, it was Jerry, the twin brother and owner of the diner. We relayed our story again and thanked him for his generosity. And when I asked how much we owed, he said any donation would do. I had no Canadian currency, so I pulled out all the U.S. money I had and placed it on the counter: a ten and a twenty to cover our three meals, and then, feeling the Christmas spirit, I added a one-hundred-dollar tip.

Thanks to Jerry Smith, his twin brother Donald, and the staff and volunteers at Mel's Diner in Kitchener, Ontario, my wife, sister and I now have a wonderful Christmas story that will always bring us joy and remind us of the kindness of strangers.

— Brian Wettlaufer —

Operation Food Package

We must find time to stop and thank the people who make a difference in our lives.
~John F. Kennedy

We were relaxing on the couch in our living room when my husband, Tom, shoved the newspaper under my nose. "This is my friend's son who is serving in Iraq," he said.

The picture showed four naval personnel dressed in camouflage uniforms. They were standing outside a makeshift tent in the desert, patiently waiting for their Thanksgiving dinner. My heart broke at the sight of the young men. Here I was in the comfort of my air-conditioned house in Miami, the day after a fabulous Thanksgiving dinner that included a turkey with all the trimmings. Sadly, I wondered what the men in the picture had eaten for dinner.

Tom rubbed his chin and commented, "This is Kevin's second tour of duty. He was a lawyer with a great job in a prominent law firm when he decided to give it up and join the navy's officer program. His father is really proud of him for serving his country."

My husband is not an emotional man, but when it comes to our service personnel, he gets choked up. He's a former Army officer.

"Being away from his family, Kevin's Thanksgiving had to be really hard for him," I said. I grabbed Tom's arm and added, "Hey, what would you say if we sent him a big food package for Christmas to let him know we're thinking of him and to show him how much we appreciate what he's doing for our country?"

"He already gets packages from his family," Tom said. "His old man, mom and sisters send him stuff all the time. Besides, Christmas is only a month away. It might not arrive in time."

I wasn't letting go of the idea. "This would be an extra present. Look, we don't have kids. And I've got plenty of time to food shop. Go on. Call your friend. Ask him what types of food Kevin would like. I really want to do this."

Tom picked up the phone and dialed his friend. I overheard the brief conversation. My husband is a man of few words; all of his phone calls are less than three seconds. Tom hung up. "He likes healthy snack foods that he can't get over there."

"Healthy Christmas snack foods?" I repeated. "That can survive being shipped to Iraq? That's going to be one heck of a challenge." I looked over at Tom, who was already absorbed in his newspaper. I started to formulate my plan of attack. "Operation Food Package" was in motion.

The next morning, I drove to the Tuesday Morning store where I scanned the aisles for healthy, transportable foods that would not perish in shipment. I noticed a display of Sclafani Panettone cake. I scrutinized the sturdy red box with the yellow ribbon. The label said it was an Italian two-pound cake, traditionally handcrafted with extra butter, plum raisins, and the finest candied Sicilian orange peels and citron. The cake certainly fit the criteria of being a holiday food. But was it healthy? Since the package listed "raisins and figs," I reasoned that was close enough. I tossed the box in my cart.

My next stop was Whole Foods, where I explored the healthy treats aisle. I chose a few protein bars, a box of Nabisco Fig Newtons 100% Whole Grain, a bag of chips made from high-fiber fruits, and a package of cranberry flaxseed cookies, for good measure.

At the last second, I saw a bar of soap made with pure olive oil. I reasoned that if Kevin had enough water to take a shower, he would appreciate a comforting soap to wash away the desert dust. At the checkout counter, the sales lady looked skeptically at my cart full of snacks and then back at me. I wondered if she thought I was a closet food addict. I shrugged and said, "I binge a little at night." Then I left the store with six bags of gourmet snack foods.

My final stop was the Publix grocery store, where I grabbed three boxes of healthy veggie crackers. In my mind, this officer was going to have a Christmas feast.

Back home, I commandeered a large banker's file box from my husband's office. I wrapped the fragile foods in bubble wrap and stuffed every inch of the box with food. Then I tucked the bar of olive oil soap into a corner. I wrote a note to Kevin telling him how much we appreciated his service. Satisfied with my work, I sealed the package and addressed it.

Later that day, when Tom arrived home from work, I proudly showed him my masterpiece.

Tom looked at the box, grinned from ear to ear, and then hugged me. "Good job, honey," he said.

I stared at the box. "I only hope it gets there in time," I said.

The day after Christmas, Tom and I had lunch at our favorite Asian restaurant. It is a tradition for us to go there since most of the restaurants in our area are closed the day after Christmas.

During lunch, Tom took out his BlackBerry and opened an e-mail message. "You'll want to read this," he said.

The letter was from his friend's son, Kevin. It was addressed to Tom and Joyce.

Kevin said that he had received our package on the night before Christmas. The airdrop had come in the middle of the night. Kevin said it was the only gift he received right on Christmas Day. The present made him feel very special, and he was grateful it had arrived at such a timely moment. He went on to say that he looked up the Italian panettone cake on Google, and he provided us a full-page description of its origin. Finally, he added that he had savored every bite of the cake.

I fought back the tears. "We did something good for one of our servicemen," I said. "I'm glad."

Tom reached over and patted my hand. Suddenly, his eyes lit up. "Let's send another package. He obviously likes that cake. Tomorrow, I'll go to our Italian bakery and buy more before they run out."

The next day, Tom came home with three more panettone cakes. I packaged them, and the box went out that same night.

A month later, Tom bounded into the living room. "You're not going to believe this," he said. "This is from my friend." He handed me his BlackBerry, and I read: "We received a message from Kevin. He said that the second package had arrived, and it was precisely on his birthday."

What a happy and fortunate coincidence that one package arrived on Christmas Day and another on Kevin's birthday. We were delighted.

Tom and I decided that it's not the size of the package, the contents or the holiday that matters. What matters is that we remember the men and women who are serving in foreign lands for us.

— Joyce Newman Scott —

Chapter
3
O Christmas Tree

A Tree from Heaven

May the spirit of Christmas bring you peace.
The gladness of Christmas give you hope.
The warmth of Christmas grant you love.
~Author Unknown

I n college, as married students with a small daughter, we could afford nothing... nothing at all. When the Christmas season arrived, I was really in trouble. We didn't even have the gas money to drive the 100 miles to visit relatives. So I thought it wise to convince my three-year-old daughter that not every house had a Christmas tree.

Starting at Thanksgiving, we walked around town when I wasn't working or in class, looking at all the decorated Christmas trees. At night, if it wasn't too cold, we walked downtown to enjoy the lights and trees. By early December, my daughter was comfortable with the no-tree explanation and enjoyed our little Christmas tree outings. But I didn't like it.

One day after class, one of the students was lamenting that he was going to be in big trouble with his landlord pretty soon. "How could you possibly be in trouble?" I asked.

Bruce was a good friend of ours, but he had been born with a silver spoon. His father owned a giant car dealership that attracted customers from several Midwestern states. Bruce was to inherit this car kingdom when his father retired. But his father insisted Bruce have a "proper" college education in business before he became a partner and eventually took over the business. One day, Bruce would have it all, but at that time he was just a car salesman when he went home for Christmas and semester breaks.

During college, Bruce lived in a really nice apartment complex close to campus. His landlord only leased to "reliable" students with references. With a complex filled with college students, he had to be strict, and he tolerated no "funny business."

One of the landlord's rules, besides no pets, parties or alcohol, was no Christmas trees or outdoor lights; it said so in Bruce's lease. So that he would not be thought of as a Scrooge, the landlord reminded his tenants they would all be going home for Christmas anyway. He didn't want a tree left to dry out and start a fire.

His aversion to outside Christmas lights wasn't the steep electrical bills the students would have to pay, but rather that the kids would hang like monkeys over the balconies to put up lights and fall to their deaths in the process. The landlord claimed he didn't have the liability insurance for that.

Bruce was not fazed by the crazy rules. He bought a nice fresh Christmas tree at Thanksgiving and all the necessary lights and ornaments for a proper Christmas display in his third-floor living room. He kept the drapes pulled from dusk to dawn so the landlord wouldn't notice.

Two weeks after Thanksgiving, Bruce was ready to go home for Christmas as soon as classes ended. "I really don't want to leave that tree in my living room in case the landlord comes to check on my place while I am gone," he said. Bruce knew the landlord was snoopy and didn't want to push his luck.

"Perhaps I could be of some help," I told him. "I haven't gotten a tree yet, so I could take it off your hands before you leave for Christmas break."

Bruce's eyes lit up. "You would do that for me?"

"Sure," I said. *Wow*, I thought. *I have a tree now, but no decorations.*

We set to plotting. Bruce enlisted the help of a couple of buddies from our class. No, the tree wasn't that heavy, but Bruce needed lookouts — "spies," we called them. We then arranged a time. I came with a couple of sheets and some rope to tie around the tree. We didn't want needles all over the nice hallway carpeting as we dragged this good-sized tree down two flights of stairs.

When engaged in this kind of espionage, sometimes things get out of control. And so it was when I arrived with my little car.

The spies (er, lookouts) had located the landlord on the premises at a time when he usually wasn't there. There would be no taking the tree down the stairs. I learned that when I went to Bruce's apartment and saw his beautifully lit tree. Bruce told me there was bad news, but seemed undisturbed by the development. He had on his car salesman smile that said, "We can make this happen!"

"Go downstairs now and wait outside below my apartment balcony," he ordered. He retrieved one of the spies from his post and told the other to be extra careful. My hopes were dashed as I went slowly down the stairs without the tree. My little girl didn't know about Bruce's tree then, but I wanted it so badly for her… and me.

Stationed below the balcony, I suddenly heard a sliding door. I looked up, and there was Bruce with one of the spies carrying his tree, which was now out of the stand and wrapped in the sheets. Before I could say anything, they tied a rope around the tree and the railing. Then they started lowering it from the balcony.

In that moment, it felt as if a Christmas tree was dropping into my arms from heaven.

Very soon, one of the spies was by my side, helping me guide the tree to the ground. Bruce disconnected the rope from the railing and dropped it. We used it to tie the tree to the top of the car. It was then that I noticed he had not even bothered to take off the ornaments or lights.

Score! I didn't have to worry about decorations now. I knew my daughter would be so delighted.

Everything was going better than expected. As I pulled out of the parking spot, Bruce and his two spies were waving. "Merry Christmas!" they shouted.

Just then, the landlord strolled up silently behind the three guys. Bruce and the spies apparently didn't see or hear him. As I shifted into Drive, Bruce yelled, "Remember, I want those ornaments and lights back."

When I put my foot to the gas, I saw Bruce and the spies talking and laughing with the landlord.

I heard later, when I gave Bruce a box of lights and ornaments back, that the landlord thought that I had just been visiting. Really, who would defy an airtight lease and have a Christmas tree?

My gift for Bruce, of course, was a little late. It was a picture of my little girl sitting by our beautifully decorated Christmas tree. She had informed me that she knew every house got a Christmas tree.

Thanks, Bruce... for the tree and the memories.

— Ela Oakland —

A Living Memory of Christmas

He who plants a tree
Plants a hope.
~Lucy Larcom

For a few years, we bought live Christmas trees from our friends, the Castranovas, who ran a greenhouse and nursery named Country Gardens. My parents said they didn't like to see a cut Christmas tree wasted by being thrown out as garbage after the holiday. My mother once allowed as how the sight "broke her heart." But I suspect that the fact that three rambunctious kids and two lively dogs played around the tree may also have had something to do with their decision. Set in its bed of earth, a live tree is much heavier and more difficult to upset than a cut tree.

I liked everything about the live-tree routine. It started with a visit to the Castranovas' Country Gardens, located about three miles from our house. My dad and I would walk in to be immediately greeted by the aroma of all manner of flowers. Mr. Castranova would sit my father down in a chair in the entryway between the greenhouse and the family's living quarters, and pour him a whiskey. The two would talk about politics while I loitered on a stool in the greenhouse, taking in the scents of the lilies, orchids, and roses. For a few moments, everything seemed to be as it should be in the world.

By the time I'd had enough of the cut flowers, the two men would have finished their drinks and would be on their way to the place where Mr. Castranova kept the live trees. Always deliberate and low-key, Mr. Castranova would quietly extol the virtues of this tree or that. After ten or fifteen minutes, my dad would make his selection and carry it out to the car. I would say "goodbye" to the greenhouse for another year.

The initial set-up of the live trees was somewhat easier than that of cut trees, since the live trees, being embedded in a big ball of earth, did not require a special stand, nor did they require watering arrangements. But any time saved on the initial set-up was more than made up for by the extra time required for decoration. The live trees had fuller, thicker branches than did the cut ones.

The trees were so rich and opulent that they didn't need ornaments. But my parents had a huge collection of lights and ornaments. You couldn't set up a tree with all this stuff in an hour. My parents could barely do it in a night, with the live trees having twice as many branches to decorate as cut trees of the same size. Between the decorating and the wrapping, it would usually be at least sunrise before the two finally made it to bed, happy but exhausted. But the waist-high pile of presents beneath the tree was always worth waiting for.

Since we didn't set up our tree until Christmas Eve, we left it up a long time — until "Twelfth Night," January 6th. There was always a little ceremony to mark Twelfth Night and the taking down of the tree. We kids would be given oranges, chocolate, and a small but interesting toy apiece. Then the stripped-down tree would be put into a corner of the living room to await the next Saturday, when it would return to the earth. Planting a live tree was too important a job to be done in the fading light of an early January afternoon.

Southern Connecticut in early January was not Minnesota or the Arctic tundra, but neither was it Florida or Jamaica. Generally, the ground had been frozen for some time by early January and was quite hard. How did my father manage to plant live Christmas trees in that hard earth? The answer is that he had prepared for this task months earlier. In October, he would dig a suitable hole in the backyard location where he planned to plant the live tree. The earth from that hole would be put into the toolshed to await the planting of the tree.

Come January, it was a simple matter of fitting the live tree into the hole and filling in with the earth removed three months earlier. At most, that earth needed a few taps with a shovel or pickaxe to loosen it up. Then Dad would give the tree a good watering and leave it to its fate. For the most part, that was a happy fate.

All too soon, the Castranovas moved out of town, and our live Christmas trees were nothing more than a memory. They were, however, a memory that lasted. When, as a middle-aged man, I took my son and daughter to visit our old house, two of those trees — a fir and a spruce — were standing sentry over the driveway. One of them was over forty feet tall; the other was between thirty and thirty-five feet. As mature trees, they possessed the same rich beauty they had in their youth, when they had ever so briefly graced our living room. Clearly, my dad had chosen and planted well. I only wish that he and the Castranovas had been there to see the fruits of their collective work.

— Jon Peirce —

Benjamin

Life is really simple, but we insist
on making it complicated.
~Confucius

When I was four years old, my dad and I were sent out to get a Christmas tree for the house. We were a bit late in the game to do so, probably the day before Christmas Eve, and when we got to where they sold the trees, they were sold out. My dad started stressing a bit. He knew my mom really wanted a tree.

My dad was not much for traditions and celebrations. He saw holidays more as days he did not have to go to work, when he would get to spend some time with us. But he knew that tree was important to the rest of the family.

So, with all the trees sold out, we just sat in the car thinking. I'm not going to pretend I was some sort of genius, but I was the type of little kid who listened more than people thought I did. I suddenly remembered that my dad grew up in Liberia, and I had been told enough about Africa and his adventures there to know that they didn't have the same trees as we did.

I looked at my dad and said, "Daddy…"

"Yes, honey?"

"You grew up in Africa." He must have wondered where that sudden realization came from, and he was probably thinking something like, *Oh, my God, child, I don't have time to tell you about my tree house adventures, odd animals and cool fruits right now.* But he said, "Yes, sweetie, I did."

"And you always celebrated Christmas on the beach, swimming, because Africa is hot and you didn't have snow."

"Mmm, we did."

"And you didn't have to wear gloves and knitted hats. You could have board shorts because you were swimming."

"That's right."

"And in Africa, they don't have our kind of Christmas trees, right?"

"No, they don't…"

"What did you have as a Christmas tree?"

I remember seeing his whole face light up.

"Palm trees!" he said.

"That's kind of like the big plants we have at home, right? Can we use one of them?"

My dad agreed, realizing that it was probably the best solution anyway, and it was already approved by one of our family, namely yours truly. So he took the money for the Christmas tree and took me into a shop to buy candy. When we got home, I walked in incredibly happy carrying kilos of candy in my arms. My dad came in without a tree, but with a giant smile. My mom must have been pretty confused. I exclaimed happily, "We bought candy with all the money!"

My dad explained: "They were all out of trees!"

"So you bought candy instead with all that cash?" my mom said in one of those I-cannot-believe-you-right-now, please-explain-yourself-before-I-burst voices.

"Yes!" I said. "When Daddy was little, they had palm trees. We are gonna use the weeping fig," I said to my mom, handing over the candy. Her face changed, and she started laughing as my dad shrugged and giggled, too.

And that is how we started our tradition of using our weeping fig, named Benjamin because it is a Benjamin ficus tree, as the Christmas tree every year. We took good care of Benjamin throughout the years and had him planted in an indoor garden. Our Benjamin grew from a tiny potted plant to being two meters high and almost as wide. Every year, we would have people over at our house to see our weeping fig with the garlands and Christmas lights, and one of my parents would retell the story of how Q (that would be me) brought Africa to Stockholm in order to save Christmas.

—Eriqa "Q" Hermen—

24

'Twas a Night Before Christmas

We are all here for a spell; get all the
good laughs you can.
~Will Rogers

I was working the overnight shift as a nurse in a twelve-bed hospice home. Lynn, the nursing assistant working with me, had been instructed by our supervisor to get the facility's Christmas tree out and decorated if our patients were stable. Thankfully, all of our patients were resting comfortably, so Lynn set out to make our workplace festive for the holiday season.

After a busy start to my shift, assessing patients and administering medications, I sat down in front of the computer to complete the most dreadful task of nursing: charting. But my charting was soon interrupted by the sound of glass shattering in the dining room. A co-worker and I hurriedly jumped out of our chairs in the nurses' station and ran to see what was going on. Since it was 4:00 a.m., we weren't expecting to find a patient or family member in the dining room, and it was too early for the kitchen staff to be there. So, that left only one possibility…

My suspicion was confirmed when I rounded the corner and found my beloved nursing assistant sprawled on the floor beside the fallen Christmas tree that she had nearly finished decorating. Thankfully, Lynn was not hurt, but being a jokester, she closed her eyes, held her mouth open, and threw her arm back for dramatic effect. We all burst into hysterical laughter!

Once we caught our breath, my co-worker and I helped Lynn to her feet. Then we all stood in disbelief, examining the destruction before us. I don't recall why or how the tree fell, but there it lay on the floor, along with hundreds of pieces of red, green, and white glass — remnants of the shattered ornaments.

Before returning the tree to its upright position, we asked Lynn to lie back down and pose for the camera, reenacting her priceless expression. Then we righted the tree and began cleaning up the mess.

Being tired often leads to "the giggles," so with this occurring toward the end of our twelve-hour shift, we were all vulnerable to sporadic bouts of laughter for the remainder of the morning. How nice and refreshing it was to cut up and laugh in an environment that is normally filled with so much sadness.

After I finished giving my patients their 6:00 a.m. medications and wrapped up all of my charting, I decided to do something to commemorate this night — one my co-workers and I were sure to never forget. Since I'm a writer who has enjoyed writing poetry since I was ten years old, I thought it would be fitting to write a funny rendition of "The Night Before Christmas" to recount our story.

I only had time to come up with a few lines before the end of the shift, but I posted what I wrote on Facebook, along with the photo of Lynn on the floor beside the fallen tree. I told my co-workers I had a surprise for them on Facebook and enjoyed watching their reactions when they saw the post. We shared a few more laughs, and we ended up getting many "likes" and comments on Facebook.

Later, when I had more time, I wrote the following lengthier version. It may be a little "cheesy," but I believe it summarizes one of my funniest Christmas memories ever!

'Twas a night before Christmas, when all through the hospice house,
Not a creature was stirring, not even a mouse;
The stockings were hung in the lobby with care
In hopes that Saint Nicholas would soon be there.
The patients were nestled all snug in their beds,

With visions of angels dancing in their heads.
My nursing assistant, Lynn, had been as helpful as can be,
So, I settled in to chart while she decorated the Christmas tree.
But at 4:00 a.m., there arose such a clatter
That I sprang from my chair to see what was the matter;
Away to the dining room I flew like a flash
To find Lynn on the floor, the Christmas tree crashed!
I offered her a hand without hesitation,
Thinking this was a scene from *Christmas Vacation*.
Then, what to my watering eyes should appear,
But the whole night shift staff hunched over, in tears.
On Dasher, on Ashley, on Lynn and Blixen,
Before Santa comes here, this tree needs fixin'!
Shards of red glass covered the floor, all the way to the hall;
Now, sweep away, sweep away, sweep away all!
The rest of the night, there was an ache in my belly
From bouts of laughter making it jiggle like jelly.
What a blessing to shed tears that were happy, not sad,
And report to the day staff what a fun night we'd had.
By the end of the shift, there wasn't a trace of the mess;
The place was nice and festive, and we all felt blessed.
Together we finished decorating the tree
In the Christmas spirit, our hearts full of glee.
Leaving work that morning, with the sun shining bright,
My soul was full, my heart happy and light.
So, as I got in my car and drove out of sight
I shouted, "Merry Christmas to all! 'Twas for all a good night!"

— Mandy Lawrence —

25

The Trashy Turquoise Tree

The Christmas tree is a symbol of love, not money.
There's a kind of glory to them when they're all lit up
that exceeds anything all the money in the
world could buy.
~Andy Rooney, Andy Rooney:
60 Years of Wisdom and Wit

It was the winter break of my final year of university, and I had run out of money. I didn't own a credit card and I had tapped out all of my student loans.

Christmas was coming, but my financial woes ensured I would not be able to get into the holiday spirit anytime soon. Pondering my situation, I started cleaning my residence for what would be my final year. When I went out to deposit the garbage inside the shed that held the bins, I noticed that someone had thrown away a small, ragtag, artificial Christmas tree. It had seen far better days and reminded me of the Charlie Brown Christmas tree I'd seen on TV. To top it off, it was a hideous hue of bright turquoise. I didn't mind the color, but it seemed more than a little garish for a holiday tree.

In any case, I felt sorry to see the poor tree lying there. It looked about as sad as I felt that holiday season. Since I was broke and wouldn't be buying any decorations, I decided to save the tree and put it up in my place. How bad could it be?

And so it was that I came to own a bent-up, trashy turquoise Christmas tree. After I straightened it up a little, I plugged it in, only to find to my amazement that all the lights still worked. Looking around my place, I found some old key chains and other doodads to hang as impromptu decorations. Overall, it didn't look too bad, blending in with the décor of my makeshift student apartment.

I propped the tree up on top of my TV so the twinkly bulbs would reflect against my window. Then I left the lights on to look at from outside, as I headed across campus to the library. Once outdoors, I was amazed to notice a group had gathered outside, looking up at my window. As raggedy and small as it looked indoors, from down below it appeared to be the top section of a tall, elegant tree. On that dark, snowy night, it was stunningly beautiful. In that unexpected magical moment, the tree and I were both transformed.

The resurrected tree immediately made me feel better and calmer, enough so that I could finally sit down and begin planning my finances for my last school term. I started filling out applications for credit cards, as well as several student bursary grants. Through it all, my turquoise tree twinkled warmly at me. It was starting to feel more like Christmas.

Soon afterward, a credit card arrived in the mail, as well as two bursary checks. I was stunned at my good luck, suddenly finding myself with enough funds to scrape through the rest of the school term. What a relief! And I owed it all to my tree. I certainly could feel the warm Christmas cheer now.

The rest of the year passed quickly, and as I planned to move on into the working world, I gave away the odds and ends that passed for furniture during my time as a student. But I couldn't bring myself to get rid of that turquoise tree, which had helped me through such a desperate, rough patch.

That tree was the catalyst that marked a turning point in my life. My epiphany came when the twinkly tree inspired me enough to change my attitude and plan my way through adversity.

So now, years later, my family still puts up that trashy turquoise tree. It reminds all of us to stay as humble as possible, and that often just a slight change of attitude can get us through a very tight spot.

Every Christmas, it holds a place of pride in our home and has always been a great conversation piece over the holidays.

— Sergio Del Bianco —

26

My Elf Extraordinaire

Children are the rainbow of life.
Grandchildren are the pot of gold.
~Irish Blessing

When it came to decorating, both my daughters teased I didn't have a Martha Stewart bone in my body. On holidays, I left it up to them to add the necessary pizzazz.

Since they planned on trimming my Christmas tree the upcoming weekend, I decided to drag out the decorations. I'd retrieved only one box from the storage closet when my younger daughter called asking if I'd babysit later that afternoon. When it came to spending time with my four-year-old grandson, the answer was always "yes."

Planning to make Randy super happy, I whipped up a batch of his favorite sugar cookies with those "little blue sprinkle thingies." Then, I set out dozens of colorful building blocks and a battery-operated toy dump truck to keep him occupied.

With a few minutes to spare before the little guy arrived, I rummaged through the closet for more boxes of ornaments and imagined my daughters working their magic on our twelve-foot, pre-lit Aspen Fir. Smiling to myself, I pictured friends and relatives spellbound by a beautifully adorned tree that would put Macy's holiday window display to shame.

My daydreaming was interrupted when Randy skipped in the door, raced past the playthings, and stopped in front of the giant tree in awe. Then he made a beeline to the open closet and pulled out a box of keepsake decorations my grown children had made when they were younger. He tugged it over to the Christmas tree and went to work.

I watched with delight as he stretched his chubby, little hands and hung a gingerbread man "just right" at his level on the lowest branch. Then he picked up a play-dough wreath with a school photo inside and studied it for several moments before placing it alongside the gingerbread guy.

He turned, wiped his forehead in exaggeration, and sighed. "Whew! I'm really tired."

Trying hard not to laugh, I asked, "Buddy, would you like some hot chocolate? You've been working awfully hard."

"Yep, and I'm gonna need some cookies, too."

After he filled his belly, I suggested we play, but Randy wanted to finish the job. I handed him a Popsicle-stick sled that his mommy had made when she was a little girl. After scrutinizing her workmanship, he nestled it between the other two ornaments.

Randy continued to hang ornaments on that one low branch. While he pondered what to do with a cardboard caboose, I reached over and moved the papier-mâché angel a little higher, hoping he wouldn't notice. Randy looked up and gave me the stink eye. "Grandma, don't touch!"

A big frown creased his forehead as he stood on tippy-toes and tugged at the cherub, sending it flying. He picked it up by a wing and put it back where it belonged. Then he grinned and meticulously added a toy drum. He must have decided the pinecones were ugly because he tossed them aside and went for a clay handprint that framed a drawing of Rudolph. When he grabbed the red-and-white-striped candy cane made of pipe cleaners, he studied it so long that I was afraid he'd try to eat it.

The magical afternoon flew by as I watched my grandson become a tree-decorating elf extraordinaire.

He saved the star for last. After turning it in all directions, he carefully placed it on top of a cotton-ball snowman in the middle of the ornament "bunch." His mother walked in just as he finished.

She winked at me and whispered, "Don't worry, Mom. We'll trim your tree this weekend."

Randy overheard. His lip stuck out in a pout, and his little shoulders slumped.

I shook my head. "That won't be necessary; it's perfect just the way it is."

The look of pride on my grandson's face was priceless.

Once or twice in the days before Christmas, I considered rearranging the ornaments. But each time I walked into the family room, a smile spread across my face, and I couldn't bring myself to disturb Randy's masterpiece.

Christmas Eve, when all our family members arrived, everyone chuckled over the mostly bare tree. One proud Grandma, I let everyone know Randy had decorated it all by himself. Basking in the attention, he'd bow and dance a little jig whenever anyone commented on his work.

When it came time for our annual Christmas photo, his mom said, "You don't expect us to stand in front of that Charlie Brown Christmas tree, do you?"

Grinning, I replied, "Only if you want to open your presents."

Although many Christmases have come and gone, no other tree has brought me half as much joy as the one decorated by my elf extraordinaire.

— Alice Muschany —

27

The Missing Ornament

I swear I couldn't love you more than I do right now,
and yet I know I will tomorrow.
~Leo Christopher

As I hung the golden harp ornament on the Christmas tree, I was transported back to my wedding day in Ireland when the gentle pluck of the strings filled our ears with heavenly music as I walked down the aisle. The next ornament, a porcelain red door, represented our first home. An ornament of a white riverboat reminded me of a weekend exploring historic Savannah. Hand-carved angels with brightly colored clothing brought back memories of our engagement in Peru. Blue starfish came from a boardwalk in Santa Barbara.

Decorating my Christmas tree is an experience that I cherish and look forward to every year, as each ornament comes with a special memory. When Dave and I first moved in together, we started an ornament tradition. We agreed to buy an ornament each year that represented an important moment or memory from that year. Most of our ornaments were from places we traveled or represented milestones in our lives.

I stepped back to admire the illuminated tree adorned with the memories from our first few years of marriage. It always made me smile to see our memory tree. But for some reason, this year felt different. There was an ornament that I had been hoping to buy for a long time. It would be the one to represent having our first baby. I always thought that after Dave and I were married, we would soon be ready to start a family. "Let's just have time to enjoy being married. We don't need to think about having kids right away," Dave said shortly after our wedding. So that's what we did.

After a few years, the topic of children was brought up again. This time, the answer was much different. "I don't know if I ever want to have children," Dave said. When I heard those words, I felt like I couldn't breathe. How could this be? The man I loved, trusted, and married had changed his mind about having a family. I was shocked and heartbroken. I was just about to turn thirty-four and my biological clock was ticking.

Dave tried to paint a picture of the wonderful life we could have traveling the world. I didn't know what to think. In that moment, I felt that I had two choices: I could stay married to Dave and try to accept that he didn't want children — knowing that one day I might regret this choice — or I could leave my husband and start over again.

After a lot of tears and discussion, we decided not to make any decisions right away. We would take some time to think about what we wanted to do. After the holidays, I took the ornaments off the tree and carefully wrapped them in tissue paper. We got back into our normal routine, but one thing was different: Neither of us brought up the topic of children.

Fast forward to the next Christmas. My excitement for hanging the ornaments had disappeared. I was even considering not taking the Christmas tree out of storage and skipping it all together. Dave asked, "Hey, how come you haven't put up the tree? It's always your favorite thing to do."

"I just don't feel up to it this year," I replied. I went to bed without even saying goodnight.

The next morning, Dave woke me up early and told me there was a surprise waiting in the living room. I went downstairs, and there it was: the Christmas tree with the ornaments hanging. The angels, the harp, the red door — all of them were on the tree.

"Not really a surprise, but thanks anyway," I said as I turned around to go back to bed.

"Wait," he said gently. "There is a new ornament that I would like you to add. It's been missing for a while now, and I want you to be the one to put it on the tree."

He handed me a small red box. I opened it, and tears filled my eyes. It was an ornament of three snowmen with the words "Daddy" and "Mommy," and a little snowman that said, "Baby." I hugged him and put the missing ornament on the tree. This small object in my hand was not just something to hang on the tree. It was my husband saying to me that he was ready to have a baby and start our family. It was one of the greatest gifts I have ever been given. To this day, when I look at my tree, it is still my favorite one. And now that I am pregnant with our first child, it is even more meaningful.

— Jessica Harrington —

28

Operation Christmas Tree Removal

The most treasured heirlooms are the sweet memories
of our family that we pass down to our children.
~Author Unknown

I n our family, traditions play an important role in celebrating Christmas. There is the rich and creamy peppermint eggnog that must be made on Christmas Eve for Santa and his helpers, along with the delicious and brightly frosted sugar cookies cut into the shape of candy canes, bells, Christmas trees, and gingerbread men. Some traditions have carried over from my own childhood, including the reading of *The Night Before Christmas*, Christmas Eve candlelight service, and the anticipation and excitement of choosing and opening one present on Christmas Eve before quickly heading to bed so Santa does not catch us still awake.

One of my favorite traditions is when our family of five piles into the car a few weeks before Christmas and heads to our local tree farm to cut down our own Christmas tree. One year, we chose a tree that was not particularly spectacular in height or fullness. In fact, it had some bare spots and some of the branches grew at an odd angle. But this tree had been chosen unanimously by our family; it was perfect for us.

Once it had been set upright in its stand in a picture-perfect setting next to the fireplace, we set to decorating it. While my husband and I tried to quickly hang the breakable ornaments in the higher branches, the kids overloaded the lower branches with their handmade toothpick stars covered in silver glitter, the thumbprint-inked angel, pom-pom snowmen, and a host of other Sunday school and preschool craft-inspired ornaments we collected every year.

As I hooked the ornaments onto the branches, I noticed a strange lump on the otherwise smooth tree trunk. When I questioned my husband about it, he assured me that it was nothing more than a minor aberration in the trunk's development as it grew. After all, this was our own version of the Charlie Brown Christmas tree, so we should expect a few oddities.

Once we got all the ornaments and twinkling lights up, our flawed tree was transformed into a stunning display of Christmas spirit standing tall in our family room. It was a thing of beauty, which was enhanced throughout the weeks leading up to Christmas Day by the growing pile of brightly patterned packages and gift bags encircling its base.

On Christmas Eve morning, I went downstairs to cook breakfast for the kids and finish up last-minute holiday chores in preparation for our fun tradition-filled Christmas Eve. As I quickly strode past the tree on my way into the kitchen, I thought my vision was a little out of focus since the tree appeared to be moving. I shook my head and continued on to my chores. After breakfast, the two older boys went into the family room to inspect the packages under the tree. This had become their daily routine to see if there were any new gifts added while they slept, and in keeping with brotherly competition, to make sure they each had the same number of gifts waiting for them.

Suddenly, the oldest screamed, "Mom! There are bugs all over the tree and on our presents!" I dropped the pan I was washing and ran into the room to see that there were indeed bugs crawling all over the tree, under the tree, on the chair beside the tree, on the wall behind the tree, on the floor — just about everywhere within a twenty-foot radius of our glorious tree! The tree did indeed look like it was moving because there were over one hundred newly hatched, tan-colored praying mantises exploring their new home looking for food.

That strange lump on the trunk had been an egg sac.

This discovery, and perhaps my loud scream, quickly brought my husband into the room, where he took charge of Operation Tree Removal. He barked orders like a drill sergeant. I boxed up the breakable ornaments, while the kids pulled all the gifts out and put them on the back deck. My husband unplugged the lights, unscrewed the tree stand, and hauled the tree out to the back deck. There it leaned against the deck railing in the cold with ornaments askew, light cord trailing, and creepy crawlies moving all over it.

I began the cleanup work inside by vacuuming walls, floors, fireplace hearth and chairs. We tried to shake out the gift bags, wipe down the wrapped boxes, and gently shake the tree branches in an effort to release the praying mantises into the wilds of our back yard.

After hours of cleanup, we brought everything back inside, knowing full well that we brought some of those little critters back inside, too. The tree stood upright once again in our family room, but it was missing ornaments and looked a bit worse for the wear. I trudged on with my chores but could not shake the feeling of disappointment that our cookie baking and eggnog mixing would now be rushed and overshadowed by the constant announcements from my kids: "I caught another one!" The boys did not want to leave the family room to make the cookies. They were having too much fun catching praying mantises and releasing them outdoors.

My Christmas spirit took a nosedive that day.

The next morning, the kids rushed downstairs and squealed with delight over the gifts Santa had left for them. As we all sat around the tree, we laughed at the praying mantises watching us from the branches and peeking out from inside gift bags. We joked that Santa probably left our house with a few in his sack, too. By the end of that morning, we were all in high spirits and having as much fun watching and learning about God's little prayer warriors as with all the new gifts we had just opened.

That Christmas was not our usual holiday. It took an unexpected turn and created a family memory. To this day, my kids reminisce about that memorable Christmas more than any other holiday story, and they cannot talk about it without laughing. We even have a special ornament that now hangs on our Christmas tree every year — a praying mantis — but it now hangs on an artificial tree!

—Grace Rice—

29

The Christmas Tree Resistance

The smell of pine needles, spruce and the smell
of a Christmas tree, those to me,
are the scents of the holidays.
~Blake Lively

Growing up, I thought that setting up a Christmas tree was an act of convenience. One simply went into the attic, hauled down a box of plastic tree branches and, within an hour, voilà! A perfectly fine Christmas tree would be standing in the middle of the living room.

It was pretty convenient. Everyone likes convenience, yes?

Well, maybe not. You see, when it comes to Christmas trees, I discovered there are two kinds of people: the artificial-tree people and the real-tree people.

I was a proud member of the artificial tribe and, quite frankly, often scoffed at the real-tree people and all their silly ways. Watching fresh Christmas trees on roofs of cars pass us on the boulevard were often met with a defiant "Pffft" from me or my brother.

Why on earth would anyone go to the trouble of getting a real tree when they could simply use the same one over and over again? Oh, those wacky real-tree people!

Years later, after I got married, my husband (from the other tribe) insisted on getting a real tree. I resisted with all my artificial-tree heart, but not wanting to be a total Scrooge, I (reluctantly) submitted.

I was surprised at how much I actually enjoyed the fresh scent of pine wafting through the house. And getting the tree wasn't terribly inconvenient, as we bought it at the corner grocer.

Once my son was born, however, my husband took it a step further, suggesting that we join a completely new tribe — an extreme-tree tribe in my book. "Let's go to Jones Family Farm in Connecticut and cut one down ourselves."

"Cut one down?" said me, the artificial-tree girl from Queens. "Are you crazy? We can just go to the corner grocer and buy one!"

Eager for "the experience," he insisted we drive an hour and a half away to the farm, climb up a mountain and cut down our very own — meant just for us — Christmas tree.

I resisted.

Each December, I tried to sway the lumberjack out of my husband. "It's such a long drive," I'd complain, "and we have to hike up the mountain, that cold mountain, just to get a tree! It makes no sense!"

As the years went by, I must admit, my resistance faded… and faded.

It was impossible to ignore the joy my son displayed when he was old enough to share in the choosing and sawing process. Seeing him and my husband sweat and smile together — positioning the saw at just the right angle under the branches — shed a new light on my real-tree prejudice. And walking behind my son as he proudly dragged his tree down the hill can only be described as a Currier & Ives moment.

My Christmas real-tree resistance is now a thing of the past.

People often refer to the "Christmas rush" and how that rush steals away their joy from a holiday that is meant to bring inner peace. My son is now in college, and with the stress of daily life, it's rare that we experience that peace. It's even rarer we get to spend an entire day together.

Choosing and cutting down our own Christmas tree takes an entire day, but it is a glorious day of making memories! The drive to Connecticut as we listen to Christmas carols, hiking the hill as nature declares her undeniable beauty, the sawing, the hauling — it's completely inconvenient… and totally worth every minute. None of us would ever want to miss this very special tradition.

I am — and will forever be — a happy member of the real-tree tribe. I am no longer part of the resistance.

— Mary C. M. Phillips —

30

First Married Christmas

At the height of laughter, the universe is flung into a
kaleidoscope of new possibilities.
~Jean Houston

Earl and I had been married barely five months when December rolled around; it would be our first holiday season together. Because I am Jewish and he is not, I told him that I didn't want him to forsake his holiday for mine: Hanukkah. We made a mutual decision to celebrate both. Then he told me that boxes and boxes of his parents' Christmas ornaments were in the garage — some of them antique — plus he had lights for decorating the outside of the house. I was excited. This was going to be fun!

The next day, Earl got out the ladder, climbed up to the eaves and arranged old-fashioned strings of lights all around the house and the bushes. They weren't the kind we see these days, with iridescent, neon colors and icicles, but the basic type with big bulbs in primary colors. As dusk descended, the house blazed with color.

That evening, we drove over to our neighborhood Christmas tree lot. We walked through the lot searching for that special, perfect tree. We both had ideas about what "perfect" meant, and eventually we found one: not too tall, too short, too wide or too skimpy. My husband picked up the tree and carried it over to the lot attendant. He set it down and told the attendant that he would bring the car around. The guy nodded, placed the tree across two wooden sawhorses, and proceeded to start unscrewing the stand.

"Wait!" I chirped at the guy. "What are you doing?"

"I'm removing the stand," he said with an impatient sigh, as though he was trying to explain something simple to a child. He reached back down to continue removing the stand.

"No!" I said a little louder. I couldn't imagine why he was removing the stand. "We need the stand."

He stopped and looked up at me, his eyes bugging out ant-like. He kept unscrewing the stand. I whipped around. Earl wasn't that far away.

"Honey!" I called. "Honey, come quick!"

He turned around and jogged back with a look of worry sketched across his face. "What's wrong?"

I pointed to the lot attendant. "He's removing the stand from the tree. I told him to stop, but he won't."

This time, the man did stop. He looked at my husband with a perturbed expression, his bugged-out eyes growing larger by the second. I thought he was going to ask Earl what planet I was from. Earl let out a rip-roaring laugh.

"It's okay, Jeffree. He's supposed to take it off."

"What?" I asked, planting my fists on my hips. "How is the tree supposed to stand up in our house if it doesn't have a stand? Maybe I don't know much about Christmas, but I do know the laws of physics. A cut tree isn't going to stand up on its own." I felt rather proud of my insight and thought that maybe the lot attendant would finally understand why he couldn't remove the stand.

"Jeffree, Christmas trees don't come with stands," he started to explain. "We'll purchase one at a store."

"Why on earth would we do that," I asked, "when it's got a perfectly good one on it right now?"

This seemed so obvious to me. I was getting a little bothered with both of them. He looked at the lot attendant, who continued to shake his head in astonishment.

"Hon, there are special tree stands that are better than these in the lot. These are temporary," he explained.

"Better how?" I pressed, not convinced that we needed to spend money on a stand.

"I'll show you; just let the man finish, and we'll go buy the stand." I could see that my new husband was trying really hard not to smile. A tiny grin escaped anyway, which was not lost on the attendant.

I was clearly losing the argument and decided to let it go. I got in the car while the attendant finished removing the tree stand and placed our tree on the top of the car. Earl paid the man and tied down the tree, and we drove over to a big discount store.

I was still unhappy about losing the stand when Earl led me to an entire row of boxes labeled "tree stands." He took down a display stand and showed me how it was like a bucket with screws protruding through the sides. When tightened around the trunk, the screws would anchor the tree and keep it standing straight up. He also pointed out that the tree would need water to prevent it from drying out, and the bucket shape would hold water. Finally, I got it. All of a sudden, I felt like an idiot.

"Why didn't you tell me this at the lot?"

"Are you kidding? That little display between you and the attendant was the most entertaining thing I've watched all week!"

I wasn't just embarrassed; I realized that I had a lot to learn about the logistics of Christmas. Walking toward the registers, we passed a display of ornaments hanging on a fake tree. I stopped and stared, pointing to one. "Look, honey, there's an ornament for people like me."

Earl gazed at all the ornaments, not sure which one caught my attention. I stepped closer and touched a shiny green one. "Look, it's shaped like a kosher pickle, even with the little bumps," I said. "They must have made these pickle ornaments for families like ours."

He smiled, and I took down the pickle, cradling it in my hand. Years later, I learned that my ornament wasn't a kosher pickle replica made for mixed families. But that evening, my husband was gracious enough not to tell me that the pickle was an old German Christmas tradition. He probably figured that I'd had enough of a Christmas education and embarrassment for one night.

—Jeffree Wyn Itrich—

Chapter
4

Making
Traditions

31

Two Trees

Family means no one gets left behind or forgotten.
~David Ogden Stiers

"Is that our Christmas tree? You have to be kidding. It's so skinny, and it has roots!" I complained as my stepdad, Galen, dragged the live tree into our home. The decorations had been brought out of the attic and sat on the floor, waiting to be hung on the unworthy tree.

"Where are the wooden ornaments?" I asked my mom.

Her reply confused and angered me. "We are not going to put those on the tree anymore. We want to start fresh with memories of our new, combined family."

In that moment, the grief over my father's death overwhelmed me. "I hate this scrawny tree. I hate my new family. I hate my new life."

My family had always bought a freshly cut tree. It was so tall that it skimmed the ceiling, and it was so plump that it took up half the room. We began with the lights, as I assume most families do, and moved onto the ornaments, recalling memories of Christmases past as we hung ornaments on just the right branches. Wood blocks cut into triangles, circles, and rectangles held our precious family photographs.

Change thrust itself upon me at the early age of twelve, and I did not welcome it. My father passed away from a malignant brain tumor, and within a year of his death, my mom remarried. My stepdad, Galen, had lost his wife in a tragic hit-and-run. I was the second-born of four children, and my stepdad had three children of his own. When my mom and stepdad married, we became a family of nine! It was so much change, so fast.

All nine of us most comfortably fit into my stepdad's home, an hour away from everything I ever knew as home. So, my mom, brother, two sisters and I packed up our lives and started over in his home, with his kids, their schools and their stuff.

Christmas came only five months after that move. Surely, I thought, there would be something familiar in this familial celebration. Instead, his family's tradition of purchasing a live Christmas tree to replant in their wooded back yard replaced the most cherished tradition I knew growing up. I didn't think I had anything more to lose from life until Galen walked in with that skinny Christmas pine. As a newly turned thirteen-year-old, I wanted nothing to do with it. And because my parents perceived this, they decided to put in place a compromise for future Christmases.

The second Christmas with my combined family ushered in new traditions again, but this time the change was easier to embrace. After my stepdad again dragged in the skinny, live tree, a second tree followed. It was tall and fat, and just like the ones I recalled from all the years my dad was still alive. The live tree found a home in front of the bay window of our living room where it held family ornaments — some new, collected for our two families combined, and some old ones from when I was a little girl. The wooden block ornaments were resurrected. The fat, cut tree became the showcase tree. It sat in our dining room where company enjoyed looking at the carefully curated way in which my mom decorated it. It was a tree worthy of a spot in the Martha Stewart catalogue.

Now that I am an adult, I appreciate and even applaud how my mother and stepdad skillfully parented us through an incredibly challenging time in all of our lives. I know now what I simply could not comprehend then — that my parents were doing the very best they knew how to do for all of us, trying to meet everyone's needs and measure out as much comfort and stability as they could muster.

Making room for two Christmas trees was no small feat, but my parents made the effort. They moved furniture. They found the money.

They made it happen. Because they loved my siblings and me, they did all they could to soften the blow of Christmases that were missing people — a mom and a dad.

Now I am the mom, and every Christmas I drag my family out to the fields to find the perfect Christmas tree. I gravitate toward the roundest, tallest one we can find to fit under our eight-foot ceilings. And every year this tradition reminds me of my mom and stepdad, two people with two big hearts, who brought two families together each December under two Christmas trees.

— Briana Almengor —

32

Mom Knows Best

When you look at your life, the greatest happinesses
are family happinesses.
~Dr. Joyce Brothers

There comes a time when every mother reaches the end of her rope. That's what happened the Christmas of 1983 when we experienced Mom's version of *Shock and Awe*.

I am the oldest of six kids — five girls and one boy. Growing up, our different personalities often clashed, and Mom found herself repeatedly refereeing petty arguments. Each of us fiercely defended our viewpoint because if Mom couldn't determine who was at fault, we all got in trouble.

That Christmas, Mom was determined to put an end to the arguing, even if it was only for a little while. She had had enough. She loudly declared we weren't going to get any presents until we said one nice thing to each other.

Cue the groans and eye rolling. It made no difference. When Mom makes up her mind, that's it.

The compliments came slowly at first, but she didn't care. She was perfectly content to sit and stare at us all day if that's how long it took.

As Mom tells the story, the compliments were random and rudimentary. We barely looked at each other, focusing instead on the presents waiting in our laps.

Begrudgingly, Mom and Dad finally gave us our presents since technically we had fulfilled her request, and Christmas went on as usual.

But that wasn't the last of Mom's big idea.

The next year, she made the same proclamation. This time, she wasn't settling for anything less than sincere. We wondered what everyone was going to say.

By the third year, we were getting the hang of it. One nice thing became many. In the months leading up to Christmas, we would take note of a kind deed or special achievement so we could use it come present time.

After a while, being nice came easier. Mom would smile proudly, taking in every word we said as we sat around the living room… hoping the good feelings would last a little longer before the next petty argument erupted.

I was thirteen when she first had that ridiculous idea. I am forty-seven now, and we still can't open presents until we say something nice to each other.

What began as a punishment all those years ago has become a beloved family tradition. Even spouses, who aren't quite sure what to make of it at first, learn to enjoy it.

Over the years, our compliments became more and more meaningful. It is the moment in our family Christmas celebration that we all look forward to most. It gives us permission to say what we don't take time to say throughout the year. It is a moment often filled with belly laughter as inside jokes and funny stories from the year are woven into a meaningful pat on the back.

We can most certainly count on a few tears as well. The tears come not just from the person to whom the kind words are spoken, but also from the giver of the kind words, overwhelmed and reminded that our family is strong and we have each other's backs — always.

The six of us, now grown with our own families, are spread out all over the country. We don't have nearly as many opportunities to argue, and we've come to terms with our differences. In fact, we love hanging out together.

Maybe it's because Mom taught us to overlook the irritating parts and notice the good in each other. Maybe it's because Mom taught us to look each other in the eye and really talk. Maybe it's because we learned we could disagree sometimes and still find reason to offer sincere praise. Thanks, Mom.

—Allison Andrews—

33

Tangerines and Walnuts

The happiest moments of my life have been
the few which I have passed at home in the
bosom of my family.
~Thomas Jefferson

I called it my "Johnny Stocking." It was made of red felt that had a white, fur-like material sewn around the top. My name, Johnny, was written in script from the mid-calf down to the ankle using glitter-on-glue.

My childhood home on Hayes Road, near Groveport, Ohio, didn't have a fireplace. Thus, we had no mantel from which to hang our stockings. So Mom placed our empty stockings on our itchy green sofa, assuring us that Santa Claus would find them. And there they lay — lined up like soldiers — three red felt stockings that boasted the names Johnny, Jerry, and Joey.

But with no chimney, how was Santa Claus going to get inside in the first place? Again, Mom reassured me, stating, "Don't worry. Santa Claus will come." And he did. To this very day, Mom doesn't know that I snuck out of bed on Christmas Eve, slipped down the hall, and unlocked the front door.

That Christmas morning of 1963 was a joyous occasion. Like any boy, I was more interested in the toys that I would find under the tree than in the contents of my Johnny Stocking. So the first thing I did was sprint into the living room and tear into every package that Mom said contained my name. I was ecstatic to get a Mr. Potato Head and a *Candy Land* board game.

Then, as an afterthought, I dumped out my Johnny Stocking. It contained the following items: a tangerine, some whole walnuts, and a chocolate Santa Claus. Two of those three contents caused me to furrow my eyebrows. While I was eager to make quick work of the chocolate Santa, I didn't pay attention to the tangerine and walnuts.

***

A few years later, my boyhood home was on Main Street in Stoutsville, Ohio. Unfortunately, that humble abode didn't have a fireplace either. So again, with no mantel, Mom placed our empty stockings on the same itchy green sofa. Thus, there they lay — lined up like soldiers — five red felt stockings that broadcast the names Johnny, Jerry, Joey, Jeffrey, and Kathy.

Again, I cornered Mom, asking how Santa Claus was going to get in if we had no chimney. Once more, Mom simply repeated, "Don't worry. Santa Claus will come."

Just to be sure, on Christmas Eve, I rolled out of bed in the middle of the night, tiptoed past Mom and Dad's bedroom, ducked downstairs, and unlocked the back door.

Christmas morning of 1967 was no different from that on Hayes Road. The first thing I did was race downstairs and open any present that bore my name. I was elated to get a jungle play set and a Johnny West action figure.

Then I dumped out my Johnny Stocking to find the same old items: a tangerine, some whole walnuts, and a chocolate Santa Claus. Within seconds, the chocolate Santa Claus was gone, and I still overlooked the tangerine and walnuts.

***

In the early 1970s, I lived in what would become my teenage home on Greist Road, near Circleville, Ohio. That house finally had a fireplace — but no mantel from which to hang our stockings. Mom placed our unfilled stockings on the brick hearth where Santa Claus would surely stumble upon them as he exited the chimney. So there they lay — lined up like soldiers — eight red felt stockings that proclaimed Johnny, Jerry, Joey, Jeffrey, Kathy, Mike, Greg, and Steve.

As for Santa Claus getting in, it was no longer a concern. With our Greist Road home having that chimney, I stayed in bed all night that Christmas.

Christmas morning in 1970 was no different from Stoutsville or Groveport. The first thing I did was dash down the hallway and unwrap any boxes that bore my name. I was overjoyed to get a set of plastic, miniature NFL helmets and a book entitled *Make the Team in Football*.

Then, as a postscript, I emptied my Johnny Stocking to find — you guessed it — a tangerine, some whole walnuts, and a chocolate Santa Claus.

But being a little older that Christmas — as I licked the remains of the chocolate Santa from my fingers — I finally asked Mom and Dad about the contents of our stockings. They both admitted to receiving tangerines and whole walnuts in their stockings as children during the Great Depression. They went on to explain how those items were considered to be magnificent treats because nobody ate fresh fruit and nuts year-round except for the wealthiest of children. And my mom and dad certainly didn't fit into that category! Lastly, Mom and Dad said they wanted to continue a tradition that signified hope during hard times.

It's funny how things work out. Now that I am a grown man with diabetes, on Christmas morning, in loving tribute to my parents, I eat a tangerine and some walnuts — but forego the chocolate Santa.

— John M. Scanlan —

34

Ryan's Gift

Love is what's in the room with you at Christmas if you
stop opening presents and listen.
~Author Unknown

I sat in front of the fireplace in early December with a red note-book on my lap, ready to make my Christmas list and hunt for the perfect presents. I printed the names of each of our children: Ross, Alexa, Maddie and… Ryan. Tears formed in my eyes as I looked at his name.

I glanced over at the stockings hanging from the mantel, landing on Ryan's. After Christmas, we'd take it down and pack it away without ever stuffing it.

You see, two years earlier, in July 2014, Ryan, our oldest, my stepson, was killed in a tragic accident.

Without him, the fabric of our family will always be frayed and torn. There will be an empty place, an empty plate at our dinner table, and a smile missing from our holiday pictures.

Turning back to my list, I traced Ryan's name with my fingers. Those letters on the page brought sorrow into this season of happiness.

Maybe we'd start a new tradition, but what? I paused, looking at his name again, and then I prayed, "Please show me something we can do at Christmas in Ryan's memory to give us a sense of hope to ease our hearts. Amen."

A few days later, I was sitting in my writing chair scrolling through Facebook when I saw a story called, "For the Man Who Hated Christmas," by Nancy W. Gavin. I clicked on the link. The story was about Nancy's husband, Mike, and how he hated the commercial aspect of Christmas and the usual gifts. So, one year she made a special donation in Mike's name. That Christmas Eve, she placed an envelope on the tree with a note inside telling him what she'd done, and that this was his gift from her. Well, Mike loved his gift so much that the tradition continued, growing with each passing year.

Nancy's story inspired me and gave me an idea for a way to honor Ryan's memory and help others, too. I decided to keep it a secret and make it a gift for the whole family. So, I did my research and planning during the day while I was the only one home.

I was able to have an ornament made with Ryan's picture on the front and a special message engraved on the back. I wrote a letter explaining the plan and placed it in a Christmas Memories book I bought. I cut out scraps of paper and put them in a bag for a drawing. Then, I wrapped it all up, hid it with the rest of the gifts and waited.

The excitement about this new family tradition had me counting down the days until our holiday celebration. It had ignited something else in me, too. For the first time since Ryan died, I felt joy in the small moments, like singing "It's Beginning to Look a Lot like Christmas," and watching *A Charlie Brown Christmas*. Once again, I was filled with the spirit of the season.

At last, it was the night before we would open our gifts. After everyone else had gone to bed, I tiptoed down the stairs and added the special box to the pile of gifts. I held the ornament in my hand, looking at Ryan's smiling face in the glow of the tree lights, and then I turned it around to read the message inscribed on the back:

Ryan Michael Wozniak
Was a gift
In his memory we give these gifts
This Christmas
And his gift goes on...
1988–2014

Reaching up, I hung it front and center on the tree. I stood for a few more moments, wondering if the rest of the family would think the idea was as great as I did. As I looked at the picture of Ryan's smiling face one more time, I wondered how he'd feel knowing his life had touched so many, and then I went back to bed with my heart filled with anticipation. I spent the rest of the night like a little kid, tossing and turning, looking at the clock to see if it was time yet.

After breakfast, we tore into the stack of gifts under the tree. The special gift was the last one opened. I had my husband Michael, Ryan's dad, open the package, but I said I would read the letter as I didn't know if he would be able to read my handwriting.

For Ryan's 28th year I donated $280 in memory of him this Christmas. Here is how the donations were made:

13 Christmas meals for people at Haven of Rest Ministries.
12 Chicken Soup for the Soul: Angels and Miracles books with the story I wrote called "Hummingbirds from Heaven" (#23) in memory of Ryan, gifted to people who have lost someone they love this year.
2 donations to the Angel Tree providing two children with a Christmas gift, the Gospel, and a loving message given on behalf of their parent in prison.
1 donation to Arts in Stark to help other artists.
28 donations made in Ryan's name.
28 more lives touched by his… and Ryan's gift goes on…

As I read the final sentence, tears filled my eyes, and I had to stop for a moment. I looked around the room and saw more tears. Pretty soon, we were all standing and hugging one another.

Next, it was time for the drawing to see who would get to decide how we would donate the money in memory of Ryan's 29th year. We would move the amount up by $10 each year based on Ryan's age, so the next year we would donate $290.

I had placed pieces of wrapping paper in a plastic bag. They all said

"NO" except for one that said "YES, Christmas 2017." The person who received the YES would get to select the charities we would donate to. I hoped we would be able to continue this tradition for years to come.

Later that night, after everyone had gone home, Michael and I snuggled on the couch eating popcorn while watching *It's a Wonderful Life*. He grabbed my hand and whispered, "Ryan's gift was my favorite gift this year. I only wish he would have been here to see it."

I squeezed his hand as tears threatened again. "Mine, too. And me, too," I said in a low voice. "Do you ever wonder if God gives our loved ones a glimpse into our homes for our special occasions, like for holidays?"

"It's a nice idea, and if so, I'm sure he smiled at what he saw. Finally, a way to remember him at Christmas." He smiled, and we watched as George Bailey learned what a blessing he'd been during his lifetime. Just like Ryan.

— Amy Catlin Wozniak —

Hats and Moustaches Christmas

> *I think the family is the place where the most ridiculous*
> *and least respectable things in the world go on.*
> ~Ugo Betti

My family's first themed Christmas happened accidentally. It was 90 degrees on Christmas morning, but my mom still made her traditional biscuits and gravy. To get out of our hot Southern California kitchen, we decided to eat breakfast on the patio. But as we sat there, it became hotter and hotter, and we were burning in the mid-morning sun.

We were having such a good time that we didn't want to go back into the house, so my brother brought out hats for everyone. He handed my mom a baseball hat. As soon as she put it on, we all started to laugh because she looked exactly like my uncle, her brother. To complete the transformation, all she needed was a moustache. We dug a pack of fake moustaches out of the Halloween box, and she stuck one on. The whole family could barely catch our breath because we were laughing so hard.

Pretty soon, we each had on hats, moustaches and pajamas, and that was how we started our new Christmas family tradition.

Every fall, we officially select a theme for Christmas. On Christmas Day, we dress in costumes and decorate the Christmas tree and dining room table with ornaments and items that go with this theme. In past years, we've had an Alice in Wonderland Christmas, a biker gang Christmas, a *Nightmare Before Christmas* Christmas, a beach Christmas, a candy Christmas, a cowboy Christmas, and more.

We spend months planning, talking about, coordinating, and shopping for themed items. To others, this might sound like a lot of work — and, to be honest, it is — but before our Hats and Moustaches Christmas, our holiday was pretty lame. We'd eat breakfast together, open gifts, sit around and watch TV, and eat. Now, in addition to those things, we put on our costumes, take family photos, and decorate. On biker gang Christmas, we even put fake tattoos on each other and then went to church.

Themed Christmases have brought my family closer. We laugh wildly, tell stories, and make long-lasting memories. Who would have thought one baseball hat and a package of fake moustaches could have such an impact on our family traditions?

— Laurie Decker —

Turkey Red, Turkey Blue

Appreciation can change a day, even change a life.
Your willingness to put it into words
is all that is necessary.
~Margaret Cousins

I n my family, Thanksgiving was not Thanksgiving without turkey notes. When I was a child, I thought every family wrote turkey notes, but later in life I discovered that most people don't even know what they are. A turkey note is a short, rhyming note written on a square of paper, rolled up into a scroll, and wrapped in colored tissue paper. It's kind of like a fancy, inedible, Iowa version of the fortune cookie.

Turkey notes apparently were invented in Davenport, Iowa, where both of my parents were born and raised. The Davenport Public Library has documented a history of turkey notes, which have been around for more than 100 years. But nobody seems to know exactly how these crafty notes were invented or by whom, just that they come from the Davenport area.

My family writes each turkey note on a small piece of white paper, and then rolls that paper up inside two longer different-colored pieces of tissue paper, ties both ends with ribbon, and uses scissors to make fringe of the tissue paper on each end, exposing both colors. When our turkey notes are placed around the Thanksgiving table, one note for each guest, they look like fancy party favors. But the fun messages inside are what really make them turkey notes.

Each turkey note is four lines long. The goal is to make it a clever rhyme or a silly poem. The first three lines usually start with "Turkey..." as in:

Turkey green
Turkey yellow,
Turkey fell
Into the Jell-O!

Turkey notes are supposed to be fun, and as kids we tried to make ours funny. We kids were great at writing silly notes, but our grandmas would be listening, so they had to be clean and nice. Or at least this nice:

Turkey orange
Turkey purple
Turkey thinks
You're going to burp-le!

Over the years, our turkey notes became more sophisticated and more personal, tailored to the recipients. The notes often focused on something that was going on in the person's life, like going off to college, starting a new job, getting married, buying a house, or having a baby. Or simply being the cousin who had brought his fake dog poop to the Thanksgiving feast the year before (more on that later!). Writing turkey notes is a good way to reflect on the past year and catch up with family members we haven't seen for a while.

Traditionally, turkey notes started off with colors, but we ventured into other themes, like:

Turkey hot,
Turkey cool
Turkey's going to
Graduate school!

and (new job):

Turkey serious
Turkey funny
Turkey's making
Lots of money!

and (new house):

Turkey wander
Turkey roam
Turkey bought a
Brand-new home!

And the one we wrote the year after my cousin Karl tried to fool us with his fake dog poop from the novelty store:

Turkey cool,
Turkey hep
Turkey says
"Watch where you step!"

Every Thanksgiving, my mom, dad, sister and I traveled from our home in Wisconsin to Davenport, Iowa to celebrate with both sides of the family. My parents both worked full-time, so there was little time to write the turkey notes before making the journey. Inevitably, we would load the car with suitcases and pumpkin pies and take the turkey-note supplies along. Dad drove, Mom navigated and led the turkey-note composition, and my sister and I chimed in from the back seat. On our way over the river and through the woods to Grandmother's house, we put our heads together and crafted the notes. We were on a mission! The countryside flew by, and the car ride went quickly as we wrote and assembled several turkey notes along the way.

At the Thanksgiving feast, each relative plucked his/her turkey note from its place by his/her plate, untied the ribbons and unrolled the note.

One by one, they read the messages aloud. Sometimes, the messages inspired hoots of laughter; other times, they elicited an "Awwwww!" or a groan from the family. If the note was incredibly crafty, the authors might even receive a short round of applause.

Turkey's single?
No, she's not!
Turkey went and
Tied the knot!

Might be followed by:

Turkey happy
Turkey glad
Turkey's going to
Be a dad!

If someone was having a very bad year, and we couldn't think of something positive to say, they might just receive the best message of all:

Turkey red,
Turkey blue
Turkey says
"I love you!"

If you're looking for a new Thanksgiving tradition, why not try writing turkey notes? Now that you know what they are, you don't have to be from Iowa to write them, or to share and enjoy them!

Turkey brown,
Turkey blue
Turkey says
"You can write 'em, too!"

— Jenny Pavlovic —

Christmas Stockings

*Christmas is a day of meaning and traditions, a special
day spent in the warm circle of family and friends.*
~Margaret Thatcher

Slumped on the couch, I watched my husband decorate
our first Christmas tree. I couldn't move. Every bit of my
body ached with exhaustion. Newlyweds of less than three
months, we should have been celebrating our first Christmas
with joy and anticipation. Instead, I cried as I rested my hand on my
flat belly. Beneath my hand, deep within my womb, our first baby
grew, and my body was roiling with hormones. Our first baby would
arrive in August, and all I could do was cry.

That first emotional Christmas, we filled a tiny stocking for our
unborn baby. As time passed, we settled into our new role as a married
couple. One child was born, then another, and another. Final tally
(including a set of twins): four girls and a boy.

Twenty-seven years later, at midnight on Christmas Eve, I found
myself filling eleven stockings. Once again, exhaustion overwhelmed
me, but it was not the exhaustion of early pregnancy. This fatigue came
from an attempt to fill needs that were all-consuming.

Earlier that year, we had made the decision to become foster parents. Then, we received a phone call in November asking if we would
consider taking four little girls into our home. They were a sibling
group that would be separated otherwise. The four girls included a set
of twins. I couldn't help thinking of our four girls, who also included a

set of twins. Our plan had been to foster two children at a time. Four would be much more than we had bargained for. Still, it felt like it was meant to be.

On a grey day at the end of November, four little girls arrived at our front door, each dragging a garbage bag of clothing behind her. They were beautiful children, but within days it was evident these children were in pain, each with her own unique way of expressing that pain. The oldest, at ten years of age, needed to care for her younger siblings and blocked my every attempt to mother them and her as well. Doors slammed, objects took flight (often in my direction), and yelling shook our house. One night, she stood in front of me crying and yelling. I noticed, at her side, a pair of scissors gripped firmly in her hand. Without thinking, I stepped forward and pulled her into my arms.

She whispered, "Cathy, I have scissors."

I responded, "I know, sweetheart."

I felt her body begin to relax, and I continued to hold her as she cried. Gaining her trust was a slow, painful process.

The second oldest frequently dissolved into hysterical giggling, her emotions riding on waves of hysteria. The twins presented an angry, united front. Individually, one would roll on the floor crying, while the other would cling to me, desperate for affection, her arms wrapped tightly around my neck. To me, they were good children stuck in a bad situation.

The eleven stockings I filled that Christmas were for our five original children, two sons-in-law and our four foster daughters. Their overstuffed bodies lounged in a row across the couch, too heavy to hang. They were mismatched stockings, some old and some new, a raggedy gathering of Christmas splendour. On Christmas morning, I listened to the cries of excitement while the smell of turkey began to seep through the house. I looked around at the faces on that Christmas morning, some old and some new. Our house was full, and so was my heart.

After the year I filled the eleven stockings, I realized I had to make some changes. Too much money and, more importantly, too much time and energy were required. I needed to find a little time for me. Raising all those children left me with a need to redefine myself. Somewhere beneath the "mommy," I had to uncover the woman who still had dreams to fill and plans to make. Gradually, I weaned the kids of the need to have me fill a stocking. I kept coming up with different rules: "When you're twenty-five, you're too old to have a stocking." "When you're married…" "When you have children of your own…" I've whittled it down, but the numbers seem to fluctuate.

Two of the four little foster girls are grown and in university. One chose to be adopted by us. The other keeps a foot in both worlds. The final two girls returned home to their family of origin. The oldest is now a young mother. A piece of my heart is with them always.

This year, I planned for two stockings — one for our adopted daughter and one for her sister, who are both home for Christmas. One of our twins, currently living in Ireland, is home for Christmas along with her twin sister. At twenty-eight, they shouldn't be getting stockings. Yet, just yesterday, she said, "Hey, Mom, Sam and I are both home for Christmas. You can fill stockings for us." She heard my hesitation and said, "How about you do one each for Sam and me, and we'll do one each for you and Dad?" Always an angle. Always the desire for one more stocking. I cave. Why do I give in? Maybe because this daughter has been living abroad for three years. Or perhaps it's because I have a hard time saying "no." Or, could it be the thought of getting my own stocking? Someone is actually going to fill a stocking for me? The mother? Christmas touches the child in all of us, and the child in me seems to be pretty excited.

— Catherine (Cat) Moise —

Hanukkah Lights

To me every hour of the light and dark is a miracle,
Every cubic inch of space is a miracle.
~Walt Whitman, Leaves of Grass

As we lit the Hanukkah menorah during the first winter at our new house twenty years ago, my daughter, who was ten at the time, wanted to know if people could see the lights from the road. I think she was sensitive to ours being the only house in the neighborhood that wasn't strung with Christmas lights and blinking Santas.

"I don't know," I said. "Let's go see."

We removed the curtain, placed the menorah in the front window, and then bundled up and went outside. In the New England snow, our house, which was on top of a small hill next to a farm with a Star of Bethlehem on the silo, looked gorgeous with the small menorah light twinkling at the window. I wanted to stay out there forever under the stars.

We got in the car and drove down the hill. Then we turned so we could pass the house from below. "There it is!" my husband pointed. But it was hard to see.

"I want it to be like the star on the silo," my six-year-old son insisted as we pulled back into the driveway. "I want to see the menorah from far away."

"It doesn't matter. We can see it." I tried to convince them. And then I had an idea. "Hey, let's put menorahs on all sides of the house, and then we can walk around and see them, and the neighbors can see them, too!"

We lit three more menorahs, bundled back into our coats and boots, and crunched all the way around our snowy yard. My daughter started to sing, and we all joined in:

> Oh Hanukkah, oh Hanukkah, come light the menorah
> Let's have a party, we'll all dance the horah
> Gather 'round the table, we'll give you a treat
> Dreidels to play with and latkes to eat.

When we got to the slope at the back of the house, my son stopped singing and flopped down dramatically, rolling all the way to the bottom of the hill. I felt my heart catch, but only until I heard him laughing.

This was so much fun that we did it again on the second night of Hanukkah, and the third, and the fourth, fifth, sixth, seventh, and eighth. Each time we got to the back of the house, my son would engage in a dramatic fall and roll down the hill. Some nights were bitter cold with wind-chills below zero. Others were slick with ice. It didn't matter; in fact, going out to see the Hanukkah lights became a test of our resolve and fortitude. A tradition was born.

The next year, we celebrated Hanukkah with a new arrival — our rambunctious Husky-Shepherd, Lefty. My husband had surprised us by suddenly allowing Lefty to join our family after insisting for years that a "dog should be accompanied by a farm." I interpreted this as meaning he would never live with a dog, not that he would suddenly agree to one now that we had a farm next door.

Lefty loved nothing more than going out for an extra romp on the farm on Hanukkah nights. He caught onto the tradition quickly and started panting the minute he saw candles. He would bark all through the lighting and the blessings, the careful placement of lit menorahs at the windows, and the long process of bundling up. The ground conditions were too unstable to try to control him on a leash, so we let him run. He'd stay with us sometimes as we circled the house, but more often than not, he'd take off across the farm fields tracking the scent of something. To bring him back each night as we were completing our circle, we would sing our song and then add a long and loud — "Left... ty."

There'd be quiet as we waited. Sometimes, we'd have to call a second time or a third, but then we'd hear a rumble in the distance. Out of the dark, he'd come bounding back, jumping on all of us over and over again as if giving an exuberant thank-you for his special Hanukkah present.

Lefty died in 2011, the same year my son left for college. My daughter had already graduated and was living in New York City, so on the first night of Hanukkah that year, the nest was truly empty. After my husband and I lit the Hanukkah candles, I insisted on going out despite the fact that it was four degrees and the ground was covered with a solid glaze of ice. We took ski poles and crept carefully down the ice-coated steps. At the front window, the small light of the menorah exuded warmth, but I felt sad. I missed the kids, even though they were coming in a couple of days to celebrate Hanukkah over the weekend. And I still missed the dog so much.

"We can walk the other way around the house," my husband said. "It's less steep."

I knew the kids would have rebelled at any break in tradition, but I humored him and our old bones. We sang the song. At the end of the last line, I added "Lefty!" Like "Play ball!" at the end of *The Star-Spangled Banner*, the word just belonged there. I even looked across the field, half expecting to see him running toward us, but there was no Hanukkah miracle.

When the kids came that weekend, they insisted on walking in the direction they'd always walked. My son stopped, as usual, at the back of the house and rolled down the hill. We sang the song, and of course they added "Lefty!" to the last line, as we've done every year since then.

With my daughter and son both adding long-term partners to the mix, it's good to see our family growing, and we make a point of celebrating at least a couple of Hanukkah nights together. But I still find myself looking across the field, waiting for that moment of rumbling and the speck of distant movement to get larger and clearer — our joyful dog coming back to us.

— D. Dina Friedman —

All's Fair...

We don't stop playing because we grow old;
we grow old because we stop playing.
~George Bernard Shaw

It's the same every Christmas. My extended family gathers, we share a festive meal, and the kids open their gifts. Soon after, the fighting starts:

"You cheated!"

"No, you did!"

"That's mine! You can't take it!"

Surprisingly, it's not the kids who are yelling at the tops of their voices or wresting gifts from each other's hands. It's the adults.

My family's been playing the Gift Game — also known as Yankee Swap — for more than twenty Christmases now. To play, everyone over age eighteen places a gift in the center of the circle and takes a seat. I pass around a bowl of folded, numbered paper slips. Then the game begins.

Number 1 goes first. He unwraps a gift and displays it for all to see. It might be a can of nuts, a puzzle, or some other generic item. At this point, we all make appreciative noises or polite comments: "Mmm, looks tasty!" or "That's a pretty puzzle." After all, the game hasn't gotten going yet. But it will. Just wait.

Now it's Number 2's turn. She has choices: She can open a new gift, or — if she wants to get this party started — she can steal Number 1's gift. If she does, Number 1 might make a mild protest like, "Hey, I liked that!" or "That's not fair!" But unless it was a really good gift (read: gift card), facial expressions and voice volumes are still appropriately calm at this point. No one has lost control… yet.

If Number 2 does opt to steal, Number 1 — now gift-less — chooses a new gift from the pile. And the game continues with Numbers 3, 4, and so on. One important rule is that a person whose gift was stolen can turn around and steal someone else's; then that person can steal someone else's and so on down the line. So the fun really starts once we reach the middle numbers. By the time we reach 8, 9, and 10, gifts are being lost left and right, everyone's shouting, and people holding the desirable gifts are shielding them with chairs, pillows, and even bodies. The kids have left their new toys to stand around our circle, gaping and giggling at the crazy adults putting on a show.

We're normally a quiet family. But this game brings out the savage in some of us. My sister Lisa, a respectable, well-behaved mother of eleven, has been known to cackle triumphantly while stealing her own offspring's gift! Lisa and her husband José must be watched closely because another rule of the game is this: If your gift has just been stolen from you, you can't turn around and steal it right back. But several years ago, Lisa and José introduced a new twist to the game — the two-way steal.

Say Cousin Cheryl steals Lisa's Caribou Coffee gift card. Lisa can't take the card back from Cheryl, but she can steal her husband's twenty-pack of AA batteries. Then he can steal the Caribou card back from Cheryl. So at the end of the game, Lisa has power in a box and José has two large, decaf turtle mochas. All they have to do is switch with each other.

The game reveals our competitive streaks, too, as each of us strives to bring the most coveted gift. Before gift cards became popular and we raised the spending limit to ten dollars, my mom held the record two years straight for her box of clementine oranges. (The third year, Aunt Sonya topped her by wrapping up *two* boxes of clementines.) Other favored gifts have been a wooden puzzle box (containing a gift card!), an animated butterfly in a jar, and a dissect-your-own-owl-pellet kit. (Some might consider bird vomit undesirable, but as a homeschooling mom, I loved this ready-made science experiment.) People have gotten creative in their choice of container, as well. In recent years, my brother Paul became notable for his prank "Earwax Candle Kit" gift box and his "Mobile Foot Rub" gift-card holder.

Then there was the most notorious gift. Several years ago, when my husband Jory's number came up, I nudged him toward a particular flat package. I was sure it was the candy my mom had told me she was going to buy. However, instead of his favorite almond bark, the box contained an Elvis Christmas ornament. A *singing* Elvis Christmas ornament.

Jory begged every subsequent number to steal his ornament. He displayed it ostentatiously and extolled its (nonexistent) virtues with Vanna-like flourishes. He even kicked it into the center of the circle each time someone stood to pick a new gift! But, shockingly, no one wanted a sparkly tree bauble that blared "Blue Christmas" at the touch of a button. At the end of the night, most of us had useful or edible gifts. A few lucky ones had gift cards. But all my husband had was Elvis. Cousin Dave finally confessed to having brought it, and Jory still hasn't forgiven him.

Even though our game always brings fun to our Christmas gathering, I never thought much about what it means to me. In fact, there were years — back when my twins were infants and I was low on energy — that I suggested forgoing it. But then, two Octobers ago, Aunt Sonya died. The next Christmas, my puzzle-loving aunt wasn't there to steal another player's jigsaw, and I felt her absence in a new way.

Suddenly, I realized that the Christmas Gift Game won't always look the same. People might move. Families with grown-up kids might splinter off to hold their own celebrations. Eventually, our number of players might shrink to the point where the game's not fun to play anymore, and we'll go back to exchanging soap-on-a-rope or salami sticks like we used to. And I will be sad because our game is more than a holiday pastime. It's tradition, togetherness and laughing so hard that my stomach aches and my eyes tear up. In fact, the game has given me some of my best Christmas memories.

In light of that, I will play the game hard while I can. I will wrap my presents cleverly. (Just wait until next Christmas when Paul sees the "Motorized Rolling Pin" gift box I found!) I will train my two daughters in the art of the four-way steal so that when they come of age, they'll be ready to compete. Heck, I might even throw caution to the wind, buy an Elvis — or Elton John, or Justin Bieber — ornament, and wrap it up in classic-car paper, in hopes of enticing hot-rod-loving Cousin Dave to pick it out of the pile.

All's fair in love and Christmas gifting!

— Sara Matson —

40

Random Yule Action Now

If you carry joy in your heart,
you can heal any moment.
~Carlos Santana

Two dozen Byers' Choice Carolers stood in snow glitter on the shelves of the hutch, mouths open, appearing to sing along to the strains of "Jingle Bells" lifting from the speaker. Twinkle lights lit the white pine standing tall in the bay window of our dining room. A stuffed Santa holding a copy of *'Twas the Night Before Christmas* kept watch by the front door while an adorned Flexible Flyer runner sled graced the back entryway.

Each room in between showcased a Christmas landscape set aglow. Our old farmhouse was decked out in all its holiday finery; everything was brimming with the Christmas spirit.

Except for us.

It wasn't so much me as it was my husband Michael. It all started in early December. Packed with the decorations, I'd found a picture of Michael's mom, Patricia, and his son, Ryan, laughing during one of our tree-decorating parties. I'd brought it out to show him, hoping to bring a smile; instead, it had acted as a painful reminder of Christmases past.

"I'm just missing everyone we've lost so much. It's hard to find the joy I usually have at this time of the year," he said one evening at dinner.

I offered words of comfort, but my efforts fell short. Seeing him so down, well, it hurt. In bed that night, I tried to come up with a plan to cheer him up and help him get into the spirit of the holidays. But as I drifted off to sleep, I still didn't have any ideas.

The next day was our day off. Walking has a way of clearing our heads. We got up early and headed out to take our dog for her morning walk at Quail Hollow, our favorite hiking spot. With no snow lining the forest and the ground solid, we took one of the trails that follow the creek. As we rounded the final curve that would take us into the open, I spotted it: a miniature pine set back from the trail. Its green branches stood out amongst the barren trees of December.

"Michael, there's that tree." I stopped and pointed. "Remember?"

"I do." He stopped alongside me. "That's the Charlie Brown Christmas tree you wanted to decorate."

"I still do." I smiled. "Today," I said as I took off in a hurry in the direction of the car. "Let's go find decorations for it." I turned back to him with a big smile on my face.

At Target, we found some tiny solar snowflake lights. Back home, we gathered small mementos from our personal decorating collection. I packed the miniature red-and-blue crocheted mittens we used on Michael's mom's tree the last Christmas she was with us, along with some buffalo plaid ribbon and a few plastic bulbs in gold and burgundy.

I didn't see what Michael grabbed, as he was waiting by the door when I came down the steps.

Up close, the tiny tree wasn't as sturdy as it looked from the trail. We wrapped the lights around it, and then placed the ribbon and mittens on it.

I'd brought along a special surprise. "In memory of Ryan," I said as I pulled the *It's a Wonderful Life* brass angel from my pocket. We'd purchased it some time ago, but hadn't found a use for yet. It's inscribed with the words, "Every time a bell rings, an angel gets its wings."

Michael had his own surprise. From the bag he'd brought along he pulled out a poster board sign that read, "We decorated this tree in memory of our son who loved to walk in these woods. Please sign here in memory of someone you miss this Christmas." He stuck the sign along with a Sharpie tied to a string into the ground beside the decorated tree.

It was still light outside when we finished our decorating. When we reached the other side of the trail, we could see the sparkle of the tiny lights shining through the woods. It made us smile. Those smiles came home with us, and so did the Christmas spirit we'd been lacking. All we'd needed was that little tree.

Soon after our decorating day, the weather turned brutal. With wind chills in the negative teens, it was too cold for us to venture out to walk.

Finally, on Christmas Eve morning, there was a break in the cold. The snow was falling; it would be a white Christmas. We bundled up and headed out to the trail. As we rounded the corner and came upon the little tree, we could see it was bent over from the weight of the snow, but the lights were still visible. When we got up close, we found it still held all the decorations.

But the most exciting part was Michael's sign. People had written the names of loved ones they had lost and notes with well wishes for us. Each signature filled our hearts. It made our whole Christmas.

I knew this was something we would continue to do each year — a new tradition. I'm already in search of another little tree somewhere to decorate. I tried to come up with something we could call these random acts of decorating, finally landing on Random Yule Action Now or R.Y.A.N. *For Ryan,* I thought.

These days when we pass that little tree, we smile, knowing that although it's small, it is mighty. Not only did it hold up in the elements, even with our decorations, but it lifted the weight from our hearts and brought joy to everyone who saw it.

— Amy Catlin Wozniak —

Chapter 5
Christmas Kindness

41

A Musical Gift

Without a sense of caring, there can be
no sense of community.
~Anthony J. D'Angelo

From my small apartment, the tune of "Good King Wenceslas" blared from my son's shiny brass trumpet. My eight-year-old son, Jimmy, was practicing for his first Christmas concert in the school orchestra. Jimmy is autistic, and his music teacher recommended he play an instrument to improve his attention span. He had noticed his musical aptitude.

The cost of the trumpet was steep for me, but by carefully budgeting and cutting coupons, I was able to make the monthly payment. No sacrifice was too great to help my son improve his skills.

School was difficult for Jimmy. He'd often get lost on the way to and from the building. Sometimes, he would mentally withdraw during class to escape from difficult social demands, typical of kids on the autism spectrum. He had special accommodations in the classroom to help keep him on target, including a personal aide.

The Christmas of 1998 was going to be lean as usual. I had been a single parent for the past few years, and my income had been drastically reduced since my divorce. Money became even tighter when I was laid off earlier that fall.

I was good at making do with what we had. We had seen hard times before. To cut costs, I packaged homemade cookie gifts in decorative tin canisters that I had been collecting throughout the year. My freezer was packed full of cherries, which Jimmy and I had picked in the summertime from my mother's orchard. Mom lived nearby, and we visited her farm home often. Putting Mom's cherries to good use, I made pies for gifts.

Focusing on the true meaning of Christmas, I thanked God for everything he had blessed us with — my parents, friends, and Jimmy's music. My mother had given me a few toys she picked up so I would have gifts for Jimmy on Christmas morning. I was truly grateful. While most people enjoyed the rush of Christmas shopping, I was content to make do with what I had.

The smell of warm vanilla and sugar filled my apartment as I frosted the last batch of cookies. And then the phone rang. I licked the buttercream icing from my fingers before reaching for the receiver.

"Hello?"

"Ms. Jagow?"

"Yes, this is Ms. Jagow."

"This is the collections department attempting to collect payment for your son's trumpet."

The instrument was almost paid off, but I had gotten behind in payments since losing my job.

"Ahh... how much is the current payment?" I inquired.

"You would need $100 to make your account current," she explained.

It might as well have been $1,000 because I didn't have it. My heart sank as I thought of having to take from my son the only source of motivation he had for going to school.

"Well, you see... I lost my job and have not been able to keep up with the payments. Will you accept a smaller amount until I can get caught up?" I asked.

"No, ma'am," the woman said firmly. "If the $100 is not paid in full, we will have to repossess the trumpet."

I hesitated a moment. "That would be just awful as my son loves playing, and music gives him a reason to go to school." I sighed. "You see, he is autistic, and school is very trying for him."

The tone of the conversation shifted. "What is his music teacher's name?" the woman asked.

"Mr. Volpe," I answered, somewhat confused by her inquiry.

"And the school I have listed here is Starpoint Central," she went on.

Was she going to send someone out to the school to get the trumpet? Then the woman asked if I would wait on hold.

Several minutes later, the woman came back. "Ms. Jagow? I just spoke with your son's music teacher, and he tells me your son is quite talented. Please accept the trumpet as a gift from us."

I hesitated a moment. Did I hear her correctly? "You can consider the trumpet paid in full," she reassured me. "Merry Christmas!"

As I hung up, tears of gratitude fell from my eyes.

The evening of Jimmy's first school concert performance finally arrived shortly before Christmas. My mother accompanied me to the show. The curtain opened, and Jim proudly walked out on stage with the rest of the band, his treasured trumpet in hand. Nervously, I twisted my purse strap around my hand as I wondered if he would remain focused and follow the bandleader's directions. Musically, he had a good ear, could read notes and had a good sense of rhythm. However, he was unable to follow the direction of his classroom teacher without the help of his aide.

The conductor raised his baton, cuing the band. All eyes were on the conductor; mine were on Jimmy as I watched with anticipation. The band broke into a rendition of "Sleigh Ride," with Jimmy following along in perfect time. Gabriel himself couldn't have sounded more beautiful to me in that moment. My mother and I, wiping tears of joy from our eyes, sat back and enjoyed the show. The band continued with many familiar Christmas classics, one after another, and Jimmy didn't miss a beat.

Many Christmases have passed since then — some more abundant than others. But I will always treasure the gift of music my son and I both received the Christmas of 1998.

Now, twenty years later, I am looking forward to attending Jimmy's Christmas concert at Berklee College of Music.

— Lori Carpenter Jagow —

42

The Shenanigator

Christmas is the season for kindling the fire
of hospitality in the hall, the genial flame
of charity in the heart.
~Washington Irving

U ncle Jim is an electrician, the father of two grown sons, and what the family refers to as The Shenanigator. He loves making people laugh and pulls kind-hearted pranks.

One year, his friends and next-door neighbors, the Millers, had to leave town a couple of weeks before Christmas to help with a hospitalized relative. This made Uncle Jim sad because his neighborhood had an annual party when they decorated the outside of their homes for Christmas, and the Millers were a big part of this celebration. So, Uncle Jim, being the kind of person he is, came up with a plan, and this time his shenanigans were full of Christmas spirit.

He called all of the neighbors and our family members and asked us to bring whatever Christmas decorations we weren't using to his house. When we arrived, he had us divide up the many strings of lights and made sure they were working. He and a few friends descended on the Millers' home with the lights and ladders. He ran a very long outdoor extension cord from his house to the Millers' so as not to run up their electric bill.

The rest of us set up an inflatable Santa, several life-sized lighted reindeer, a nativity scene complete with Mary, Joseph, Baby Jesus, a camel, and a three-legged donkey. There were several large snowmen and two large, lighted angels. We all watched as Uncle Jim plugged in the main connection, and the Millers' house lit up so bright that I was fairly sure it could be seen from outer space!

Uncle Jim had driven the Millers to the airport and volunteered to pick them up upon their return. Their flight was due in at six o'clock in the evening — perfect timing because it would be dark when they arrived home, and the light show would greet them. My Aunt Mary had organized a few women who cooked a ham, candied yams, green beans, a large salad and homemade rolls, as well as mince, pumpkin and apple pies! They set the table at the Millers' and had the food heated and ready. My cousin brought his boom box and put on a CD of Christmas carols to add to the mood.

The look on Mr. and Mrs. Miller's faces when they arrived home was wonderful. The relative they'd tended was on the mend, but the Millers were weary and not looking forward to a cold, dark house and preparing a meal. They arrived in front of their very festive-looking home and were escorted inside to find a feast prepared for them. Imagine coming home from a long trip to such amazing sights, sound and scents! I learned from Uncle Jim, The Shenanigator, that doing for others is the key to great happiness and joy.

— Patricia Merewether —

43

Snow Angels

Open your presents at Christmas time but be thankful
year round for the gifts you receive.
~Lorinda Ruth Lowen

After retiring and moving from Florida to rural Denver, Pennsylvania, we were enjoying our first Christmas in our new house. But then, unfortunately, my husband Bob spent the week after Christmas in bed with the flu. So I had mixed feelings about the weather forecast. I was excited that it was going to snow, and eager to send all those snow photos to my friends back in Florida, but I was concerned about the need to clear snow from our driveway and from the sidewalk around our corner lot.

In the morning, I walked gingerly to the end of the driveway to pick up the newspaper, which was almost completely buried in snow. I watched with fascination as individual snowflakes fell on my black jacket; I could see their individual lacy designs before they melted. I even made a video of the falling snow.

It was beautiful, yet foreboding, because I had no idea how we would clear the snow. My husband was too ill to operate the snow blower.

Around noon, Bob stumbled out of bed. Even though we were required to keep our sidewalk clear, I didn't want him to go outside. Then I heard an unexpected knock on our front door. As I walked to answer it, I was surprised to see children through the glass.

Three bundled-up boys stood outside with snow shovels. The boy in front spoke for the group. "Could we shovel your driveway? We don't want any money. We're going around the neighborhood, and yours is the first house we came to that needed shoveling." Immediately, tears of relief and wonder filled my eyes as I looked at three small snow angels! I didn't have to worry about Bob going outside after all. I put on my jacket, hat, and gloves to get to know the boys while they worked.

Having retired from forty years in various educational positions, the last twenty-two years as an elementary school counselor, I missed interaction with children. Talking with these boys filled my heart. I learned they were neighbors from two homes in the next block and were all fifth-graders. The boys worked hard, even competed with each other a bit, and had my driveway, sidewalk, and mailbox area cleared in no time. Thankfully, I had made lots of Christmas cookies and could send them off with a package to share. I went inside warmed by their generous good deed and happier than ever that we had moved to Lancaster County, Pennsylvania.

— Shirley Redcay —

44

Potato Prayer

How beautiful a day can be when kindness touches it!
~George Elliston

I thanked my brother for his Christmas Eve hospitality and hugged him before I stepped into the drizzly darkness. "Will we see you tomorrow?" I asked.

"I'll be there," my brother said between coughs. "Can't wait for some scalloped potatoes!"

As I hurried to my van, cold raindrops pelted my face like icy tears. I hated to disappoint my sibling. The recent death of his wife already made the holidays difficult. Now he was fighting bronchitis and looking forward to a dish I hadn't planned to serve. Laced with butter and minced onions, scalloped potatoes represented the ultimate comfort food in our family. But where would I find potatoes at eleven o'clock on the night before Christmas?

Few vehicles trolled along the four-lane road that led to the highway and home. I whispered a tiny prayer, "Please, help me find my brother some potatoes." I reached for my phone, pressed the center button, and spoke to Siri.

"Call Kroger," I said. Closed.

"Call Walmart," I said. Likewise.

The answering machines at two more local food stores informed me their employees had left at 7:00 p.m. to be with their loved ones. I appreciated the family-friendly policies, but I still needed potatoes.

I pulled into a gas station with a shop behind the pumps. The clerk frowned when he heard my odd request. They didn't carry produce, he told me. However, their competitor a few blocks down sometimes did. I got back in my vehicle and hoped.

The clerk in the second convenience store said she might have a few wrapped baking potatoes. She poked her nose into a refrigerated case and moved some things around. When she reappeared, she shook her head and apologized. Sold out.

Feeling frustrated and defeated, I headed toward the expressway. I passed a few restaurants, all closed — all except one. Lights twinkled inside a twenty-four-hour coffee shop, which served breakfast around the clock — bacon and eggs… and hash browns! I zoomed into the parking lot. Maybe the manager would sell me a few raw potatoes.

Several people waited in the lobby for to-go orders or a table in the main dining area. Cranking up my courage in front of the crowd, I told the hostess about my brother, the loss of his wife, and his wish for homemade scalloped potatoes on Christmas Day. The girl nodded, bobbing the festive reindeer antlers in her hair, and told me to wait while she asked the chef. She thought for sure they could spare some spuds. I hoped again.

Everyone in the foyer watched me — the strange lady begging for potatoes at midnight on Christmas Eve. A tired-looking woman made room for me on the take-out bench, and I engaged her in conversation. Her children were away for a week, and her best friend was keeping her company in their absence. We chatted until the manager appeared with dismaying news. They didn't use whole potatoes. The hash browns came already hashed and pre-packaged for cooking. Disappointed, I thanked him and turned to leave, but my seatmate stopped me.

"I might have some potatoes at my house," she said. "I think I had four big ones left in the bag. If my kids didn't eat them, you are welcome to them."

I hesitated for only a second. Desperation overcame my natural inclination to distrust. With gratitude, I accepted her generosity. I tried to pay for her to-go order, but she waved me off. She said she lived a couple of miles down the road. She just hoped the bag was still in her fridge.

Like the wise men trailing a star, I followed her home where a strand of old-fashioned, colored lights outlined the roof. Her friend opened the front door and held back two little barking dogs. A Christmas tree glowed in the den. The woman shuffled into her kitchen and opened her refrigerator. I prayed again, "Please, please."

She emerged triumphant, holding an open mesh sack filled with four large, yellow potatoes. I threw my arms around her shoulders and offered again to compensate her. She wouldn't hear of it. "Merry Christmas," she said.

"Merry Christmas Potatoes, thanks to you," I replied. As I drove away, I realized I never even asked her name.

On Christmas afternoon, the smell of scalloped potatoes and ham hung in the air like a sweet fog. The stranger's simple gift touched our entire family with a poignant reminder. Sometimes, the smallest kindness can be the answer to someone's prayer — even a prayer for potatoes!

— Andi Lehman —

Twelve Days of Christmas

*Christmas is the season of joy, of holiday greetings
exchanged, of gift-giving, and of families united.*
~Norman Vincent Peale

Hunter and I spent our first Christmas as a married couple in Ann Arbor, Michigan, where he was in graduate school. We were far away from our families, it was bitter cold, and Hunter was busy with his studies. I was expecting our first child in a few weeks, but the Christmas season seemed drab and uninviting.

Doing our best to make Christmas merry, we decorated a Charlie Brown tree cut down from the yard and strung lights around our tiny cottage. We had a little jar of cash saved for gifts, but it wouldn't go far.

Hunter and I talked about the Christmas traditions we wanted to start as a new couple. Hunter's family had a tradition that appealed to me. Starting December twelfth, the family would act as Secret Elves and give a small gift to another family each day for the Twelve Days of Christmas, increasing the number of items in each gift box to match the number of days. The first day, there was just one item; the second day, two; the eighth day, eight; and so on. It took effort, creativity, and a bit of cash. But I knew how much it had meant to Hunter when he was young. Even with our small budget, we wanted to do the Twelve Days of Christmas for a family that needed some extra cheer.

Choosing the family was easy. I worked as a nanny for Kelly, a single mother with two adopted sons. Like us, she was a transplant from the West and had no family and few friends in Michigan. She worked twelve-hour shifts at the hospital and was often exhausted at the end of the day. Her sons Kevin, age eight, and Aaron, age four, would love this.

Hunter and I made a list of the Twelve Days and the things we could afford to buy. Our gift ideas ranged from toothbrushes and cold cereal to socks and dollar-store toys. The crowning gift for our Twelve Days was a handmade Christmas nativity set, which we carefully sculpted using clay that we baked in our oven. We prepared twelve gift boxes and planned to deliver them anonymously, one each day, after sundown.

The first few days, the task was easy. The boys were not expecting anyone at the door after dark, so we had an easy time ringing the doorbell and running to our car before the gift was discovered. Hunter and I giggled as we drove by the house and watched the boys jump up and down with their little presents.

As the days went on, the boys became more vigilant. They stalked the windows and leapt for the door at the slightest noise.

One night, when I was scheduled to work, Hunter had to make the drop alone while I was in the house tending the boys. Since the boys were starting to suspect my involvement, I would have to feign surprise. I was nervous about playing my part, but happy to witness the boys receiving a delivery.

Bless them! They waited with the greatest eagerness for the plop on the step, the doorbell, and the running footsteps. Hunter was fast, and it was a good thing. Those boys had the door open in seconds. They brought in the present and did something that surprised me beyond anything I could have imagined.

"Look! Look! It's the present from the Secret Elves!" Kevin hollered, his hazel eyes glowing with excitement.

"Oh, it's a pretty one!" Aaron cried.

"Wow! Should we open it up?" I asked.

Aaron grabbed at the gift and shook it, his huge brown eyes bulging and his arms protectively hugging the package. "Oh, no, Nanny.

We don't want to open it now."

I was puzzled. "Why not? It's for you, isn't it?"

Kevin shook his head and pointed at the tag. "It says 'to the family.' Momma's not here. We wouldn't be a family without her."

He was right! She had fought to adopt her boys and keep them.

Aaron nodded solemnly. "We wait for Momma!"

Kevin guided his brother to the living room. "We'll open it tonight when she gets home from work — or in the morning."

Kelly's little boys took the package and lovingly placed it under the tree. They looked at it with reverence, and we left it sitting there, unopened, waiting faithfully for their hard-working mother.

Getting back well after midnight, Kelly didn't wake her boys. I'm not sure how they liked the gift. Young and curious as they were, their mother's presence was more important to them than the gift. They waited to share the gift with the person they loved best, the mother who had adopted them and made them a family.

We had given them Twelve Days of little surprises, but they gave us the spirit of Christmas that we had been wanting so desperately. Far away from our families in that wintry place, Hunter and I felt love warming our hearts, and the spirit of the giving season filling our souls.

Years later, we visited Kelly's family over Christmas. The same loving feeling surrounded us in Kelly's home. But can you imagine my delight when I noticed the mantel? Above the fireplace, the boys had set up the little handmade nativity scene we had given them as the last gift of the Twelve Days of Christmas.

I couldn't resist asking Aaron where they had gotten it. He remembered with perfect clarity.

"Oh, it was from the Secret Elves a long time ago. They gave us the best Christmas ever."

— Kate E. Anderson —

A New York City Christmas

*My idea of Christmas, whether old-fashioned or
modern, is very simple: loving others. Come to think of
it, why do we have to wait for Christmas to do that?*
~Bob Hope

I
t's an undeniable fact that the Christmas season in The Big
Apple is one spectacular show — the gigantic Christmas tree at
Rockefeller Center, the kicky Rockettes at world-famous Radio
City Music Hall, and all manner of beautiful and bright deco-
rations around town, from fabled Fifth Avenue to the tiniest back
street in Greenwich Village. It was there, in all that icy splendor one
Christmas, that my family and I experienced a very warm New York
moment. To this day, more than thirty years later, it is our fondest
Christmas memory, and one heck of a story.

Back then, we had a cherished family tradition of attending a
Nutcracker performance at the New York City Ballet just before the Big
Day. We had established this truly awe-inspiring holiday outing so that
our children would see world-class dancers perform the quintessential
Christmas theater program. We had also persuaded two of our closest
friends to bring their families along with us every year.

An excellent dinner at a fine New York City restaurant always
began the festivities. Then, we'd relish watching our collective five
youngsters — ages four through eleven — displaying their very best,

if not quite impeccable, manners in the distinctly grown-up world of Lincoln Center.

Christmas magic for us was seeing the sparkle and dazzle in their faces as the Sugar Plum Fairy danced across the enormous stage, and later as young Clara and the prince sailed off in their magical carriage above our heads.

But before the party dresses and navy blazers appeared, there was the more mundane task of procuring eleven tickets for this performance. Since this was a once-a-year treat, we opted for the best seats that we could find. And that was my job.

The year of our remarkable experience was 1983, if memory serves me well. That year, I worked for Citibank, and they had a wonderful employee benefits program, including an on-site store, which was a great source for children's Christmas presents, both the fun kind (toys) and the practical variety (clothes). In addition, I could order tickets to important, in-demand events in the city. My assigned task was so much easier that year!

"Are you really ordering eleven tickets?" the benefits manager said, opening her mouth a bit wider than normal. "That's a bucket load of money right there."

I assured her that I was just the point person, with the individual families paying for their seats. I'm sure I saw relief on her now-smiling face.

The big day arrived, and there we were in the sumptuous and festive lobby of the New York State Theater in Lincoln Center, home of the New York City Ballet. After our wonderful dinner, and with the kids' excitement rising rapidly, we were happily floating through the crowds of theatergoers. And then, a ticket-taking attendant looked askance at our precious tickets and directed us to... the box office. Huh?

Trying not to panic, I checked the date on the tickets — it was indeed the right day. For the record, it was a Saturday night, the busiest night of the season. What could be wrong? Perhaps they hadn't been validated properly through our company employee program, and so we needed a brief consultation with the front office.

Well, it was a speedy business to discover this simple and

devastating fact: It was the correct day; it was not the correct performance. Unbeknownst to me, our eleven tickets were for the matinee performance earlier that day.

What to do? Rallying my composure and marketing experience, I politely requested to see the General Manager. Now, the GM of a Lincoln Center theater is not an insignificant personage in New York City. Classy, articulate, and very, very smooth, he took in this contingent of devastated ballet fans in his busy lobby. With great aplomb, he assured me he would address our dilemma.

He rallied his house staff and scurried about with them, first finding eleven chairs and then carefully crafting space for them at the ends of various rows in the orchestra section, all the while keeping his eye on the fire codes and other City of New York regulations.

Remember, this was my mistake, and this was the busiest night of the year. It was well within his purview to regretfully and firmly turn us away. He did not. His easy courtesy and splendid efficiency were beautiful gifts to eleven harried holiday souls. He accomplished a monumental rescue without a moment's hesitation. And then he said, "Merry Christmas to all of you. I hope you will be comfortable in your new seats. Enjoy *The Nutcracker* tonight."

And we did.

Footnote: In the two other cities where we have lived since our years in New York, we've continued our cherished Christmas tradition, recently introducing three of our young grandchildren to this revered family outing. This year, another five-year-old will join the fold.

But never again have we interacted with such a gracious gentleman as we did that December night in Manhattan.

And I read my tickets diligently now.

— Maureen FitzGerald O'Brien —

47

The Christmas Witch

Peace on earth will come to stay, when we live
Christmas every day.
~Helen Steiner Rice

Every kid in my neighborhood knew about the Christmas Witch. She was an elderly woman who left her Christmas decorations up all year long: a twinkling tree in the living room, a plastic wreath on the front door, and giant candy canes hanging in the windows. One kid told me the decorations were meant to coax youngsters closer to the house so the Christmas Witch could kidnap them.

I promised myself I would never go near that place, but when I turned fourteen, I got a newspaper route and discovered I'd have to deliver papers to the Christmas Witch.

"Stop worrying," my mother advised. "Just deliver the newspaper. She won't bother you."

My first day of delivery was a dark, frosty March morning. The sky was just turning pink as I approached the last house on my route… that of the Christmas Witch.

Inside, the house was dark, so I tiptoed up the porch steps and placed the newspaper by the door.

I'd done it.

Then I quickly turned around, not seeing an icy spot on the step. I slipped, fell and slid down the stairs, landing on the sidewalk. I got up and stumbled, unable to walk. I'd sprained my ankle.

The porch light blinked on. The door opened. Someone shuffled out.

It was the Christmas Witch.

"I'm sorry," I said. "I…"

"Dear me," said the Christmas Witch. "Are you alright?"

Speechless, I pointed at my ankle.

"Come in; make sure you're okay." She smiled — not a wicked-witch smile but a nice smile, like she was concerned.

I didn't have any choice; I couldn't walk home. Holding the railing, I hobbled up the steps into her house. She turned on a living room lamp as I limped to a chair.

"Relax. I'll get something to warm you up." She hurried into the kitchen and returned a moment later, handing me a steaming mug. "Have some tea while I call your parents."

I told her my number as she dialed.

"Hello," she said. "This is Mona Wright on Pine Way Avenue. Your son slipped and hurt his ankle." She nodded and hung up. "Your mother will be here shortly."

"Thank you, Mrs. Wright."

"You're welcome." She sat down across from me, and then whispered, "You don't have to call me Mrs. Wright; you can call me Christmas Witch."

I was flabbergasted.

"It's alright." She shrugged. "I hear what people say. It doesn't matter."

"You do have lots of decorations," I said.

"I think it's pretty," she replied.

I said, "People think it's… weird."

"They don't understand the reason I leave up my decorations," she responded.

Like most teenagers, I just blurted out the next question. "What is the reason?"

Mrs. Wright took a deep breath. "Well, in 1970, my son Anthony was drafted and sent to Vietnam. He kept in touch with me as often as he could. My husband had died years earlier when Anthony was little, so the only family we had was each other. Anthony was scheduled to come home on leave on January 10, 1972. He called me on New Year's Eve and told me to leave up the Christmas decorations. He would help me put them away when he got home."

"So what happened?" I asked.

"Three days later, Anthony was killed in a helicopter crash," said Mrs. Wright. "My boy never made it back home. And even though I know it doesn't change anything, I can't bring myself to take down those decorations, even after all these years. I guess I just like to pretend that Anthony will be home soon to help me with that chore."

I didn't like myself at that moment. Mrs. Wright wasn't a witch. She was a sad, isolated person struggling with a terrible loss.

"I'm sorry," I said quietly.

Mrs. Wright sighed. "It felt good to talk about Anthony again."

The doorbell chimed.

"That's your mother," said Mrs. Wright, wiping her eyes.

My sprained ankle healed quickly, and my first morning back to delivering newspapers, Mrs. Wright met me at her door.

She smiled as I handed her the paper and said how much she enjoyed our visit.

Over the next couple of years, I saw Mrs. Wright occasionally, and I would always wave hello or stop to chat. Funny, I didn't think of her as the Christmas Witch anymore.

When I came home from my first semester of college, I learned that Mrs. Wright had passed away. I didn't get to see her again, but I never forgot her story.

After all these years, that experience has always helped me remember that ageless lesson: be a little less judgmental and a bit more understanding toward others.

— David Hull —

48

Space Mountain at Midnight

*Don't you wish you could take a single childhood
memory and blow it up into a bubble
and live inside it forever?*
~Sarah Addison Allen, Lost Lake

I f I close my eyes, I can still smell the sweet scent of the air that night thirty years ago. It was different from Florida daytime air — crisper, cooler. And somehow, because it was at Walt Disney World's Magic Kingdom, it smelled that much sweeter.

After a long day at the parks, my mom, dad, younger brother and I had just finished a late dinner at our hotel restaurant. As we walked to our room, my dad, carrying my already sleeping brother, shot me a "break the rules" smile and whispered, "Let's go back to the Magic Kingdom and ride Space Mountain one more time."

So my roller-coaster-loving, always-up-for-the-next-adventure partner-in-crime and I boarded the bus that most vacationers were getting off. I remember walking through the gates, not believing how amazing this was. It was far past my bedtime, and as I walked down Main Street holding my dad's hand, the whole park looked like a bright fairy tale. We exuberantly rode Space Mountain, and the wind made our hair dance as we threw our hands high in the air.

Flash-forward thirty years, and I am standing in a long line at our Disney hotel about to make a $1,000 frivolous request to a complete stranger. I close my eyes and contemplate whether I should keep standing there or just be smart and leave, saving myself the heartache of another rejection. Just a few days earlier, I had pleaded my story through tears but the Disney employee on the phone said, "I'm so sorry for your situation, hon. Adding an extra park day for everyone in your family would cost $1,000. And if you don't arrive until the evening, the park may be already be sold out the day before Christmas Eve. I wouldn't recommend it."

I was mad at myself—at us all. We should have planned this trip better for my dad. This was his very own "Make-a-Wish" trip, as he jokingly called it. Diagnosed with Stage 4 metastatic pancreatic cancer a few months earlier, he was not expected to make it to Christmas. But he decided he would—and he would fund a Christmas trip to Disney to celebrate my parents' 40th wedding anniversary with my brother and me and our families.

The two park days that we planned were chosen by my dad for the grandkids' special interests—Animal Kingdom for my nieces and Hollywood Studios for my boys, with their recent *Star Wars* obsession. The third and final day, my dad had planned for my mom to visit her extended family in Florida—leaving us to return to the hotel at night just in time for our early flight the next morning. It was typical of my dad to make the trip perfect for everyone else. I wished I had fought harder to incorporate his beloved Magic Kingdom into the schedule.

Just like that, a cast member named Michael, holding an iPad, walked up to me and snapped me back to reality, smiling. "Happy holidays. What can I help you with today?"

The floodgates opened. I let it all out. My anger that my fifty-nine-year-old dad would not get to see my young boys grow up. Or grow old with my mom. Or retire and enjoy all he had worked for. Anger that I hadn't even been able to buy a Christmas gift for him yet this year. How do you choose what you know will be the last Christmas gift you ever give your dad? Anger at the suffering that I knew was coming for him. Anger at this black cloud of terminal cancer that I could see closing in on us, closer and closer each day.

The angry tears came out so fierce I couldn't get my story or my reasons out, just, "I need to get my dad back to Magic Kingdom tonight to ride Space Mountain. And there are ten of us. And we won't be able to arrive until late. And we don't have tickets."

And somehow my eyes must have told the rest of the story because he returned thirty minutes later and smiled magically, saying "Merry Christmas," and informing me that we all had tickets for the Magic Kingdom and fast passes to Space Mountain that night.

I watched the four cousins giggle together, wide-eyed with adrenaline and excitement. My brother and his two girls, and me and my two boys — with our memory-making dad. I knew they'd recall every detail of their night-time adventure, even thirty years later.

As we walked down Main Street with my boys holding my dad's hands, the whole park looked like a bright fairy tale lit up for Christmas. The crowds slowly shuffled out as we rushed in. The air was invigorating. The crisp, cool Florida air smelled sweeter in front of the spectacular lit-up castle. Once again, I was with my roller-coaster-loving, always-up-for-the-next-adventure partner-in-crime, riding Space Mountain late at night. The wind made our hair dance and we threw our hands high in the air.

— JL Kennedy —

49

Neighborly Miracles

Christmas is not as much about opening
our presents as opening our hearts.
~Janice Maeditere

When my husband and I were first married, we lived on a quiet cul-de-sac. Across the street, there was a house with a ten-foot-high hedge that obscured all but the path to the garage. These were clearly neighbors who wanted privacy and weren't interested in any "neighborly" behavior. They kept to themselves, and we kept to ourselves.

My husband had discovered that an elderly brother and sister lived in the house. The house belonged to the sister, and the brother helped around the house with things like getting the mail and setting the trashcans out on trash day. They were both very old and unfriendly. In fact, they had even called the police on my husband for playing music too loud with his band in our garage one afternoon.

One autumn, the brother had a stroke and passed away. We noticed our diminutive neighbor — the tiny sister, who was actually older than her brother — trying with all her might to pull her trashcans to the curb. My husband went to her rescue, and from that day until the day we moved, he took her trashcans to the curb every week.

Fast-forward to Christmas Eve, a few months after my husband first started helping the neighbor. It was our first Christmas as a married couple, and we didn't have much. We had no gifts, and no party to attend. We didn't even have any special holiday treats to share at home.

I confessed to my husband, "I wish we could have our own Christmas Eve party — just the two of us. When I was a kid, we always had our own family Christmas Eve party. We would have a cheese-and-meat tray, cookies and candy. It always felt like a feast to me as a kid."

I understood that Christmas wasn't all about cheese trays and cookies, but it just didn't feel like Christmas without a party. My husband seemed to feel the same way. "Next year, we'll have a party," he told me, trying to be cheerful.

There was an unexpected knock at the door, and a large package was dropped off. It contained a glorious Christmas food basket. There were cookies and truffles, nuts and fresh fruit, and even cheese and sausage. It was the feast I had been missing! Everything looked delicious. What a Christmas miracle!

We discovered a note at the bottom of the basket: *Merry Christmas! From, Marie.*

Our neighbor — who we thought was unfriendly — had sent us the perfect Christmas gift. And that wouldn't be the last time. She sent us a Christmas gift basket every year we lived across from her. She even sent us one the first year after we moved away. I think that, to Marie, my husband's help with the trashcans was a miracle, too. But that was nothing compared to the miracle of that first Christmas gift basket on a Christmas Eve when we had nothing.

— M. Ellison —

50

The Norway Spruce

The best time to plant a tree is twenty years ago;
the second best time is now.
~Author Unknown

It was our first Christmas in our little cabin, and the mountain air was sweet with holiday spirit. Our enthusiasm soared when my husband's extended family accepted our invitation to stay at our cabin and spend Christmas Eve and Christmas with all of us.

Even though money was tight, we made every cent count in order to host an unforgettable occasion. At the craft store, I found a sales remnant sprinkled with holly leaves and berries — enough to sew a festive tablecloth. I bought miniature stockings for everyone along with tiny treasures to stuff inside. Shopping the sales, we filled the refrigerator and freezer in advance. I made candy, cookies, and loaves of sweet bread so that we had plenty of goodies to eat, plus enough to send home with our company. Each family member, including my brother-in-law's dog, would have a homemade present under the tree.

All we needed was a tree.

We drove down the mountain to the quaint town of Woodstock and visited several tree lots, but couldn't find the right one. Across the road, my husband spotted the local nursery and suggested we check them out. Of course, the nursery had a nice choice of trees, but they cost considerably more than the trees we had seen earlier, deservedly so.

Winding through the paths of cut conifers, we inhaled the glorious essence of pine that saturated the air. Suddenly, my husband gasped. "Look!" he squealed. "They've got live trees!"

Now, my husband was a certified conifer-loving tree nut, but unfortunately the "live" trees wore price tags that were way out of our budget.

As he stroked a lush Norway spruce, I knew my husband had landed in tree heaven. It was a beautiful tree for planting in the yard, but I didn't think it looked much like a true Christmas tree.

After a quick glance at the price, my mouth flew open. "We can't afford this," I reminded him.

"Think of our first Christmas tree growing next to our cabin for the rest of our lives," my husband said in a dreamy tone. "A tree we can enjoy the entire year. A tree that brings back all the sweet memories of spending our first Christmas at our cabin with my family."

Nothing I said changed my husband's mind, and so with great trepidation on my part, we bought the tree.

The nursery's owner handled our transaction and gave us instructions on the tree's care. The spruce could only stay indoors for a few days, and then we needed to plant it right away. I'll admit I felt disheartened about wasting money for a tree we couldn't bring indoors and immediately decorate or enjoy throughout the holidays.

As instructed, we cared for our tree outside. However, a week before Christmas, we experienced unusually balmy temperatures, and our tree started to droop. Even though the tree had no warranty, we headed to the nursery, hoping the owner might replace it. Unfortunately, he had sold out of live trees.

The owner urged us to go home and plant our tree. If we did, he felt certain it would survive. He also insisted that we pick out a beautiful white pine to take home at no extra charge.

Grateful for the replacement tree, we thanked him for his generosity and headed home. I'll admit that I had grown attached to the spruce and looked forward to finally bringing it indoors, but mostly my heart ached for my husband. Now, the expensive tree of his dreams would spend Christmas outside.

Judging from the tree's appearance, we had little hope. Still, we planted it in a spot where we could view the spruce from inside our cabin, and much to our surprise and delight, it perked up shortly after Christmas.

Whoever thought my husband's dreamy sales pitch would come true?

The following Christmas, and every Christmas after that, we dressed our outdoor tree in colorful lights until we could no longer reach the tree's top.

Now, twenty-three years later, our Norway spruce towers over our cabin. From our "Norway Room," named in honor of our beloved tree, we have a spectacular view. Throughout the years, the tree has grown up with our family, and we can't imagine our place without it.

We have enjoyed the spruce's majestic beauty through every season, but especially during the winter when its lush green branches are blanketed in fluffy snow. The scene is breathtaking!

As far as those first family Christmas memories that my husband envisioned when we bought the tree, we've got memories all right. His entire clan canceled on us that Christmas Eve morning, and so we packed the presents and children and drove two hours to spend Christmas at his parents' home.

Today, when we gaze at our magnificent tree, we find ourselves reminiscing about the fun and anticipation we felt that first Christmas and can't help but chuckle over how our grand plans fell through. But we've never forgotten the nursery owner's kindness and feel grateful that he encouraged us to plant and save the tree.

—Jill Burns—

Chapter
6
The
Perfect Gift

51

The Countdown before the Countdown

Patience is not just about waiting for something… It's about how you wait, or your attitude while waiting.
~Joyce Meyer

"Mom, look at this *Star Wars* LEGO set," my eight-year-old son Nathan said. "Can I get it for my birthday?" Before I could answer his first question, he continued, "If you've finished shopping for my birthday, can I get it for Christmas instead?"

I smiled. My son had definitely figured out how things work in our house. Nathan is the youngest of five, and all of his siblings are teenagers. Two of them are girls, and they are extraordinarily difficult to shop for, so if they find something they like, I will often buy it and set it aside for the next holiday. It does eliminate the element of surprise, but at least they are happy on their birthdays and on Christmas morning.

I looked at the LEGO set in question. "Nathan, this isn't just a regular LEGO set. It's an Advent calendar." At his questioning look, I explained, "An Advent calendar counts down the days until Christmas. Starting on December 1st, you open one box each day. And each box contains one small LEGO toy."

He smiled. "That's a lot of LEGOs."

"Well, there are twenty-four, so I guess that is a lot."

"I want this really badly, Mom. Can I get it for my birthday?"

"Yes, but here's the problem with that, Bud. It's August right now, and your birthday is in September. If we bought this for your birthday, you couldn't start opening the toys until December 1st. That's a long time to wait to play with a new toy."

He shrugged. "Then can I have it for Christmas?"

"Well, that's not going to work either because it's an Advent calendar. If you get it for Christmas, you won't be able to count down the days until Christmas."

He thought for a minute. "Okay, then I'll just choose something else."

After much deliberation, he picked out a different LEGO set. "So you can wrap this and give it to me on my birthday, and I'll pretend to be surprised," he said with a smile.

I nodded. Like I said, he knows how things work in our house.

We left the toy department so that I could grab the groceries and other items we needed. We were heading toward the checkout when Nathan said, "Mom, I changed my mind. I really want that *Star Wars* Advent calendar."

"Even though it would be two and a half months before you could start using it?"

"Yes, I really want it."

So we bought the calendar.

On Nathan's birthday in mid-September, he opened his presents, including the Advent calendar. He acted as surprised and pleased with it as he did with the gifts that were actually a surprise. And then he started to open it.

"Bud, remember that's an Advent calendar. That box contains one small toy for every day from December 1st until Christmas Eve. So we can't open it yet."

His shoulders slumped. "Oh, yeah, that's right."

We put the box in his closet. I hoped he'd forget about it, but that was wishful thinking.

"How many more days until I can start opening the toys in the calendar?" he asked the day after his birthday.

"Well, you've got the rest of September, plus all of October and all of November."

"Can't I just open it now?"

"Well, it's yours, so if you want to do that, you can," I said. "But I think it would be really fun to wait and use it to count down the days until Christmas."

"Okay, I'll wait," he said.

But just a few days later, he asked about the calendar again. "How many more days, Mom?"

"Nathan, you've got until December 1st. That's two and a half months."

"I don't think I can wait that long."

Again, I told him that it was up to him, and again he agreed that it would be better to wait until December 1st.

But just days later, he asked yet again. I gave him a pocket calendar, and we counted how many days until December 1st.

"It's just so long, Mom," he whined.

At this point, I regretted that I'd ever bought the calendar. "Nathan, every December, we count down the days until Christmas," I said. "But this year, we're counting the days until we can count down the days until Christmas."

He smiled. "It's the countdown before the countdown, Mom."

I looked into his smiling face and realized that he was enjoying this. I found it frustrating, but for Nathan, this was just making the fun of Christmas last even longer.

So I joined in. We marked off the days on his pocket calendar and talked about how fun it would be when he finally got to open the first box in his Advent calendar. When the waiting got tough, I reminded him how glad he'd be that he'd waited.

"I wonder what the first toy will be," he wondered aloud, turning the box over in his hands. "I hope it's R2-D2."

"We'll find out in just thirty-eight days, Bud," I said.

"I can't wait that long," he said, even though he'd already decided that he would.

The countdown before the countdown became a daily ritual for us. Finally, it was December 1st. Nathan's hands were practically shaking as he opened that first box. It was an R2-D2 figure, just as he'd hoped. For the next twenty-three days, he opened another box and was delighted with each one.

"I'm so glad I waited, Mom," he told me nearly every day. "This is the best countdown to Christmas ever."

People say that Christmas starts earlier and earlier every year. I know these complaints are about the over-commercialization of the holiday, and I see their point.

But this year, Christmas came to our house very early, and it was so much fun. It taught my son patience and the power of delayed gratification.

The countdown before the countdown made the most wonderful time of the year even more special.

—Diane Stark—

52

The Best Christmas Present I Ever Bought

Intuition is a spiritual faculty and does not explain,
but simply points the way.
~Florence Scovel Shinn

I heard my husband asking for something in the men's clothing department. I whirled around just in time to hear him announce, "This is the one, Margaret. This is the one I want."

I burst out laughing. Normally, getting my husband to go clothes shopping was impossible. This must be something special.

We were in a crowded department store where I was trying to find a Christmas present for my father-in-law. Keith was supposed to be helping me; instead, he was asking a salesperson to unlock a leather Ohio State jacket from its hanger so he could model it for me.

He did look good; in fact, the jacket looked like it had been tailor-made for him, and I told him so. He beamed back at me. I knew a coat like that had been on his wish list for years, but he'd never gotten more specific than "leather jacket," and I'd never asked.

There was only one problem. I knew it even before I flipped the dangling price tag. The jacket cost several hundred dollars.

"Um, honey…"

Before I could say anything else, he was shrugging it off.

"I know, I know, but I couldn't resist; I just wanted you to see it on me."

We'd agreed we weren't going to buy each other Christmas presents that year. We'd just made a big move to Columbus, Ohio thanks to a major job promotion for Keith. And although his company had paid for the move and he'd received a wonderful raise, there had still been plenty of expenses.

We'd just bought a house. Within a week of moving in, my minivan required a major repair. Also, the move had come right before Christmas, so we'd begun shopping right away for our family and our three young children.

Keith loathed shopping, especially since he worked in retail; the only reason he was with me was because I was pregnant with our fourth child. Since I was tired all the time, he'd agreed to come along and help so it wouldn't take me as long.

We found a sweater for his stepdad and continued on our way.

But even after all the presents were bought and wrapped, I couldn't stop thinking about that Ohio State jacket.

Keith was a huge Ohio State football fan, and he'd been away from his beloved team for a decade. He'd worked so hard, for so long. I wanted him to have something special, something that showed how proud of him I was.

He deserved that jacket. But I told myself it could wait a few months, until after we were settled and had paid down some of our bills.

Still, something nagged at me. Every time I thought about it, about the look on his face while he was wearing it, I felt a sense of urgency. It was a feeling I couldn't shake.

Why was I still obsessing over it when Keith had probably forgotten all about it?

One afternoon, a few days before Christmas, I buckled my toddler into his car seat and headed to the mall. I had to get that coat out of my head. Maybe it wasn't as nice as it had originally seemed; I'd only really looked at it for about thirty seconds.

Anyway, it probably wasn't even there anymore; surely someone had bought it by now. Or the store no longer had it in Keith's size.

Of course, the mall was mobbed. I had to park far from the entrance, and I began to question my wisdom in making the trip as

I transferred my cranky two-year-old from his car seat to his stroller.

I made my way through the crowds until I finally found the section of the men's department where Keith had tried on the jacket. And, lo and behold, it was still there. There was just one left, and it was in Keith's size. It looked every bit as fine as it had when he'd tried it on the first time.

Woody, named for Ohio State coach Woody Hayes, started to fuss. I gave him a pack of gummies as I waited patiently for a salesperson.

I was buying that jacket for Keith. I'd put it on a nearly maxed-out credit card and pay it off. What was a few hundred more dollars? The store wouldn't have the jacket if I waited a few more months as I had originally planned.

As Woody and I left the mall, I noticed I didn't have that sinking feeling I'd sometimes get when I bought something expensive and began having second thoughts. I actually felt great about what I'd done.

I could hardly wait until Christmas morning.

Keith was stunned when he opened his present. He didn't know what to say, even as he leaped off the couch, shrugged off his robe and put on the jacket.

He wore it just about every single day for the next four months, and then, in late April, just months into his new job, Keith suffered a fatal heart attack while he slept. He was only forty. Our baby girl was born three weeks after he died. She's now eighteen.

Had I put off my purchase, Keith would never have had the chance to wear that jacket.

And I wouldn't have the memory that I treasure to this day of my husband's ecstatic face — not just on Christmas morning, but every time he wore his leather Ohio State jacket.

— Margaret Jan Feike —

53

The Pillow

We can only be said to be alive in those moments when
our hearts are conscious of our treasures.
~Thornton Wilder

Christmas was only days away, and my preteen thoughts were fixed on a shiny black boom box. I knew my family was having a rough year in terms of cash flow, but I had my heart set on that boom box.

It didn't seem like too much to ask. All my friends had boom boxes. And it wasn't as if I was asking for a top-of-the-line model. Certainly my parents could find a way to get me this one gift. Besides, Christmas was magical, so for one day I wouldn't have to be the girl with the hand-me-down clothes and the curtains made from bed sheets. It was the day when impossible was made possible

I knew this because a few years earlier, when I should have been in bed, I heard a knock on the door on Christmas Eve. When my parents opened it, a garbage bag full of toys and other gifts for the Christmas season sat on our porch. It was Christmas magic! So even when my parents warned us that this year was particularly tight and that we would have a light Christmas, I still expected to receive the boom box.

Christmas morning came, and I was surprised by the small number of gifts under the tree. I made my way through the festively wrapped packages and found the one with my name. It was not a shiny black boom box, but a homemade pillow sewn in the shape of a heart. It was obvious my mother had worked hard on it, and she had even added a special fluted ruffle around the edges to make it extra girly. My siblings each received their own pillows, unique in color and shape. One was square, another a triangle, a third, a circle, and so on.

"That's it?" I distinctly remember thinking the harsh words when it finally sank in that this pillow was my "big gift." The last thing I remember about that Christmas was picking up my stocking, sitting on the old grated heater in the corner of the living room, and eating my candy, sulking.

Years have passed. I have my own children now. Two of them have grown and moved out, one is fourteen, and the other is hitting the age that I was when I was so ungrateful. That memory, of my behavior on that Christmas morning, resurfaced and really started to bother me.

I started to see it all: my mother staying up late into the night, using her talents, energy, and fabric scraps to make a Christmas with the little she had. I saw her carefully setting each handmade pillow under the tree. I understood the heavy weight she carried knowing she couldn't provide the store-bought gifts her children put on their wish list.

I cringed as I imagined her heart breaking as she saw my response to her gift. I didn't even say thank you to her.

So this afternoon, I decided to make an important call, thirty years later. When Mom answered, I froze for a moment. Silly, I know. I'm a grown woman, and I talk with her often. But today I was that twelve-year-old girl again. I took a deep breath, and my voice shaking, I told her I was sorry. I thanked her for the beautiful heart pillow. I told her how much I loved it, and even more importantly, how much I loved her for her effort. She, gracious and loving, accepted my apology.

I cried.

She cried.

It was as if I had finally decided to open the porch door on Christmas Eve, to find the Christmas treasures waiting for me — my mother's love and forgiveness.

— Christine Shultz —

54

The Last Gift

Christmas is most truly Christmas when we celebrate
it by giving the light of love to those who need it most.
~Ruth Carter Stapleton

The way we open presents has become something of a family joke. We have a precise set of rules. We go from youngest to oldest, one at a time, and the presents get better and better each round. Every time it's your turn to open a present, you have to ask the room: "This one now?"

So, you may open socks first, but in a later round you'll open that gift you've been hoping for all year. But there's never any doubt which one is the absolute last gift — the grand finale. And it comes in a simple, white envelope tucked into the tree.

Years ago, when my sister Kallie and I were very young, our dad asked us to take the money our family would have spent on him and use it to bless others instead. Our mom began giving anonymously to a different cause or family each year. She told him what we did in a Christmas card that he would open last, after all the presents had been unwrapped.

One year, Kallie and I decided we wanted to do the same. We asked Dad to devote some of our Christmas present budget to someone who really needed it. This also turned into a tradition. Through the years, he's given such gifts as a donation to a foster-care nonprofit, a refrigerator to a school in Africa, and emergency food and clothing to a disaster-relief network. All the time, we donated anonymously because, as he said, "There is tremendous power in self-sacrifice for the sake of others through giving in secret, as we read in scripture."

That line is from one of those Christmas letters he writes to tell us what he did in our honor. Those letters are as dear to us as the generous acts themselves. Our dad, the strong, silent type who always wanted to be John Wayne, suddenly becomes a big, old softie in these eloquent, expressive essays. He starts by recapping our year and telling us how proud of us he is, and then reveals what he did to give back.

One gift in particular sticks out in my mind. Our family has always been connected by music. I played the very same trumpet that my dad did when he was in high school, and my sister and I both took piano lessons while growing up. She still plays the same two Christmas carols each year. That's why my dad reached out to a neighborhood piano teacher to see if she knew of any students who could use a little help.

The instructor told my dad about a twelve-year-old girl we'll call Yesenia who was very talented and dedicated to her lessons. Her dad was also very devoted to her learning. Working in a local feedlot, he didn't make a lot of money, but he still managed to pay for her weekly lessons. Yesenia would practice every day at home, but her little electronic keyboard was less than ideal. It didn't have a full range of octaves, the pedal wiring kept breaking, and the keys weren't weighted to provide the touch of a real piano.

That's when my dad got the idea to give her a real studio piano. After scouring the city for an affordable, pre-owned upright in very good condition, he found one that a church nearby was selling. It was perfect. He was able to give it to Yesenia's dad, under the pretense that my dad was the middleman for someone else who wanted to do a good deed. Her dad was moved to tears. He said Yesenia wanted to play piano in college, and this piano would help her improve her skills immensely.

My dad told us all this in his Christmas letter, the last gift to be opened. I keep these letters and read them from time to time when I need some encouragement. Five years later, when we were thinking of what to give my dad that Christmas, Yesenia popped back into my mind. Was she still playing the piano?

I reached out to her piano teacher and I was thrilled to hear she had continued her lessons and was doing great in school. I asked if there was anything we could do to help, and her teacher said they had been struggling to pay for lessons. So this time around we got to bless my dad by blessing Yesenia. We were able to pay for her monthly lessons until she graduated high school.

We wrote up that gift, put it in an envelope and placed it in the tree. The look on my dad's face and the quaver in his voice as he read it told us exactly how much it meant to him. We really did save the best present for last.

— Traci Clayton —

55

Paperback Christmas

Books are a uniquely portable magic.
~Stephen King

There were deep snowdrifts around our house, and sharp icicles glittering from the eaves like tinsel on a tree. There were daily sledding runs down perfect hills. The nativity scene was made from snow, even Mary and Joseph, and the manger was made of sheets of ice through which a candle twinkled brightly.

This is what my childhood Christmases were like because my family lived way up north in Canada, up in the sub-Arctic.

In some ways, it was picture-perfect. But, winter also meant waking up in the dark, going to school in the dark, getting out of school in the dark, playing in the dark. Climbing back into bed, and… it was still dark.

When you live up where the sun shines at midnight in the summer, it means that you also live where the sun barely rises above the horizon in the dead of winter.

To fight the depression and boredom that everyone in our town fought during the winter, my parents employed a unique strategy: They bought books.

This was before the days of the Internet. We couldn't just order the newest novel online and have it arrive at our house two days later. We couldn't even go into town to buy books — there was no bookstore. We were lucky there was even a grocery store!

So, every summer, on our yearly trek down south, my parents

hit the bookstores. Used bookstores mostly — we were not wealthy.

And they'd buy books — *boxes* of books, as many as they could afford. After all, these books had to last all winter. All the long, long, dark winter.

I'm telling you this so you can understand *why* the best Christmas present I ever received *was* the best Christmas present I ever received. Why it mattered.

Why it made me cry.

Books were light and hope in the dark for my family. Books were reminders that the sun would come up again, and that the night could not last forever.

And certain authors became very, very dear. My parents had just a short amount of time each summer to scout out the stores for the books they loved. They'd crow when they'd find an omnibus of their favorite mystery writer or an out-of-print copy of a favorite romance author. Those finds were treasures, and they snatched them up and brought them back with us to fill the long winter days.

Those books meant "home" for me.

But when I left for college, I left all those books behind.

College was wonderful. It was challenging, exciting and eye opening. But it wasn't home.

As I came to the end of my first semester at college, the dorm began buzzing with preparations. Yes, the holidays were coming in a few weeks, but we decorated the dorm anyway. Christmas preparations were everywhere, and everyone was excited.

And the "residence life" staff had planned a party. That was what they told us, anyway. They were planning a party, and they wanted us all to come.

What they didn't tell us was that we weren't the only ones they'd told about the party. They'd told our parents, and they'd asked all of our parents to send gifts.

I went to the party not expecting anything special. I was in the middle of papers and finals, and while I liked the people in my dorm, I was a bit cynical about big planned events. They didn't mean much, I thought. I'd just stop in for the beginning of the party, stay long enough to be polite, and then go back to my room. After all, there was still a lot of studying to do, and I was determined to do it.

But then they called my name and handed me a gift. "This is from your parents," they told me.

It was a small rectangle, beautifully wrapped.

Curious, I peeled down the corner of the paper.

It was a book.

And not just any book.

It was my favorite. My favorite historical romance, by one of my favorite authors.

And, I knew, it was my mother's only copy.

It was a copy she'd found during one of those summer trips to a used bookstore, those desperate trips when she and my dad gathered up all the reading material they could, to guard themselves against depression on those dark, dark winter days.

It was my favorite—and it was one of hers, too. And her only copy.

She'd given it to me.

Suddenly, there in the dorm, far from the warm light and full bookcases of my childhood, I was home.

—Jessica Snell—

56

Unpacking Christmas

The best of all gifts around any Christmas tree:
the presence of a happy family
all wrapped up in each other.
~Burton Hillis

M y mother, a later-in-life humor columnist, died in July 2006 at age eighty-one after a long illness. My dad, a year older than Mom, was in failing health, requiring much care, and he agreed to move to an assisted living residence. We found a lovely place for him just a few miles from where I was living.

It was up to me to get their condominium emptied and then sold, so we rented a nearby storage unit so we could properly go through everything later when we had more time. It all happened faster than I expected, and before long we had a scheduled move date.

The task was enormous. I was working full-time and raising a teenager, so I enlisted the help of the woman who had helped care for my parents, plus family members — my teenage son and my brother (who lived an hour away). I was grateful when my sister Laurie said she'd come to Maine from New York to help out during the final weekend before the big move.

In the previous few weeks, we'd discovered nearly every drawer, bin, and shopping bag in the condominium was filled with all kinds of paperwork. We found dress shop receipts, Playbills from shows they'd seen, hotel notepads, take-out menus from restaurants — and copy after copy of my mom's columns from a career spanning more than three decades.

During the final "push" weekend we all went to the condo to do what I called a quick-and-dirty sorting, prior to moving everything to storage. I was disappointed that I hadn't found some kind of a note for us from my mom. I knew she loved us with the strongest of a mother's love, but it seemed inexplicable that there was no goodbye note. After all, she was a writer!

Yet, we were in a hurry, so what mattered most was getting the job done. So when I glanced over at my sister, I couldn't help but feel quietly annoyed, seeing her parked next to Mom's desk, going through one paper at a time, slowly and methodically—a perfectionist trait she'd inherited from our dad. Meanwhile, I was hurriedly packing one thing after another.

My sister seemed to be spending an inordinate amount of time on the trivial, even though I had made it clear we had a deadline. But in those early days and weeks of grief, I had often found myself fluctuating between anger and tears, so I tried to let go of my anger for the time being. After all, Laurie had her grief, too, and had traveled a long way to help. She was doing the best she could. We all were.

The move was accomplished, and I spent chunks of time in subsequent weekends going to the storage units for the sorting process. It would be months before this was completed, and I was resigned to it.

As the December holidays approached, I overdid everything. In the sadness of missing my mom, I wore myself out shopping, rushing to holiday and church activities, and shopping some more. I was throwing my grief into purchasing inanimate objects to show my love for family and friends.

On Christmas Eve, I was at home, upstairs, speed-wrapping gifts and feeling anything but Christmas-y, when I heard the front doorbell ring.

"Ted!" I shouted to my trusty sweetheart, who was downstairs. "Can you get that?"

A minute later, he called up to me.

"Kath, can you come downstairs, please?" he asked.

"I'm busy! Can't you take care of it?" I called back.

"I think you should come down," he said. "There are some carolers at the door."

By now, I was just plain grumpy. Carolers? Ugh. Setting aside the wrapping paper, ribbons, and labels, I went downstairs, through the dining room, and into the kitchen.

"You have to see this," he said, as I walked through the kitchen and headed to the door.

And singing "We Wish You a Merry Christmas" were my nieces Christie and Kathy, my nephew Tommy — and my sister Laurie! They had come from New York to surprise me.

"Don't worry," called out my sister above the singing. "We have a hotel room, and we brought food!" She laughed, pointing to a large cooler. Later, she told me that my facial expression was indescribable, somewhere between shock and joy, with my mouth open, unable to say a word.

The bounty they'd brought for Christmas Day was wonderful, including a pre-cooked turkey. And although Mom's absence was palpable, the presence of my loving family moved me in a way I could not have imagined. The pre-Christmas rush had stopped. I was filled with emotion — the good kind. Anger and angst had given way to what felt like a truer meaning of the holiday.

On Christmas Day, we all had a lovely and lively time with Dad, with laughter, singing, way too much food, and family stories. Then we all moved into the living room to open gifts.

"Don't open these yet," said my sister, as she passed out small packages to each of us. When we all had them, she let us unwrap them together.

It took a minute to take it in. We each found an exact reproduction of a note, on soft cream-colored paper trimmed with a simple design at the top, each one framed. They were the words from my mom that I had prayed for. In her own handwriting, she had written:.

If anything should ever happen to me, I want my children &
grandchildren & now great-grandchildren to know how much

I love them all. They have been the joy of my life. And also — I love & have always loved my husband Larry.
I have a wonderful life. *
Mom, Gaga, Marge
*Even better than "Jimmy Stewart's!"

It was a Christmas I would never forget, as I looked again and again at the sweet, flower-outlined paper. It was the note Laurie had found on that day so many months earlier as she'd sat at our mother's desk... words I'd longed to see and read, now forever belonging to each of us, imprinted in our hearts, a reminder of the love our mother had for us, and of our family's love for each other.

— Kathy Eliscu —

57

I'll Be Home for Christmas

I know for certain that God does not make mistakes,
but he does make miracles. I am one. You are, too.
~Nick Vujicic

On December 11, 1984, my life was forever changed. I was relaxing in the tub and my four-year-old son gently knocked on the door to tell me I had a phone call. He said it was my dialysis nurse. I had been on dialysis for two and a half years after my kidneys failed due to a childhood disease. I told him to tell "Mike" I would call him back. When my son, Kevin, replied that "she" was calling from Northwestern Memorial Hospital in Chicago, my mind did a complete reversal. "She" meant it wasn't Mike. Northwestern meant it wasn't my local dialysis center. Was this "the call"?

Back in 1984, we didn't have a cordless phone. I hastily ended my bath, put on my robe and took the call. The "she" on the other end was indeed the nurse from the Northwestern transplant center and she was calling to inform me there was a matching kidney for me if I wanted it. Did I want it? Yes, of course, I wanted it! She gave me my instructions, and when I hung up I feverishly began my preparations.

My husband would take me there. My mom would watch Kevin. My bag needed to be packed. I contacted my place of employment to let them know the wait was over, and I called a few friends to share the exciting news! Before an hour had passed, my husband had picked me up, Kevin was snuggled in at my mom's house, and I was off to Chicago on that crisp winter morning to receive my precious "gift of life."

Upon arrival, everything happened so fast. I was admitted, taken to X-ray for pre-op testing, given my first dose of an anti-rejection drug and wheeled down to the operating room. As I lay there awaiting this new chapter in my life, so many things went through my head. I wondered about the person who had died and the family who so generously agreed to donate precious organs to help others. I prayed for them silently as I knew they were mourning this tragic loss, but I couldn't help but feel the elation of not having to be on dialysis anymore. How my life would change! Maybe I could have another child.

My thoughts were suddenly interrupted when the curtain was whisked back, and a tall, gregarious, gray-haired man with a wide, toothy grin bellowed, "Hi! I'm your surgeon. We put new kidneys in the lower side of your abdomen. What side would you like yours on? And, by the way, would you like to see it? It's right here in this ice cooler."

I declined the offer and explained to him that I had a dialysis catheter tube protruding from my left side and a hernia I had had from birth on my right. With a twinkle in his eye, he said, "No problem, we'll fix that hernia while we're in there!"

Wow, a two-for-one situation. It really was my lucky day!

I knew the transplant was successful when I woke up in the recovery room desperately having to go to the bathroom. I hadn't had that feeling in years!

Next stop, my own room and more anti-rejection drugs. As the days went by, my energy returned, my color was again rosy, my appetite was enormous, and all my lab-work numbers were great! Soon, it was time to go home.

I went home on Christmas Eve! Welcoming me was a brightly lit Christmas tree adorned with all of our sentimental ornaments. They dangled joyously, beckoning to me as I came through the front door. The strong pine smell and festively wrapped presents under the tree added to the expectations of my new life that lay ahead. My eyes filled with tears as I hugged my little family in a tight huddle, so grateful for this wonderful Christmas gift.

That was thirty-three years ago. I am so blessed to still have this gift! I cherish the memory when Kevin, now thirty-seven, took that most important phone call. Since then, we have adopted beautiful twin girls, and one of them has a little boy of her own.

Every Christmas is special in one way or another, but for me, the Christmas of 1984 was the best one ever!

— Debby Kate Stahl Ramsey —

A Perfect Exchange

An aunt is someone special to remember with warmth,
think of with pride, and cherish with love.
~Author Unknown

The unexpected, tube-shaped gift from Aunt Maisy was wrapped in familiar paper — the same wallpaper that had graced her outhouse walls. I giggled to myself thinking how my thrifty aunt had saved that scrap of leftover wallpaper in her attic for years.

Hard as I tried, I couldn't imagine what Aunt Maisy, who was not one to spend money on store-bought "gifts," would possibly be giving me for Christmas! We had never exchanged gifts before. In fact, we only saw her and Uncle Chill a couple of times a year in the summer when Dad would drive us nearly a hundred miles to visit them.

But Uncle Chill was gone now, and Mom and Dad had coaxed Aunt Maisy into coming to spend Christmas with us. They hoped she might stay since, according to Mom, she wasn't well enough to live on her own anymore.

I hadn't planned on fitting a gift for Aunt Maisy into my Christmas budget, but Mom insisted I buy her something. I browsed through Eaton's and drooled over the boxed chocolates, thinking what a great gift they'd make since she would have to share them with me! But I remembered Aunt Maisy was not supposed to eat anything with sugar because she had diabetes.

I sprayed my coat with perfumes from the test bottles, but I knew

Aunt Maisy would scold me for wasting money on store-bought toiletries that she claimed were "far too expensive" and "good for nothing but making you sneeze."

I rummaged through bins of scarves, shawls, and handkerchiefs, but nothing seemed suitable for Aunt Maisy, who wasn't one to wear frilly or fancy things. She only had one good dress, which she wore to church or when she was having company.

I admired an endless array of jewellery, but all the glistening strings of beads, chains, earrings and bracelets seemed far too flashy. The only piece of jewellery I ever recalled seeing my aunt wear was a tiny, enamelled strawberry brooch, which Uncle Chill had given her when they were young and courting. Whenever she wore her good dress, the little brooch was pinned to its collar.

It was nearing noon, but I still hadn't found anything suitable for Aunt Maisy! I figured I'd pop into the drugstore and buy myself some bubblegum before meeting Dad.

As I stood in line while people were getting their prescriptions filled, I spotted the cutest little jars of jam I had ever seen! There were three little jars per set, nestled in a pretty red tartan box with a cellophane front. But what really caught my eye was the word on the sign above the boxes. It read "diabetic" and stated that the jams were "sugar-free" and "doctor approved."

My heart was pounding with excitement as I remembered hearing Aunt Maisy tell Mom how much she missed her "sweets." I eagerly chose the box that contained three of her favourite backyard fruits: gooseberry, strawberry and currant. I paid the cashier, who talked me into buying a red bow with my leftover change from the purchase.

To this very day, I can still picture the look of delight on Aunt Maisy's face as she opened her gift from me! She fussed and fussed as though the box of jams was the finest gift she had ever received. I hadn't expected my gift to give her such pleasure, and I was even more surprised at the unexpected joy I felt in watching her open it. She even asked Mom to pin the red bow onto her collar, and it was only then I noticed Aunt Maisy was not wearing her beloved strawberry brooch.

Finally, my turn came to peel the outhouse wallpaper off the funny, tube-shaped gift. Tucked inside the tube were several old, yellowed notebooks, which we call "scribblers" in Canada, rolled up and bound with rubber bands, along with a tiny box that rattled when it was shaken.

I slipped the bands off the scribblers and found the fragile pages were filled with Aunt Maisy's handwriting. In her journals, she had recorded all of our summer visits and the things we did together — things I took for granted. I never realised, until then, how much she and Uncle Chill had cherished the time we spent together. And inside the tiny box was Aunt Maisy's beloved strawberry brooch.

Today, the scribblers and the precious little pin are two of my most prized possessions. And that Christmas of so long ago still holds a special place in my heart.

— Linda Gabris —

59

The Writing Desk

Some gifts are big. Others are small. But the ones that
come from the heart are the best gifts of all.
~Tinku Razoria

There are good gifts, and then there are the gifts that have an impact that lasts far beyond the holidays. I received one such gift the year I realized my dream was to write. Despite being told that everyone has the same dream, and that I was aiming too high for a small-town girl, I was determined that I would be published one day. I worked on my craft whenever my busy schedule as a wife and mom allowed it, but my fear of failure kept me from ever sitting down to complete anything that I wrote.

One day, I came across a little antique writing desk in a local shop. I fell in love! I decided this was exactly what I needed to keep me focused on my goal. I went home and described the desk to my husband, telling him I would only allow myself to purchase the desk as a reward if my writing was ever finally published. He thought my plan sounded great. At last, I had an incentive to focus on my writing!

But that Christmas, as our family exchanged gifts, the man I love presented me with my writing desk. I was surprised, touched, and confused.

I asked him why he had bought me the desk before I had anything published, when he knew I only wanted it if I became successful. He smiled. He explained that if we ask God to bless us by fulfilling a dream, we need to step ahead in faith that He will do it, not sit back in doubt and wait to see if He might. My husband gave me that desk to help me view success not as a question, but as the certain result. He believed I would become a writer one day, and he wanted me to believe it, too.

I guess I shouldn't have been shocked when my very first story was chosen for publication less than two months later, but I was. While my husband was thrilled for me, his calm smile told me that it came as no surprise to him.

That gift was wonderful, but my husband gave me so much more than a writing desk that Christmas. He gave me the gift of faith, knowing we need to move forward as if our prayers have already been answered. One might call it the gift that keeps on giving.

—Jaime Schreiner—

60

The Best Christmas Ever

Blessed is the season which engages the
whole world in a conspiracy of love.
~Hamilton Wright Mabie

My father was in the Air Force, and we were stationed in Louisiana. We had been shopping for the enormous Christmas feast Mother always made and had just finished bringing in the groceries. We were sitting at the kitchen table having milk and cookies when she first mentioned Mrs. Neuwirth and her children.

"We really must do something for the poor woman. Five children to feed, and it looks like they'll be having no Christmas at all." I was twelve years old, and I couldn't imagine anything as terrible as having no Christmas.

Mother snapped her fingers, stood up suddenly and began to pace across the floor. "I've got it! We'll give them their own Christmas, right down to the tree, stockings for the children, and dinner!"

It sounded like a great idea, but before I could ask how we were to accomplish this miracle — for we weren't rich ourselves — Mother was on the phone talking to some of our neighbors and arranging a get-together to discuss the problem.

That's how I found out why Mrs. Neuwirth needed help. It seemed Mr. Neuwirth had a drinking problem, and there was never enough money for what the family needed.

One of the neighbors suggested we invite them to Christmas dinner or just show up with food for the family. My mother reminded her of how embarrassing that would be for the poor woman, and that we should allow her a little dignity.

"How about if we give them Christmas anonymously, and I mean everything, right down to the tree and gifts, and even wrapping paper with bows?" Mother suggested.

"None of us is rich, my dear. Just how are we supposed to give that family Christmas?" This was from Mrs. Smith from down the street at the corner.

"If we all pitch in, it won't be very much for each of us. All of us can buy extra canned goods; we'll just pool our resources when it comes to the food. It won't hurt to bake an extra pie or an extra batch of cookies. We share with each other, so why not with them?"

But how were they to provide gifts for the children? Again, Mother had the answer. "Everybody, look through your attic and basement. How about all those toys you've packed away? They don't necessarily have to be brand-new."

One lady even volunteered to provide a tree for the family. The meeting broke up soon afterward, and the ladies scattered to do their part. I'll bet a lot of attics and basements got cleaned up as women scoured their dwellings for things to share with the Neuwirths. We all had to hurry; Christmas was only a week away.

My father produced an enormous box, which sat at the far end of our kitchen. Every day, a neighbor would drop something into it to add to the pile of goodies intended for the Neuwirths. There were canned goods and baked goods, wrapping paper and bows, and stuffed toys and dolls for the younger children. Mother even found a watch still in its box. It was one my father hadn't liked and refused to wear. It would be perfect for Mrs. Neuwirth's oldest son, who was thirteen. Soon, the box was full to overflowing with wondrous things, except a turkey.

Two days before Christmas, my mother began to despair about not having a turkey in the box. Even if the whole neighborhood put the money together, there were no turkeys left at the commissary;

Mother had checked. She was standing in the kitchen pondering the problem when Mrs. Smith appeared at the back door with a huge bag. Up to this point, Mrs. Smith had only contributed a few cans of peas and some napkins.

Mother opened the bag, and inside was the biggest, fattest turkey ever! Mother's eyes grew large, but she quickly recovered and hugged Mrs. Smith.

"Oh, my dear, that was the last item we needed for the box. Thank you so much! Where on earth did you find one? The commissary was completely out."

Mrs. Smith turned a startling shade of red and seemed at a loss for words. Then she patted her hair straight, coughed and said, "Not at all, not at all. It was no problem whatsoever. I discovered it in the back of my freezer — didn't even realize I had it. I was defrosting the freezer, and there it was." And all the while, she was gesturing with her hands and seemed quite flustered. She wasn't used to being caught making a generous gesture, I guess.

Mother just smiled and thanked her again, and the woman beat a hasty retreat back to her own house.

By Christmas Eve, the box was ready and wrapped as a giant present. The neighbor who had provided the tree helped my father cart everything over to the Neuwirths' front porch.

They snuck over and began hauling that cumbersome box up the steps to the front porch, trying to be quiet so Mrs. Neuwirth wouldn't hear and catch them. Finally, everything was ready. They propped the tree against the house. My father rang the bell, and then sprinted off the porch like a small boy playing a prank to join his friend behind a bush. The rest of the neighborhood was watching from their windows.

Mrs. Neuwirth opened the door and stared for a moment at the huge box, and then quickly shut the front door. Perplexed, my father was about to go up and ring the bell again when the door opened slowly. Mrs. Neuwirth came back out on the porch and walked around the box, no doubt looking for some clue as to where it had come from. She peeked inside, curious about the contents, and gasped as she saw all the goodies so lovingly placed inside.

She stopped at the side, put her hands up to her face and began weeping. I knew she had read the note tacked to the box that said: *Merry Christmas to the Neuwirths, From Santa Claus.*

To my knowledge, Mrs. Neuwirth never discovered who had left that gigantic package on her doorstep that Christmas Eve. But to me, that was the best Christmas ever, for I had watched a community come together to show the true spirit of Christmas to a family in need.

— Alanna Parke Kvale —

Chapter
7
Holiday
Hiccups

61

Hands Up

The thing about family disasters is that you never
have to wait long before the next one puts
the previous one into perspective.
~Robert Brault

It was Christmas 1979 and I was eleven years old. We were in our family van heading from California to Nebraska to spend Christmas with relatives. My brother, mother, stepfather and I were excited about this adventure.

By the time we entered Flagstaff, Arizona, it was dark outside, and we were pleasantly surprised by the snow that was everywhere. I looked out the window and thought how pretty it was, and then I lay down in my seat to sleep.

I was startled awake by screams. Then everything went dark, as if I was forced back to sleep.

Then I awakened again. This time, I was confused. People were yelling my name and I seemed to be sleeping on the ceiling of the van. I heard my mother tell me to crawl out the window, and I realized my family was standing outside the windshield yelling for me to come to them. In shock, I crawled out.

A helpful bystander who witnessed the crash explained what he saw. He kept telling us, "I can't believe you all made it out!" He shared that we began to skid on black ice on the road, and it spun our van quickly into a nearby field. He pointed to a large rock and said, "You hit that on the nose, and it just lifted the van into a flip upside down!"

He still couldn't believe we were alive, with no major injuries. We thanked him for his help and gathered as many of our belongings as we could. Eventually, after the police and tow truck did their jobs, we spent Christmas Eve day on Greyhound buses returning to California.

We arrived home around 5:00 a.m. Since our house key was lost in the accident, we had to enter through our garage instead of the front door. I changed into my pajamas, and my mother and brother picked up doughnuts as a quick Christmas morning breakfast. Soon after, I was sleeping on the living room floor, and my brother was asleep in his room. My parents decided to get cleaned up in their room.

As I began to wake up from my deep sleep, I heard voices down the hall in my parents' room. I could tell there was some excitement happening, and I wanted to know what was going on. When I walked in and asked, my family could only laugh. I was confused, and this is what they told me.

Since we had planned to be gone for Christmas, my mother had asked our elderly neighbors across the street to watch the house. That Christmas morning, our diligent neighbors had seen two people going into the garage with what they thought were ski masks on their heads, and the neighbors immediately called the police to report our house was being burglarized. What our neighbors didn't know was they were seeing my mother and brother bringing home the doughnuts.

When the police arrived, they assumed a robbery was in progress. They silently went around to the back yard to enter the house through the sliding glass door to the living room. As the officers approached, they saw me lying on the floor, lifeless. This was now, to them, a possible homicide, and the officers drew their guns and slowly entered the house, walking down the hallway looking for the criminals. First, they passed my brother's room and saw a boy lying on his bed, lifeless, on Christmas morning when every boy in California would be awake. They continued down the hall to my parents' room with guns out and saw my stepfather sitting on the bed reading. They yelled at him, "Get your hands up in the air now!" One officer kept his gun pointed at my stepfather as the other walked into the bathroom where my mother was taking a shower after the long, hard journey. He opened the shower curtain and demanded that she get out.

My mother put her hands in the air, confused by their presence. She tried to ask for a towel to cover up while the officers yelled at both of them to explain who they were. My stepfather tried to explain the journey we'd all just been on, and the officers insisted on seeing IDs. My parents looked at each other with the realization that they didn't have any IDs since they had been lost in the accident. As time went on, and the adrenaline in the officers began to wear off, they started to get the bigger picture. Right then, my brother woke up from the noise and walked into the room. The officers realized that this had all been an enormous misunderstanding.

Once my mother was covered up and apologies were flowing all around the room, the officers left. When all the shock and confusion wore off, my parents and brother began to laugh at the whole experience. Then, I woke up and walked in and they realized that I had been the first "victim" that the police had spotted.

When we started our Christmas adventure, we had no idea what an adventure it truly would become.

— Steffanie Brooks-Aguilar —

62

On Our Way to Bethlehem

*Christmas, my child, is love in action. Every time we
love, every time we give, it's Christmas.*
~Dale Evans Rogers

A few Christmas seasons ago, when my sons were four and two, my wife and I heard about a nearby church that put on an interactive living nativity scene. They had live farm animals in a stable and a real baby portraying the newborn Jesus. Even though our kids were too young to fully grasp the Biblical Christmas story, we knew they would be engaged by the spectacle of the costumes and animals, so we decided to attend a performance one evening.

When we arrived, we were greeted by a guide who directed us through the scenes of the story on our own trek to Bethlehem to see the newborn Jesus. The church grounds were bustling with characters in Biblical garb. Groups of sheep trailed behind their shepherds. A choir of angels sang about the birth of a new King. The three wise men with their gifts passed us as they followed the great star leading them to a special manger in the distance.

The part of the story that usually gets lost is that this miraculous event took place when a census of the entire Roman world was ordered by Caesar Augustus. The census was conducted to account for all the Empire's citizens, to ensure taxes were being paid properly to the government. The very reason Joseph was travelling from Nazareth was to get to his hometown where he was required to register because he belonged to the house of David in Bethlehem. Mary was soon to become Joseph's wife and had to make the journey with him to take part in the census.

This church's re-enactment incorporated the audience members into the census, and we were assigned official papers to indicate we were registered under the family name of Daniel. After being told there were no more rooms at the inn that had turned away Mary and Joseph earlier, we entered a village scene where Roman guards demanded that everyone present their registration papers. Our guide announced that we were the family of Daniel and had census papers to prove it. I pulled mine from my pocket when the guard requested it. He read it aloud: Abraham. But then he said something was amiss.

"This man does not have the right papers," the guard snarled. "We are taking him to jail."

Apparently, I had been handed the wrong paper on purpose so the guard could act out an arrest. Not knowing what to say, I went along with it as the Roman guard started manhandling me. My four-year-old, Ethan, however, started screaming.

"Leave my Daddy alone! Leave my Daddy alone!"

The Roman guard may have been acting out his part, but my son was being serious. With tears streaming down his cheeks, Ethan grabbed my free arm — the one that was not being pulled toward the jail by the guard — and started pulling me the other way. I was in a tug-of-war between a fake guard and my real son. The poor guard did his best to stay in character, but probably sensed his power was dwindling.

"He must have his papers," he continued. "We have to take this man to jail for one night."

With a blood-curdling scream, Ethan yelled, "Noooooooo!"

Realizing his gig was up, the guard loosened his grasp, saying, "Okay, we'll let him go this time."

Ethan grabbed the arm that the guard had just released and pulled me the other way toward his mother and brother.

"Is everyone okay now?" my wife asked, still a bit stunned by our son's reaction.

"Daddy's not going to jail now," Ethan blubbered.

"Thanks, buddy," I said. "You just saved me."

I have never felt more loved.

Ethan was far too young to understand role-playing. Based on his actions, I believe he would have acted no differently if that had been a policeman, the FBI, or the devil himself trying to drag me away. Springing me from jail on our way to Bethlehem was one of my four-year-old son's greatest achievements.

Ethan will be nine this Christmas, and he still talks about the time he saved his daddy from going to jail when we went to see the baby Jesus. Hearing the pride in his voice, I don't have the heart to tell him just yet that it was pretend.

— Darin Cook —

63

Busted

Do I forget, or do I refuse to remember?
~Craig D. Lounsbrough

ecently, I read *The Girl on the Train*, racing through it as I tried to figure out if the alcoholic, seemingly harmless protagonist, Rachel, was indeed a murderess during her blackouts. Of course I knew that booze can lead to bad judgment, or worse — you might slay someone and then forget you did, having to search for clues the next day to determine whether you'd committed the dastardly deed.

That fact is that I am not a lush. Usually, it's just two glasses of wine at most if we're out socializing..

But there was that one time…

We went to our friends' annual holiday party with our children, who were in their early twenties. The kids scattered as soon as we crossed the threshold, and my husband disappeared into a throng of men. I slipped from one gaggle of gossiping women to another. Each time I tried to mingle, I found myself grabbing a libation beforehand, hoping it would make me more jovial and more relaxed. The more meaningless chatter I heard, the more I gulped down liquid courage and the less I minded the giddy silliness of the conversations I was trying to join.

It was a Christmas party, for heaven's sake, and I strived to be "of good cheer." Long after midnight, my husband corralled our besotted kids as I teetered toward the guestroom to find my black coat. It felt heavy on my shoulders, and I struggled to put it on. My husband helped me climb into our high SUV. Even so, the hem of the coat tripped me and I tumbled in while the kids watched me from the back seat. Nevertheless, I lectured the kids about their drinking on the way home — until I zonked out.

I don't remember the rest of the night, but the next day, I awoke feeling groggy. I dragged myself down the stairs to grind coffee beans. That annoying noise was more than I could stand, so I decided to leave the coffee preparation until later. Instead, I'd fetch the paper. I fumbled with the closet door to locate my coat.

I donned the black wool overcoat. The sleeves draped past my wrists. The garment hung to my ankles. And the coat was so wide.

I trudged into the den.

"Does this fit me?" I inquired.

My husband glanced away from the TV and said, "Seems long."

I shrugged and reached into the pocket to get my gloves. Instead, I pulled out a key ring with a BMW logo. I dangled the keys in front of my husband.

"Better call our hosts," he said.

I phoned our friends. After the pleasantries and before I could inquire about the coat and keys, my pal said, "You know that new, young lawyer in town — the one who's about six-foot-two?"

"No."

"Well, someone stole his overcoat last night at our Christmas party, and his brand-new car keys were in the pocket! He had no way to get home. It was too cold to walk. Can you believe that?"

"Awful," I said. "Any suspects?"

Just call me Rachel.

— Erika Hoffman —

64

Christmas Upside Down

To slow down is to be taken into the soul of things.
~Terry Tempest Williams

The first Christmas with our baby daughter was pure bliss. At nine months and not walking yet, Jana posed no immediate danger to the Christmas tree, and the cat easily escaped her exuberant curiosity. I snapped photos of her opening presents with a bow perched on her head at a jaunty angle.

The next Christmas stood in sharp contrast. Shrieks and feline yowls filled the air as Jana and kitty streaked by the tree, making the ornaments jangle. Chasing fueled my toddler's delight, so I stood near the tree to grab her while she writhed and whined, "Down!"

My exhaustion stemmed from more than mothering. As a minister's wife, I faithfully attended every party celebrating the season. I dragged Jana to each event, primped and dressed to perfection. I scoured *Southern Living* magazine for scrumptious recipes. The church ladies' accolades heightened my determination to make the parsonage family appear perfect despite my fatigue.

A church-wide dinner on the Sunday evening before Christmas was the last event for this pastor's wife. As Dale and I stood in the kitchen discussing the dinner, Jana scampered by. Dale swung her up into his arms as she giggled. She threw her arms around his neck and nuzzled.

"Honey," Dale said to me, "you're wearing yourself out. Let me get a bucket of chicken for the dinner."

"No! That's cheating. I can make a taco salad. Everyone raves about it. I know you're trying to help, but I'd be so embarrassed if people knew I didn't make something myself."

"Okay," Dale said, "but you worry me. One woman can only do so much."

That Sunday began with morning worship. I trudged the fifty yards from the parsonage to the church juggling Jana, a diaper bag, my Bible, and a purse. I taught Sunday school, sang in the choir, and attempted to appear engrossed in Dale's sermon, although I fought off sleep.

That afternoon, I wrangled Jana into an all-too-brief nap, prepped the salad, and sent it ahead to the church with Dale. He liked to arrive early, and I assured him I could make it on my own.

Taking extra time to prepare Jana, I underestimated how long I needed to dress myself. Fearing tardiness, I wriggled into a one-piece dress with a green velvet vest and adorned it with my "HO HO HO" brooch. Opening my lingerie drawer, I waffled between pantyhose and knee-highs. Knee-highs would be faster, and my mid-calf dress would cover them. I donned a pair of knee-highs, threw on my heels, and clomped down the hall just in time to keep the cat and the toddler from upending the tree.

I wrestled Jana into her hooded coat and tied a flawless bow under her chin. Slinging the diaper bag and purse over my shoulder, I picked her up and scurried toward the door, only to discover a downpour had made the church almost invisible. I seized an umbrella and slogged out into the rain.

Jana wailed as I tried to cover us both, to no avail. Hair blew in my face, obscuring my view. The purse and diaper bag slipped from my shoulder to my elbow. The door to the fellowship hall beckoned, but I became aware of a mortifying problem.

The knee-highs I had chosen in haste had passed their prime. They were sliding down my legs and would be around my ankles with a few more steps.

I finally wrestled my umbrella, screaming toddler, and bags in through the door, and swung around to discover the person I most dreaded seeing at that moment. Marge always dressed immaculately, and I desperately needed her approval. She had helped me many times to divert unwanted criticism from the church ladies. I shuddered at the picture we presented, especially with my knee-highs now only ankle-highs.

Marge smiled kindly. "Let me take this little darling off your hands." She reached for Jana, who quieted in the arms of a capable adult. "Why don't you take a minute to yourself?" She avoided stating the obvious. It would take more than a minute to right myself.

I slipped inside the ladies' room, tugged up my hose, and checked my reflection. The woman in the mirror was a frazzled mom on the verge of tears, not a competent pastor's wife. I rearranged my hair, smoothed an errant smudge of make-up, and took deep, calming breaths. Then, I plastered on a smile and marched into the fellowship hall.

I felt the warmth immediately. With sly grins, every woman I greeted smiled broadly and refused my offers to help. Eventually, I relaxed into my role for the night — a pampered pastor's wife.

Dale helped me carry our belongings home, and thankfully the rain had subsided. I set Jana free and decided I didn't care if she and the cat demolished the tree. I stumbled down the hall to change into my robe and slippers. When I reached to unclasp my brooch, I discovered something odd — the clasp was not on the side where I expected it. I had worn it upside down the whole evening, and it merrily communicated to everyone a message that likely led to all the pampering I'd desperately needed: "OH OH OH."

— Rhonda Dragomir —

65

Glam-ma's Red Christmas Suit

In order to be irreplaceable one must
always be different.
~Coco Chanel

M y sister was thrilled when I told her we were going to make the trip to her house for Christmas. She explained the Christmas tradition she had started shortly after Mom passed away. "We're lining the walkway around the house with luminaries. We'll light a candle as we call out the names of our loved ones who have passed on. When we're finished, we'll have a moment of silence. Then, in unison, we'll say the short prayer that I've printed out. Finally, we'll sing the first verse of "Silent Night," and then go in to have our Christmas Eve dinner. Dress warm because we're expecting snow."

She was so excited that we were coming. After Mom passed away, we had gotten into a nasty fight and didn't talk to each other for a few years. Now that we had finally put aside our differences, it seemed as if we couldn't get enough of each other. We had spent Thanksgiving together and now, for the first time in years, we would also be spending Christmas together. I was just as thrilled as she was.

While running around to pick up last-minute gifts, I came across a two-piece outfit that I thought would be perfect for staying warm during the outdoor ceremony. It was bright red, and the jacket had a hood. It fit me perfectly. I couldn't believe how lucky I was to find such a warm, fuzzy, beautiful red Christmas suit when I wasn't even looking for one. I loved everything about it.

As we prepared to leave, I put on my red suit with a white turtleneck. I looked great. When my husband came in, I asked excitedly, "How do you like my outfit?"

He stopped short, and then he said, "Well, well, I… Yeah, it's nice. We better get going. We have a long ride ahead of us."

When we finally drove up my sister's long driveway, I was excited to see my sister, brother-in-law, nephew and another family member smiling and waving. I pulled up the hood of my jacket so I wouldn't get cold, and then got out of the car with open arms, yelling "MERRY CHRISTMAS!" For some reason, everyone looked completely shocked!

Still smiling but somewhat confused, I repeated, "MERRY CHRISTMAS!" My sister walked over and gave me a hug, and then stood back. My brother-in-law stood with his head tilted to the side. My nephew looked like he was half smiling, half smirking.

Finally, my sister broke the silence by yelling, "WHAT THE HECK DO YOU HAVE ON? IT LOOKS LIKE SHAG CARPET!" Before I could say anything, she bombarded me with questions. "WHERE DID YOU GET THAT THING? YOU LOOK LIKE AN ELF. NO, YOU LOOK LIKE A BIG RED SHEEP. All YOU NEED IS A TAIL! DO YOU SHEAR, VACUUM OR WASH THAT THING?" Then everyone burst out laughing. I tentatively joined in the laughter but thought to myself, *You ought to be glad I'm not an elf because I'd be helping Santa put some names on his naughty list right about now.*

Slowly, I walked over to my very tall nephew, who hugged me. With my head barely reaching his chest, I looked up and whispered, "What's wrong with them? Is my suit that bad?"

He broke out in a laugh and said, "You look like Elmo!" I should've known better than to ask a nineteen-year-old.

The luminary ceremony was touching and absolutely beautiful, but for some reason everyone burst out laughing before we even finished singing "Silent Night." I've often been told that I'm a Glam-ma, but even Glam-mas are allowed to make fashion mistakes. And according to everyone's reactions, I made a big one.

I must admit, that Christmas was one of the best I ever had. I knew we were going to have a great time, but I had no idea that my warm, fuzzy and beautiful red Christmas suit would add to the merriment.

—Francine L. Billingslea—

66

All Around the Table

Against the assault of laughter, nothing can stand.
~Mark Twain

I t began like any Thanksgiving, with silver polishing, airport pick-ups, grocery trips, and more. We knew better than to fool with our traditional menu — it was Norman Rockwell all the way, including Aunt B's famed secret-ingredient pumpkin pies and her baked beans made from scratch.

The day before Thanksgiving was a frenzied one, and our stress levels were up. In addition to all the normal issues of cleaning, shopping, and prepping, there was one big problem: the missing dining room table.

Said table had undergone a mishap — a three-inch slice gouged from the surface. A refinisher with a fine reputation and long experience had hauled it away weeks before, assuring us his repair would be invisible, and promising to return the table by the Monday before the holiday.

But Monday had passed. And Tuesday.

By Wednesday, we were close to canvassing the neighborhood for card tables and TV trays to borrow. But then, at noon, the doorbell rang. And there stood the repairman with the tabletop so perfectly mended we truly couldn't spot the damage.

Soon, the table was back in its place. Dressed for the holiday, it was picture perfect.

Thanksgiving Day dawned. The scent of roasted turkey wafted

through the house. Sweet potatoes were baking, Yukon Gold potatoes were boiling, and cranberry sauce was cooling in the fridge. Our holiday crowd had gathered.

Aunt B, with her dyed red hair, was the relative everyone should be so lucky to have. She lived as if she, not Mister Rogers, had coined this memorable line: "I like you just the way you are." No matter what we did or said, we were loved. She just cared the socks off us, and we knew it.

Unfortunately, smoking had caught up with Aunt B. She'd quit more than twelve years earlier, but she was now in a wheelchair and using oxygen, thanks to COPD.

Another guest, our friend Faye, was also frail. We'd always thought of her as bigger than life — the jokester with hoop earrings, bright, bold outfits, and the loud laugh. But she was also a smoker and now dealing with lung cancer. We all knew this was probably her last Thanksgiving.

We were thankful to be with these two larger than life women as we squeezed in around the table, now groaning with goodies.

Using what energy she could muster, Faye waggled black olives on her fingertips, making the toddler next to her burble in delight. Then she flung some olives around the table. One landed in a water glass. Typical Faye.

At that moment, a strange sound emanated from the dining table. The highly recommended refinisher with the fine reputation and long experience had accidentally screwed the metal bracing back onto the underside of the table using the wrong screws.

Shorter screws.

Slowly, the middle began to sag. We watched open-mouthed as the table transformed in slow motion from a smooth, flat surface to an ever-deepening V.

Creaks, groans, and the sound of metal hitting the stone floor stirred us from our stunned stupor. We flew into action, whipping the baby's highchair and Aunt B's wheelchair to safety. One son dived underneath, bracing the table like Atlas holding up the world.

As if rehearsed, every person grabbed something, and then with all the food and wine and glasses safely away, our son eased out from underneath and we watched the table fully give way. We were speechless. Then came a chortle — Faye's, of course. It spread. Soon, we were all laughing till we couldn't breathe.

With nothing broken, nothing spilled, and no one hurt, we adjourned, shifting from a formal sit-down feast to a casual buffet. The meal itself was perfect, right down to Aunt B's beans and the grand finale — her succulent pumpkin pie with real whipped cream.

We lost our friend Faye that spring and Aunt B not long after. Over the years, many Thanksgivings have melded into one. But in the Family Tales Department, that surprising Thanksgiving stands out.

Each Thanksgiving, sights and scents take us back in time. We even figured out how to duplicate Aunt B's pie. It was her handwritten recipe card that revealed the secret pie ingredient: scorched butter stirred into the pumpkin mix.

And that's how we make them today.

— Edith Hope Fine —

67

Almost Perfect

The only thing faster than the speed of thought
is the speed of forgetfulness. Good thing we have
other people to help us remember.
~Vera Nazarian, The Perpetual Calendar of
Inspiration

Our fourth child arrived in November 1984 — a sweet, healthy girl with dark, fuzzy hair and big, blue eyes. I was very glad she arrived in November because Christmas would soon be upon us, and I needed every day left to organize and prepare.

That year, more preparations were required than usual, as eight additional people were joining us for the holidays — my parents, an aunt and uncle, their daughter, her little boy, and their newly married son and his wife.

Our families had always been close. With our homes a few streets apart, we were together a great deal and shared many good times. So, although there'd be a few more people that year, they were all special to me, and I was excited to have them join us.

Snow was falling in huge, quarter-sized flakes as the crowd arrived on Christmas Eve day. Parcels galore were carried in, and our kids checked every tag as they crammed them under the tree. Extra shaking and sniffing took place when their names were on the tags.

"Okay, everyone is assigned a room, so find the door with your name on it and make yourself at home." I did my best to direct everyone, with my new daughter tucked tightly under one arm. "And when you're settled in, come down for hot chocolate or tobogganing in the back yard."

Squeals of excitement ricocheted from the walls, and the celebration was suddenly in full swing.

At supper, the table was surrounded by rosy-cheeked kids smelling like the great outdoors. The men chatted as the women reviewed the traditional menu for Christmas dinner.

"Do you have all the vegetables, dear?" my mom asked sweetly. "And were you able to get the jellied salad started so I can finish it tonight?"

"It's all done, Mom," I answered.

"What about buns? Did you find those nice soft ones?"

"Yup—fresh as I could get."

"And the turkey is defrosting in the garage?" asked my aunt. "We'll stuff that right after dinner."

Complete silence hung in the air as my face turned red. "Ahhh… the turkey is still in the freezer. I forgot it needed to thaw."

Both my aunt and my mom gave a soft gasp. "Oh, dear." Mom sounded calm, but her brow was furrowed. "How are we going to manage that?"

"Good grief!" my aunt added. "You always defrost the turkey a day ahead." She didn't sound quite as calm. "It's impossible to stuff now."

Years later, I realized I could have just cooked that turkey from frozen, but at the time, dealing with "new baby brain," I panicked.

"My microwave isn't working," I said. "I don't know what to do!" The ladies stared at my stricken face, obviously thinking the same thing.

My husband overheard our laments and pitched in. "We have a microwave at the office. I'll take the guys there, and we can enjoy a sauna while it defrosts."

The plan was brilliant! Within minutes, the men were all loaded in the car, with my newlywed cousin securing the twenty-five-pound turkey on his lap. While they were gone, we cleaned up dinner, corralled the antsy children to listen to *The Night Before Christmas*, tucked them in their beds, and then continued preparations for the next day.

Nervously, we watched the clock. The men finally returned, entering the kitchen carrying a greasy bag, with faces reflecting something akin to fear.

"What happened?" I asked.

"Well," my husband said, "I forgot that the microwave was just a tiny one. The turkey was double the size of the oven, so we crushed it as best we could and squeezed it into the opening. It took every muscle we had to do it, and… you may not like the results." He opened the bag and pulled out an object that had no resemblance to the bird they left with. "By the time we got it crushed and into the microwave, it was squished up against the sides and top, filling the whole space."

"Got a little fried," my cousin said with a grin.

I looked at the squashed, leathery turkey and could only imagine what had taken place inside that office. Perhaps muscles had been used, but by the look of it, I suspected the heel of a shoe had been involved. "Well," I said, "we can go to bed now, since stuffing it is out of the question."

We dropped into our beds, and it felt like we had just fallen asleep when we awoke to a horrific noise. Squinting at the clock revealed it was 4:00 a.m.! The noises were getting louder, so I left my warm covers to investigate and discovered our six-year-old son had found the tool set that was waiting for him under the tree. He'd opened it and was trying out the hammer and saw, in the dark, on what I could only hope was not our furniture.

Soon, the whole house was awake. With sleepy shouts of "Merry Christmas!" everyone staggered down the stairs. I fed the baby while we watched the kids open the rest of their presents. In spite of the chaos, something niggled at the back of my mind. There was something I was forgetting, but I couldn't put my finger on it. Knowing it would eventually come to me, I let it go and enjoyed the morning.

After the torn paper and candy wrappers were cleaned up, the men were snoring where they sat, so we ladies finished preparations for the Christmas dinner, making sure everything would be perfect. It was nice to have the extra help as we worked together in the kitchen. I reviewed the menu. The veggies were cooked, the gravy was made, homemade cranberries awaited in a fancy dish, the buns were cut and buttered, the jellied salad turned out perfectly, and Mom had prepared a beautiful cabbage salad. I found and cooked some stove-top stuffing to make up for the traditional stuffing, and even the mutilated, overcooked turkey didn't look too bad sitting on an elegant platter.

It was all there. We'd done it! The dinner bell rang, and the hungry herd charged to their places at the table. I hadn't figured out what had been bothering me earlier, but the joy of the day quickly replaced any worries. I smiled at my family sitting on either side. Nothing could possibly spoil this.

The aroma of deliciousness filled the room, and we could almost taste that turkey as we joined hands for prayer.

After giving a heartfelt grace, my husband declared, "Well, it's been quite an adventure, but everything looks amazing. Let's eat!"

We started to load up our plates when our nine-year-old daughter leaned over and asked, "Has anyone seen the potatoes?"

Well, it was almost perfect!

— Heather Rodin —

68

Dad's Christmas Rant

A lovely thing about Christmas is that it's compulsory,
like a thunderstorm, and we all go through it together.
~Garrison Keillor

I sit in my chair at the end of the day.
Before too long, I'm asleep where I lay.
I've a right to be tired, of my fête I am proud.
I've been to the mall, battled traffic and crowd.
The gifts are all strewn at my feet on the floor.
If my wallet weren't flat, I'm sure there'd be more.
I drop in my chair at the end of the day.
Before too long, I'm asleep where I lay.
I've a right to be tired, I feel long in the tooth.
I've been in the yard and up on the roof.
From upstairs to down, from gable to eve,
Endless strands of lights to hang, wrap and weave.
I plop in my chair at the end of the day.
Before too long, I'm asleep where I lay.
I've a right to be tired, I sure need a nap.
There were thousands of gifts that we needed to wrap.
My wife and myself, we wrapped up a storm.
From boxes to bags, and some without form.
I fall in my chair at the end of the day.
Before too long, I'm asleep where I lay.
I've a right to be tired, the tree's finally done.

The hunt for the tree was nowhere near fun.
We looked east and west and saw hundreds or more.
The one we selected, too wide for the door.
I glance at my chair just before dawn.
I've exhausted my toolbox, my brain and my brawn.
No time to relax, must get to my room.
I feel I could sleep Christmas Day until noon.
As I've said many times, I've a right to be tired.
Due to three scary words… "Some Assembly Required."

— Michael Fulton —

69

Locked Out

*Family. A little bit of crazy, a little bit of loud
and a whole lot of love.*
~Author Unknown

Christmas lights have always fascinated me. As a child in the 1960s, I eagerly awaited the holidays. Colored lights on a tree or around a window could turn even the most mundane house into something magical!

Back then most people didn't rush to decorate like they do today. My parents waited until the week before Christmas to put up our tree. These days, it's a race to see who can be the first in the neighborhood to decorate, with some lights even going up before Thanksgiving!

In our small town in North Carolina, decorations were slow to appear. There was one exception in our neighborhood, and it happened to be right across the street from our house. Much to my delight, an aluminum tree, complete with a color wheel, began to glow at the beginning of December. Night after night, I propped my elbows on my windowsill and watched that tree change colors. I thought it was beautiful!

Our own decorations were beautiful, too, and after making it through the agonizing wait for them to go up, I couldn't get enough of them. Sparkly fuchsia fabric embedded with tiny, bright blue lights outlined the picture window of our living room, creating the perfect frame for our fuchsia decorated tree. Round and teardrop-shaped glass ornaments adorned the tree, along with lots of silver tinsel and a couple of strands of lights. To my eight-year-old eyes, it was fabulous.

One night, shortly after our tree went up, our parents left to go shopping. While they were gone, my sister and I ran out to the front yard to see how the tree looked through the front window.

After a few minutes of gazing at the beautiful lights, we got cold and decided to go back inside. We ran up to the front door and grabbed the knob, only to find that it wouldn't turn. In disbelief, we tried it again. Same story. The door was locked. We'd been so intent on going out to see the lights that we forgot to make sure we could get back in!

We ran around to the back of our bi-level house and tried the door to the basement. It, too, was locked, as was the sliding-glass door to the family room. We'd locked ourselves out of the house.

Cold and scared, we went back around to the front of the house and tried the doors on our mother's car. Fortunately, the car was unlocked. And though it wasn't a great deal warmer, we were able to sit inside it to wait for our parents to come home.

About an hour later, we saw the lights of our father's car. We got an earful about how careless we'd been.

Three years later, our father was transferred to Columbus, Ohio, and we experienced Christmas in the north, where it was truly cold. It took us a while to adjust, but it finally became home. Life moved on, and soon we were measuring our time in Columbus in years instead of months. My sister went away to college, and I entered high school. We looked forward to Christmas even more because we knew we'd all be together again for a couple of weeks.

Our family loved driving through the neighborhood to see the lights on Christmas Eve. On one particularly cold Christmas Eve, we almost didn't go because of the weather, but I begged my dad to take us anyway. Finally, he gave in. Since my sister's car was in the driveway, he grabbed her keys, and we all headed out.

The neighborhood looked beautiful and we thoroughly enjoyed ourselves. After the drive, Daddy parked my sister's car, and we spilled out into the bitter night. We were all shivering in front of the door when my dad looked at the keys in his hand and realized his mistake… my sister didn't have our house key!

We had done it again! We were locked out after looking at Christmas lights! No one had thought to bring a purse or another set of keys. Our dad frantically searched his pockets, but the only keys he'd picked up were my sister's. We didn't waste time trying the back door — we knew it was locked. Since this was long before cell phones, we couldn't call a locksmith, either. Daddy finally decided that the only way in was to break one of the small windows beside the doorframe and reach around to the handle. Reluctantly, and grumbling all the way, he went in search of a rock so he could break into his own house!

That lockout, like the one ten years before, became a favorite family story. We all learned a valuable lesson: Never, ever leave the house without making sure you actually have a way to get back in!

— Rita Warren DeFoe —

70

Holiday Perfection

What matters is who sits around the table,
not what's on it.
~Author Unknown

The mustard-yellow oven looked like an artifact from the 1970s. I glared at the offensive appliance, roughly the size of a child's Easy-Bake Oven. Next week, our entire family would arrive for Thanksgiving dinner in our new home. I wanted everything to be perfect, but there was no way to fit a turkey in that tiny oven. Who had lived here before us — elves?

My husband Jake shuffled into the room. "It's midnight. What's wrong?"

"Why did the builders put a miniature oven in a large home? I can't make a perfect Thanksgiving turkey in this stupid thing."

Jake rubbed his eyes and yawned. "Let's replace it."

"We just moved. We don't have funds for a new one."

Jake wrapped an arm around my shoulders. "We'll buy a used one." He gestured to my nemesis. "We can rip this out now if you want."

At midnight, the idea made perfect sense. We grabbed tools, removed the old built-in appliance, and cleaned the decades of greasy dirt left behind.

The next morning, we found an online ad: "New stove for sale. $60."

Hopping into our pickup, we drove over for a look. A friendly young couple met us at the door and led us around back to a large shed. The husband said, "We bought this stove back home in Iowa, but there was already one here when we moved in last year. This one's just been sittin' in the shed, so we figured to sell it."

I swiped a layer of dust off the appliance with my finger. Underneath, the white stove gleamed. It looked perfect. Even though our entire remodel budget was sixty dollars, we bought it. The two men loaded it into the truck, and Jake and I drove home, congratulating ourselves on finding a bargain.

Once we maneuvered the stove into the kitchen, we noticed an odd smell.

"It probably just needs a good cleaning," I said. We scrubbed every inch we could reach, inside and out, but the odor got worse.

As the stench permeated the entire house, Jake shared his horrible realization. "I think a dead mouse is stuck in the insulation, but I can't get to it without ripping apart the stove."

"Holiday guests expect aromas like pine boughs or gingerbread. Our house reeks of rodent carcass. We need to do something," I whined.

So we ran the self-cleaning feature repeatedly every day.

By Thanksgiving, the stink had dissipated. Mostly. I felt confident that by the time our guests arrived, the delectable scent of perfectly roasted turkey would cover any lingering odor.

Humming, I stuffed the turkey, slid it into the new range and inspected the side dishes. Ruby-colored cranberry sauce, potatoes waiting to be mashed, and pumpkin pies from the bakery all passed inspection.

The freshly cleaned house looked perfect, so I dressed, put on make-up, and did my hair. I wanted to look perfect, too — or as perfect as possible despite wrinkles and acne.

As family members arrived, we greeted them, gave them the house tour, and then sat together, chatting and laughing. After a time, Jake pulled me aside. "Honey, the turkey isn't cooking."

I hurried to the kitchen and opened the stove door. The huge raw turkey perched sadly in the cold oven.

Agh! Had I burned out the stove with repeated mouse cremations? I stood paralyzed, dismay tap-dancing across my brain.

My eagle-eyed mom glided into the kitchen and pointed out the problem within seconds. "Sweetheart, it will cook faster if you turn on the oven." She tapped the knob, firmly fixed in the "off" position.

Panic set in. "What are we going to do? We have a house full of people, and nothing to feed them except raw turkey!"

Jake sauntered downstairs and brought up a large ham from the basement fridge. At my questioning look, he winked. "I wanted it on hand just in case."

And he was perfectly right, as usual.

That Thanksgiving, our family ate ham sandwiches — and ribbed me unmercifully about not turning on the stove.

Although far from what I'd envisioned, that Thanksgiving was perfect in its own way. While munching my sandwich, I realized I didn't need to strive for magazine-perfect food presentations or a picture-perfect house.

My focus didn't need to be on perfection, but rather gratefulness. I looked around the table and thanked God for the people in my life: my husband, who showed me love in unexpected ways, like ripping out a stove because it bothered me, and having the foresight to tuck away an emergency ham; my mother, who was still teaching me cooking basics — like flipping the knob to the "on" setting; and our precious daughter and grandson, siblings, and cousins. I silently thanked God for the perfect blessing of having family together.

We invited everyone back for Christmas. This time, rather than trying to make everything perfect, we decided to skip the fancy turkey dinner and offer Crock-Pots of soup instead.

I even made sure to turn the dials onto the "high" setting so the soup would cook in time for Christmas dinner. Only one thing would have made those Crock-Pots of soup more perfect — if I'd remembered to plug them in.

— Jeanie Jacobson —

71

Three Bags Full

After a good dinner, one can forgive anybody,
even one's own relations.
~Oscar Wilde

I had baked the pies early that morning — apple, pumpkin, and mincemeat. There was a cherry cheesecake in the fridge. The side dishes were put together and ready to go into the oven. Candied yams, stuffing, mushroom casserole, green-bean casserole, and baked beans had been prepared. As always, I wished I had a double oven!

I stopped for a moment to realize how lucky I was to have an oven at all. A scant thirty-six hours before, I had turned it on to bake a casserole for dinner, and nothing happened. It just sat there, cold and silent. I was on the phone early the next morning, already bracing myself for the probability that Thanksgiving dinner would have to be take-out. But my landlord surprised me — they had guys knocking on the door with a brand-new oven in just a few hours. The day before Thanksgiving? No problem.

And now that shiny new oven was full of a big bird and the kitchen was beginning to smell like a combination of turkey and heaven. The cats wandered in, noses twitching in the air. I laughed and shooed them out, promising them they would get a special treat later.

I checked the mound of dough in the bowl on top of the refrigerator — yep, it was ready! I got out my muffin pans and poured oil into a small bowl. I dipped my fingers in the oil and rubbed my hands together, coating them. Then I realized I was still wearing my rings. Sighing, I washed my hands and removed the rings, wrapping them in a piece of paper towel, which I put on my desk. I congratulated myself for remembering *before* I dived into the dough this time!

When the pans were full of dough balls that would soon become dinner rolls, I put them back on top of the refrigerator to rise a second time. Then I turned my attention to the sink full of dirty dishes. It was hard to keep up when I was cooking a giant holiday meal, but the kitchen wasn't big enough for leaving them to be an option.

I could hear my husband vacuuming in the living room. He had already cleaned the bathroom. After the vacuuming was done, he started dusting the knick-knack shelves. Just as he finished that, we heard a knock on the door. Our company had arrived. My brother, my sister-in-law, and two of our friends were there for Thanksgiving dinner.

They came in, and my husband visited with them in the living room while I finished the mashed potatoes and gravy, all while rotating the side dishes through the oven and, lastly, the dinner rolls. While they were baking, I put down some canned food for the cats so they wouldn't be tempted to join us at the table. They looked insulted — meaty pâté isn't nearly as appetizing when a real turkey is sitting on the counter! Again, I promised them they could have some later. "Just stay off Daddy's lap while we eat, okay?"

Finally, only twenty minutes past my target time, the turkey was on the table, surrounded by pretty dishes full of tasty sides and a heaping bowl of perfectly browned rolls. I snapped a couple of pictures and called everyone to the table. We gathered around and said grace, and then my husband carved the turkey. We were laughing and joking, telling stories, and keeping one ear tuned in to the football game on the TV in the living room.

We were gathered around the table and wondering if we had room for dessert, when I realized I had forgotten to put my rings back on. I walked over to my desk in the living room. The rings were gone.

I turned around and asked my husband, "Have you seen the paper towel that was on my desk?"

He replied. "Yeah, I threw it away."

"YOU WHAT? THAT HAD MY RINGS IN IT!"

Every mouth dropped open. My husband's face turned a sickly shade of whitish green. I loved my wedding and engagement ring set, and I was pretty damn fond of my anniversary ring, too. Losing them to overzealous cleaning was not cool. Through clenched teeth, I asked the dreaded question: "Where is the trash?"

Of course, it was in the Dumpster, somewhere in three bags of wadded-up paper towels because my hubby had cleaned every surface he could find—something I would normally appreciate, but not when it meant a treasure hunt through the garbage! Mixed in with the paper towels were empty cans, eggshells, the turkey wrapping, cat litter, and all the other "stuff" that normally goes into a trashcan.

Just as I was wondering how I could tactfully shoo everyone out the door, my friend Diane stood up and said, "Well, let's get started on this." Going through one's own garbage is bad enough, but this lady was willing to go through someone else's!

Dessert and football forgotten, we spent the next hour with chairs gathered around the three thirty-gallon trash bags, painstakingly unwrapping every single wadded-up paper towel. We laughed and joked, but there was an undercurrent of concern. At one point, I excused myself to wash the raw pumpkin off my hands, using the time to wipe away tears I didn't want anyone to see. I was simultaneously wracked with guilt and furious with the idiot who didn't check to see what he was throwing away!

As we neared the bottom of the last bag, I asked my husband if he was sure there were only three. He looked like he wanted to be somewhere else, but he nodded in confirmation. Seeing the desolation on my face, he volunteered to Dumpster dive if we didn't find it—just in case the rings had fallen out.

And then there it was—a paper towel unfolded to reveal shining gold and sparkling diamonds. I yipped loudly and snatched them out of my sister-in-law's hand, nearly scratching her in the process. I glared at my husband as I put them back in their familiar place on my fingers. I held out my hands for everyone to see. They applauded. My husband said, "Next time, put them in a better place!"

I threw a dinner roll at him.

— Linda Sabourin —

Chapter 8

There's Nothing Like Family

72

The Other Wife

From home to home, and heart to heart, from one
place to another. The warmth and joy of Christmas,
bring us closer to each other.
~Emily Matthews

It was a few days before Christmas and the temperature was below zero. While frost coated the insides of the windows, our small kitchen was warm, steamy, and scented with the vanilla of freshly baked cookies. As I pulled each batch from the oven, our toddler daughter, Molly, adorned them — and the floor — with frosting and multicolored sprinkles. Seasonal tunes floated from the radio, and Molly happily added her lisping voice to "Dingle Bells" and "Fwosty the Snowman."

The holiday spirit was alive and well in our home, though this year my widowed father was away, so our Christmas Day celebration would include just the three of us — me, Molly, and my husband, Tom. Christmas was Tom's favorite holiday, and he began preparing months in advance, hiding presents in drawers, stirring up his traditional homemade spaghetti sauce, and triumphantly bringing home boxes of decadent chocolates or a bottle of some exotic liqueur for a Christmas Eve treat.

The one negative about Christmas was that Tom's four older children, from his first marriage, always spent the holiday with their mother. They had done so since the divorce, years before I had met Tom. But though they were in high school and college now, he remembered carrying the little ones outside on his shoulders to search for Santa among the stars before they went to bed. He always paused for a moment on Christmas Eve to gaze up at the nighttime sky, and I knew he was with the children then for a moment.

On this particular icy day, the phone rang, interrupting our holiday sing-along. I was under the table chasing cookie sprinkles, but I crawled out, brushed the sugar crumbs from Molly's round cheeks, and picked up the receiver. "Hello?"

The person on the other end hesitated for a moment. "Hello? This is Lori," I repeated, as I handed Molly the next bare cookie, ready for her artistry.

"This is Jackie." The voice on the line was familiar to me in spite of its unusual hesitancy. Jackie was Tom's ex-wife. Although we had met only in passing at a few child-related functions, she did call occasionally to discuss co-parenting issues with Tom, and I often answered the phone. Their calls were always brief and to the point.

"Jackie, hi! Tom's still at work. You can probably catch him before he leaves the office," I said.

"Actually, it is you I wanted." This was new. Startled, I sat at the table. Molly handed me a gooey snowman cookie, and I accepted absent-mindedly. "Me?"

I could hear the inhalation of breath on the other end of the line and steeled myself for bad news. Illness? An accident? Had one of the children been injured? What could it be that she wasn't speaking directly with Tom?

"I'm just going to come out and say it," she continued. "Tom and I have been divorced over ten years now." Confused, I mumbled an affirmative. "Well, anyway, it was an ugly divorce, and we were both pretty angry for a lot of years. I blamed him, and I'm sure he blamed me, too. But looking back on it, I think there was plenty of fault on both sides, and I've had ten years to think it over.

"The thing is," she went on, her usually energetic voice subdued, "I know Tom loves his kids, and though we didn't get along when we were married, he really is a great dad. The way we've been doing the holidays… well, the kids don't see as much of him as they should. I'd like to put an end to it, but I need your help."

Transfixed, I clutched the phone as Jackie explained, "The way I see it, it all boils down to you and me. We could avoid each other because the world expects us to. But if we are willing and able to get together for the sake of our kids, they can all have their father, and they can have each other.

"There is no reason for us to pretend to dislike each other. We don't even know each other. Maybe, if we did, we could actually be friends. I'd like to give it a try if you're willing. Would you, Tom and Molly like to join us at my house for Christmas Day? It might be the best gift we could ever give the kids—all five of them."

A picture flashed before my eyes for a split second—my impression of Tom's face when I informed him that we would be spending Christmas Day at his ex-wife's house. Normally, a decision like this would have been a topic for discussion and mutual decision, but… "That sounds wonderful," I said. "I'll let Tom know. I'm sure he'll be… amenable." A giggle of combined relief and amusement from the other end made me laugh, too. We didn't know it, but in that moment a family was re-born.

Tom's expression was indeed a memorable mixture of surprise, suspicion, excitement and dread. But to his credit, he recognized the olive branch and accepted it. It wasn't simple. Everyone was nervous when we arrived, carrying chocolates, liqueurs, and cookies with sprinkles. But the irony of the situation brought about great amusement, and the day was a true success.

It was followed in turn by other family events and holidays over the years—sometimes at Jackie's house, sometimes at ours. Memories were made over board games, lively poker games, charades, and jokes. Pictures from those days preserve the laughter of a family united. The five children—six, with the addition of youngest sister Kathleen—became a group of siblings loving and fiercely loyal to one another, bonded by their mutual memories and their pride in a truly unique, unconventional and quirky family.

The tradition continued until Jackie's sudden death. At her funeral, Tom gave the eulogy. It was one of the rare times I'd seen him cry. And in a tip of the hat to what transpired between two mothers on that bitter December day, their son Danny remembered that "for all these years, Christmas finally meant something again."

None of us ever learned what inspired that Christmas call after a decade of strained relations. Tom has since joined Jackie, leaving me widowed. All the children and grandchildren are mine now, and the spirit of that long-ago call remains. The six siblings travel miles across many states to be together whenever possible, making memories for their own children as their parents did for them so many years ago, when a hand extended in friendship created a family.

As for me, on Christmas Eve I step away from the loving, rambunctious family. I take a moment to look up at the nighttime sky and be with Tom. And I ask him to wish Jackie a Merry Christmas, from me, with thanks for our Christmas legacy.

—Loreen Martin Broderick—

73

My Obsession

The family — that dear octopus from whose tentacles
we never quite escape, nor, in our inmost hearts,
ever quite wish to.
~Dodie Smith

"**O**kay, enough is enough. Will you guys please straighten up? Is asking for one decent Christmas photo too much?"

My scolding and whining only made them laugh harder and act sillier.

The most challenging — but also the most rewarding — part of the holidays for me has always been trying to capture perfect family photos. To say it's an obsession might be putting it mildly — it's more like a matter of life or death.

Every year, all family members must help to fulfill this obsession — which they do, but only after considerable begging, bribing and pouting from me, and usually from them as well.

The little ones are delightful and such a joy to photograph; however, my five grown children (ranging in age from forty-two to fifty-five) are an entirely different story.

This past Christmas Eve was the most challenging of all. After getting individual pictures of everyone with Santa, we needed group photos of adult grandchildren, younger grandchildren, great-grandchildren, couples, and five generations with great-great Granny. Whew! We were all exhausted from forcing smiles and striking novel, yet traditional poses while simultaneously trying to appear spontaneous.

The moment I put my camera out of reach, family members knew they were finally free to loosen up and relish the rest of the evening. But, to everyone's dismay, just as the festivities got into full swing, the dreaded words escaped my mouth: "We forgot to get a group photo of you five kids!"

My untimely announcement was met with cries of disgruntlement from said kids:

"I'm hungry; let's wait."

"Can't we miss just one year?"

"You can do it without me."

"I need a drink first."

"We can't find Jeff."

Oh, how I wished I'd gotten their picture out of the way at the very beginning of the evening.

In drill-sergeant fashion, I grabbed the brood, lined them up, and shouted orders right and left: "Chris, stand up straight. Tim, put the elf back on the shelf. Jeff, please take off your coat. Darren, you're too tall. Jacqui, why in heaven's sake are you holding a banana?"

They howled in unison as six-foot-five Darren challenged, "What do you want me to do — cut off my head?"

My thoughts exactly. "Whatever it takes to get this photo."

In frustration, Tim finally urged, "Mom, just put us where and how you want us."

And that's exactly what I did. Then I pleaded, "Please don't move a muscle; just smile and look natural."

That conflicting comment had everyone in the room roaring with laughter.

When all was said and done, after a hilarious half-hour, we ended up with one or two decent shots. Oh, how I love these kids!

Excluding the time that two of the boys were serving in the military, our children have never lived more than a few miles away from us. We are so blessed to be surrounded by the five kids and their families year 'round, but it's extra special when we're all together to celebrate the holidays. So it's reasonable, in my mind, to want to preserve these occasions forever, even at the expense of my loved ones.

The photo albums I've compiled over the span of fifty years—a nostalgic journey into our priceless Christmases past—are enjoyed by everyone in the family, from the youngest grandchild to ninety-seven-year-old Granny.

As icing on the Christmas cake, our tree is always beautifully adorned with precious photo ornaments that multiply as our family continues to grow. It probably comes as no surprise that I've been trying unsuccessfully to get last year's group photo of my five kids to fit within this year's special ornament—without cutting off Darren's head!

— Connie Kaseweter Pullen —

74

The Labels

The more we're willing to accept what is,
and not what we thought, we'll find ourselves
exactly where we belong.
~Meredith Grey, Grey's Anatomy

One morning close to Christmas, a deliveryman stood at my front door with two boxes from Amazon. Puzzled, I asked, "Who are those addressed to? I don't think we ordered these."

Then I looked at the labels: JoAnne Duffy Bennett. Bennett was my married name, but Duffy had never been my maiden name, because I didn't know my real birth father.

For more than twenty years, I had been led to believe that a certain man was my late birth father. No one could possibly imagine how shocked I was to have a stranger contact me this past year through a DNA site where we had both tested. He showed up as my half-sibling. I was so confused. This very close DNA match and I are only four months apart in age and had been born at the same hospital. How could this be when I knew the identity of both my late birth parents, and his mom and dad weren't either of them?

My new brother was amazingly patient as I tried to figure this out. I couldn't have asked for a nicer person to be related to me. I started building a new family tree on AncestryDNA using his dad's name as my birth father, and all his relatives started connecting perfectly, which had not been the case with the man I had been told was my biological father.

It was my understanding that he was going to tell our two siblings about me when they attended a concert together. But then I started receiving Facebook messages from total strangers. One said, "Hello Sister." Another said, "Hi, I am your little brother." And the next one said, "Hello, um, I'm not sure how to say this but to just say it. I hear that you are my mom's sister. It's nice to officially meet you. I'm twenty-four." I can't explain how relieved I was that, in the end, this incredibly kind family was truly from my paternal side.

I had substitute fathers, but they didn't give me their last names. No one understood how much I wanted a "real" father's last name that I could call my own. But now I was seeing my real father's name in black and white — on these two boxes. After all those years of having a non-identifying birth certificate, no birth announcement, a few baby pictures, four "absent" fathers and two mothers, I finally felt a sense of belonging.

Through my tears, I kept looking at my name: JoAnne Duffy Bennett. Duffy fit so perfectly between my first name and my married name. Whoever sent these special packages knew how significant reclaiming this missing puzzle piece had been in my life journey.

I will always save those two simple address labels as if *they* were my gifts, but I was also tickled to see what was inside the boxes. So much thoughtfulness went into picking out two of the cutest LED bears — one from my brother, and the other from his dog, Speedy. Ever since I was in the sixth grade and wrote my first term paper on the "The Bear Facts," I have loved collecting stuffed bears.

My three birth siblings gave me what I most desired: to feel that deep sense of acceptance and belonging from a family that I can call my very own.

—JoAnne Bennett—

75

Thanksgiving with the Family

Some family trees bear an enormous crop of nuts.
~Wayne H.

I spent this Thanksgiving with my mother, my father, my brother, my dog and my cat in our house in the suburbs with its white picket fence. My brother flew in from Texas to spend the holiday with us. While my mom prepared Thanksgiving dinner, my brother and I watched the Macy's Thanksgiving Day Parade on TV, followed by *The National Dog Show*. As my brother snuggled the dog and cat, I told him he should have been a veterinarian instead of a doctor.

My parents argued over how to serve the turkey, and my mom was driven crazy by a mysterious beeping sound, the source of which took a while to find. We took those snafus in stride, though, as they're pretty par for the course. When my brother was a kid, he was given a school assignment that involved describing his family's Thanksgiving routine. He wrote that before his mother prepared the meal, she covered the fire alarms with tinfoil.

Once we discovered that the beeping noise was coming from the oven, we gathered around the table to enjoy our meal. It included turkey, stuffing, sweet potatoes, asparagus and a dish my brother and I dubbed "junky corn mush" as children. Dessert was pumpkin pie with whipped cream. We reminisced about the past, pondered the future and enjoyed the present. My dad promised to sweep the leaves off the porch later, and my mom reminded him that next week he needed to bring her to the train station.

After we finished the meal, we squeezed together on the sofa, smiled and took a family photo. Then we turned on the television and laughed over a sitcom together.

We're like the stereotypical Norman Rockwell portrait of a loving, cookie-cutter family, except for one small detail: My parents have been separated for twenty-five years and divorced sixteen years ago. The mom in this picture-perfect portrait recently left her second husband and now has a significant other in Chicago. The dad has a significant other in France who has two teenage children of her own and is around the same age as his daughter from his first marriage. The child of the mom's second husband died of a drug overdose. The son in this portrait has some questionable political views. The daughter has some pretty severe mental-health issues.

The dog is currently at the center of a custody battle between the mother and her second husband. The cat, well, I guess the cat has the cleanest record of us all, but he did begin life as a stray and has a chunk missing from his ear to prove it.

For the past fifteen years or so, my brother and I have gone to Connecticut with our father to spend Thanksgiving at my sister's house, while my mother spent the holiday with our stepfather's family. This Thanksgiving was her first after leaving my stepfather. She didn't want to spend Thanksgiving alone, so we decided the four of us would celebrate Thanksgiving as "the original gang" in her new house. (She shares the house with me. Another mark against the daughter is that she's failed to become an independent adult.)

My dad was already well acquainted with our new house. In fact, he paid for half of it. Sure, he was a little frustrated the last time he bought my mother and me a house so we could escape my stepfather, and we returned a month later (right after our last dog died tragically and unexpectedly), but he was willing to take the risk again. This time, we would be living closer to him. To my father, family is everything.

It actually means a lot to all four of us. We all know that life doesn't turn out as planned. We've never been the most conventional family, and we've had our fair share of conflicts with each other. But through all the hardships, hospitalizations, deaths and divorces that life has thrown our way, we've been there for each other. That is something to be thankful for.

Besides, even when life throws you lemons and curveballs, even when it breaks your heart, fractures your family and becomes abnormal in a thousand different ways, in the end you still get to enjoy a lovely holiday with your first husband, your children and your pets in your cozy little house with a white picket fence in the suburbs. Just ask my mother.

— Kira Popescu —

Ashley's Angel

...and a little child shall lead them.
~Isaiah 11:6

Decorating at Christmas has always been a big deal at our house. The children help pull ornaments and garland from boxes while their dad sets up the tree and wrestles with the lights. Christmas music plays while we decorate the tree and sip hot chocolate.

"Here's the sleigh Aunt Debra gave me for my first Christmas!" yells Joseph.

"Look, Mama," says Rebecca. "Here are Grandma's crocheted snowflakes."

"I found the angels Mrs. McGrath made for us," Rachel announces.

Carol McGrath's angels. I remember the day Carol's minivan pulled into the driveway. As I greeted her at the front door, I noticed the shoebox she carried.

Seated on the edge of my brown sofa, Carol lifted the lid of the box and pulled out a small ceramic angel. Four more angels peeped at me from a nest of shredded newspaper. "Arlene, when my ceramics instructor showed our class these angel ornaments, I knew I had to make a set for your family."

This sweet, bubbly woman with a quick smile continually thought of others. My children had enjoyed her as their Sunday school teacher a few years earlier. We all adored her.

I reached for the angel. Carol had carved "Mom" into the hem of her red robe and painted her hair dark like mine. I glanced at the angels in the box. Carol had painted their hair to represent the members of my family. Each wore a distinctive robe of red, blue, green, pink, or silver. Two sang from songbooks, two held candles, and the hands of one were folded in prayer.

"I'm sorry I've only finished four of your angels," my friend apologized.

I looked from the angel in my hand to the box. "But, Carol, I see five."

She pulled back the shredded paper so I could read the names carved on the robes: Dad, Joseph, and Rachel. The final angel had no name.

"Rebecca's angel hasn't been fired in the kiln yet," Carol explained. "She's painted a soft brown, and her hands are folded in prayer like Joseph's angel. I'll bring her over in about a week."

Ah, I thought, *the nameless angel serves as a filler.*

Before the gift-giver could even back out of my steep driveway, I arranged the angels on the tree. I knew I would always treasure this gift from a dear friend.

When Carol delivered Rebecca's angel the following week, I hung it on the tree and thanked her profusely. But when I offered her the nameless angel, she insisted I keep it.

What would I do with an extra angel? In the end, I left it in the small box I labeled "Carol McGrath's Angels."

Each Christmas, we carefully unwrapped the angels. Sometimes, we hung them in a tight cluster, sometimes in a straight row, and sometimes scattered all over the tree. It seemed a shame to leave the silver angel in the box, but there was no reason to hang her up as she did not represent a family member.

And then something happened.

While putting away the decorations one year, I removed six angels. "How did the extra angel get on the tree?" I wondered.

The same thing happened the next year. I never seemed to think about it in the midst of decorating, listening to Christmas carols, and drinking hot chocolate. And no one was ever around when I put away the decorations.

One year, while rearranging ornaments to fill in vacant spaces on the tree, I discovered the nameless angel. Tucked deep in the branches on the back of the tree, other ornaments strategically hid her from view.

When the children came home from school, I ambushed them. The silver angel dangled from my fingertips. "Who's been sneaking the extra angel onto the tree?"

The look on ten-year-old Rachel's face gave her away, but it took several minutes to get the story out of her. In a near whisper, she confessed, "That's Ashley's angel."

"Ashley?" I asked.

"Ashley is your baby who died, Mama," Rachel explained. "I saw the angel in the box and thought about Ashley. She should have a place on our tree, even if I never got to know her."

Tears trickled down Rachel's cheeks and mine. Her older brother and younger sister stood in respectful silence. They knew my first pregnancy had ended in a miscarriage. They had heard how devastated I was over the loss of that child, but I had no idea Rachel also felt a sense of loss.

"Where did you get the name 'Ashley'?" I managed to ask.

"You said you didn't know if the baby was a boy or girl. A boy at school told my friend Ashley her name could also be for a boy, like the man in *Gone with the Wind*. So I figured Ashley was a good name for the baby."

I stepped into the kitchen for a napkin to wipe my eyes.

"Did I make you sad, Mama?" Rachel asked.

"No," I said between sniffs, "I'm glad you thought of it, sweetie."

I blew my nose and then said, "Ashley. What a lovely name! And a beautiful silver angel with a lovely name shouldn't hide on the back of the tree. Let's find a place for her with the rest of the family."

Ashley has enjoyed a place of prominence on our tree every Christmas since that day.

— Arlene Janet Ledbetter —

Thanksgivings with Grandpa

Surely, two of the most satisfying experiences in life must be those of being a grandchild or a grandparent.
~Donald A. Norber

In 2008, I graduated from college at the beginning of a recession. Although I graduated with honors and had plenty of solid recommendations from professors as well as collegiate work experience, finding a job proved to be a near-impossible task. Eventually, I stopped focusing my search for jobs in my field and broadened my reach to other entry-level jobs. Thankfully, I landed a job a few months after graduation with a golf club back home. The pay was low, but it was a job, and it would provide enough to pay the rent and other bills.

As the months went by, I proved myself a hard worker and was rewarded with more responsibility. This responsibility included taking on multiple duties outside the scope of my position, but unfortunately it did not come with more pay. Due to those extra responsibilities, it was necessary that I work on-site not only after hours, but also most holidays. For the first time, I found myself facing the reality that I wouldn't be with my family during the holidays.

When November rolled around and I was asked to work on Thanksgiving, I couldn't help feeling deep disappointment.

Then, a week before Thanksgiving, I received a call from my

paternal grandfather. He had decided to stay in town and wanted to know why I wasn't with the rest of the family. I explained to him that my job required that I work on Thanksgiving, and that my benefits didn't include paid time off. He asked, "Want to go to Thanksgiving lunch with me?"

I thought about it for a minute. I didn't have to be at work during the lunch rush; it was only for dinner. "Sure, I'd love that. Do you want to come over, and I'll cook?"

"No," he laughed. "Don't go spending any money. We'll go out. Cracker Barrel is open for Thanksgiving. We'll go there."

"Oh, okay. That sounds fine then. Thanks, Grandpa!"

I was a little dismayed at the prospect of going to a restaurant for Thanksgiving. After all, I was used to home-cooked meals for the holidays. I was a decent cook myself and happy to cook dinner, but I didn't dare argue with Grandpa!

Grandpa arrived at my apartment on Thanksgiving morning. We watched a bit of the Thanksgiving Day Parade on TV, something I always enjoyed doing as a child, and then ventured out to Cracker Barrel. The parking lot was packed. Thankfully, we found a spot, and I squeezed through the large crowd to put our names on the waiting list. While we waited, we went outside and sat down in the rocking chairs to chat. I found myself laughing and trading stories with Grandpa, and realized after every chuckle and creak of the rocking chair that it was a very familiar and calming experience. As a child on warm summer days, Grandpa would always take me out to the front porch, and we would rock away in his homemade rocking chairs, guessing which color car would drive by next. I'd forgotten how much fun I had playing such a simple game with him, and how much I cherished the one-on-one time with my grandfather.

Fortunately, we only waited a few minutes before our name was called, and we were feasting away on the Thanksgiving special.

"Now see," Grandpa laughed between bites, "this is every bit as good as any other food."

I nodded, my mouth full.

"And this way," he continued, "you have no dishes to clean. We can just go back and relax."

After we ate, we browsed the country store for a bit, and then Grandpa paid for our lunch.

"Oh, Grandpa, you didn't have to do that! I can pay for us." I tugged on his arm.

"Oh, hush," he laughed. "I've got it."

I thanked him, and we made our way back to my apartment. We sat down for a while, and talked about how great the food was and how much fun we had. After an hour or so, Grandpa pulled himself up and stretched.

"All right. Come on with me!" he shouted. I laughed. Any time Grandpa took his leave, he always invited me along.

"I'd love to, but you know I have to go to work." I smiled.

He smiled and chuckled. "Oh, I know. You be careful tonight, okay?"

I nodded and wrapped my arms around him in a tight hug. "Thank you so much for today."

"Oh, you're welcome."

"Seriously, thank you. It means a lot." I squeezed him just a bit tighter. "I love you."

"Love you, too," he said quietly. He gave me a tight hug back and headed out for the evening. I headed off to work, feeling happier and more uplifted than I expected.

The following year, I was still at the same job and still had to work the holiday. Not wanting me to be alone that year either, Grandpa invited me out to Cracker Barrel again.

In 2010, I found myself a new job within my field of study. However, I was pulling long hours because I wanted to prove myself a capable employee, and the pressure was really high in those first few months. Although I had paid time off as part of my new benefits package, I elected not to travel out of town with the rest of the family. Grandpa didn't go out of town either. Instead, he invited me out to lunch again that Thanksgiving.

As the years passed and I built a career path for myself, I had more than enough vacation time to take if I wanted to travel out of town. However, I realized that I had a new tradition that meant the world to me: spending Thanksgiving with my grandfather.

Every year, we spend Thanksgiving at Cracker Barrel together. We rock in the rocking chairs, swap stories, browse the store, tell each other secrets, and playfully argue about who is going to pick up the tab. I always lose. It's our special time, just the two of us, and I cherish and look forward to Thanksgiving with Grandpa every year. Sometimes, the best traditions are made when you aren't even trying.

— Whitney Woody —

78

Home for the Holidays

Call it a clan, call it a network, call it a tribe,
call it a family: Whatever you call it,
whoever you are, you need one.
~Jane Howard

We were on a romantic weekend getaway when we got the call. Julie, our eighteen-year-old niece, had been hospitalized with pneumonia. It was her first semester at college. What had started out as a nagging cough had quickly morphed into difficulty breathing, turning what should have been an exciting new chapter of her life into a nightmare.

As I listened to my husband, Joe, speak with his sister on the phone, I knew what we had to do. I watched through the window of our cozy cabin as the fiery orange maple leaves drifted to the ground. My heart went out to Julie's parents, Keith and Amy. Julie was their only child; their world revolved around her. And while her going away to school was a difficult change for them, they knew Julie was well prepared, and they were looking forward to seeing her blossom on her new adventure.

Julie was studying to be a nurse. But now, she was receiving around-the-clock care from a dedicated team of nurses at a hospital in the state where she was attending college.

Joe and I rarely took vacations. We had scrimped and saved up for this trip all year, but my husband's family needed our support. So we checked out of our cabin and drove the four hours to reach them, spending the rest of our weekend in a hospital waiting room, offering our comfort and prayers.

It was a scary situation, but there was a lot of hope at the hospital that day. Keith and Amy had been through rough spots before and come out stronger on the other side. Julie's story would be the same, they felt sure. We returned home feeling optimistic.

But over the next couple of weeks, Julie's health went from bad to worse as the fluid filled her lungs, and she fought for every breath. Before long, a breathing tube became necessary. Term papers and semester exams fell to the wayside.

Keith and Amy rented a small apartment in the city where their daughter was hospitalized so they could be near her at all times. They went on family medical leave, putting their jobs on hold. Family and friends did what they could to support the struggling family from afar, sending well wishes, groceries, gas cards—anything they thought would be useful. Amy called daily with updates.

Knowing what they were going through, Thanksgiving passed quietly. We missed them at our table.

As the weeks went by, Julie's condition continued to deteriorate. Her temperature soared. By December, her doctors had induced a coma. They were using a tilt table and physical therapy to keep her muscles healthy in hopes she would have use for them again. Twice, the phone rang in the middle of the night at Keith and Amy's tiny apartment. Hospital staff was calling because they thought the end was near for Julie. But Julie clung to life.

No one wanted to talk about Christmas, but it was approaching quickly. The rest of the world was preparing to celebrate. Our neighbors were stringing lights on their porch rails; store windows glittered with shiny gifts. Everywhere we looked, we saw the signs of the season.

My heart hurt every time we saw a car drive by with an evergreen tree tied to its roof. Not only was part of our family dealing with a sick child who might never come home, but they were separated from the rest of the family at the time of year when people come together. Our support felt far away. None of us felt much like celebrating.

Then Joe had an idea. What if we could take Christmas to Keith,

Amy and Julie? It wouldn't be fancy, but it would be heartfelt. The extended family united behind the idea, and soon we were busy with the planning.

It wouldn't be the same kind of Christmas we looked forward to each year—with roasted turkey, piles of presents and the whole family gathered by the fireplace. And it would mean a lot of work. We would have to pack up our small children, travel hours to get there, and stay in a hotel. It would be a subdued celebration, but at least we would all be together.

As we began to put our plan in motion, Amy called with a bit of good news. Julie's temperature was going down. The medications were beginning to work. We prayed for a miracle.

By the time Christmas week arrived, Julie had made even more progress. She wasn't out of the woods, but she was awake and talking. A couple of us at a time were able to gown up and spend time by her hospital bed, sharing a few small presents.

But mostly we shared a different kind of gift: our support, laughter, and the kind of casual conversation we all take for granted. True, she wouldn't be home for Christmas, but our hearts were full of hope that someday soon she would be.

Back at the hotel that night, we ate Chinese food as our kids played with their cousins at the indoor pool. Our only Christmas tree was the one in the hotel lobby. It wasn't a conventional Christmas, but it was a hopeful one.

After months of intense therapy, Julie was eventually able to go home. Inspired by the amazing care she received, she went on to finish college and become a neonatal intensive care nurse. And while some scars, like the ones in her lungs, remain, she was able to marry and have a precious child of her own.

Since then, we've had many merrier Christmases with our dear niece. But I'll never forget how close we came to losing her, and how we all came together as a family on that Christmas so many years ago.

—C.L. Nehmer—

79

The Joy in Giving

Christmas waves a magic wand over this world, and
behold, everything is softer and more beautiful.
~Norman Vincent Peale

My sixteen-year-old son asked, "Mom, would it be alright for me to try to sell some of the overgrown Christmas trees out back?"

"I'm sure that would be fine with us, Jeff. Where are you planning to sell them?"

"I was thinking of asking Dad's chiropractor friend in town. He has plenty of extra parking space at his office."

I agreed with Jeff's idea. It's always nice for teens to earn some extra spending money, especially around the holidays.

We'd planted the noble firs and Scotch pines to offset some of our taxes after purchasing the property on which we planned to build our new home. Most of the trees were overgrown since we'd been too busy to do anything with them. Therefore, any extra money they could generate at this time would be like icing on the cake.

The following Friday, Jeff used his dad's chainsaw to cut down about two dozen of the best trees and made several awesome signs with plywood he found in the old shed on the property. After stringing the colorful lights he found in the attic around the tree lot, he was bound to attract locals as well as weekend commuters on their way back from skiing at the mountain. His dad's friend let him use the lot without charge since he appreciated and encouraged good work ethics for teens.

Jeff sold most of the trees he'd taken to the lot on Saturday, and several people said they'd come back on Sunday if he could restock. He got up early Sunday morning and talked his younger brother into helping him cut more trees before heading into town to set them up.

The following weekend, Jeff got both his brother and sister to help him, since business was booming. He was a good salesman, keeping his prices fair.

All three kids learned a lot about kindness while selling trees. The money became less important to them than making certain everyone left with a tree, regardless of how much they could afford to pay.

They shared with me about a man and his wife who were thrilled when Jeff sold them a fifteen-foot tree for ten dollars. They needed it for a home where they cared for elderly men and women. The lovely couple was so appreciative, and thanked the kids over and over. Somehow, Jeff could sense when someone really needed a break, and he'd make certain the price was affordable even if it meant giving away the tree.

They learned how to be responsible as well as charitable, making sure to help the customers load and secure the trees to their vehicle. They always said "thank you" and wished everyone a "Merry Christmas."

But nothing warmed my heart as much as what Jeff bought with the $900 he'd earned. It had been his secret goal since he began this venture three weeks before Christmas.

Without telling anyone except his brother and sister who helped at the tree lot, he bought a brand-new Honda ATV for his youngest brother, age six, and had it sitting next to our beautifully decorated tree on Christmas morning.

Chris was the only one of the five siblings who didn't have a cycle to ride on the acreage. He was ecstatic!

It was the best imaginable Christmas gift for our youngest son, and the most heartwarming surprise for my husband and me. We couldn't have been more proud of our kids. They had worked hard together to make Christmas amazing for their younger brother, and also a little brighter for many customers who might not have otherwise had a lovely tree for their home.

Perhaps more importantly, they'd learned the joy in giving to others — the greatest gift we can give ourselves.

— Connie Kaseweter Pullen —

80

Quiet Christmases

Christmas is the day that holds all time together.
~Alexander Smith

We moved to the Northwest during our third year of marriage. Most of my husband's family is in California and most of my family is in Maine, so we found ourselves alone on Christmas Day. The people in our church, who were welcoming and friendly, felt sorry for us, so we did get invitations to their homes, but we chose to enjoy that Christmas alone. We were actually looking forward to that time together with our two toddler boys.

We soon decided that Christmas in our home would be done that way every year... quietly, with only our immediate family, simply enjoying the day together. We buy gifts that can be shared and enjoyed by all: puzzles, games, books, and activities that bring us closer as a family. We've gone sledding and snowshoeing, sipped hot tea, roasted marshmallows in the wood stove, and enjoyed many other simple activities on Christmas Day.

We always have a fun breakfast, like homemade cardamom buns or a buffet of homemade pies. I prepare our meals ahead of time so the whole day can be enjoyed together. We eat holiday foods and we set the table with our "fancy" things to make the day even more special for our children.

To me, Christmas isn't about presents or shopping; it's about making memories with the people I love most in this world. This past

Christmas, we got a solar-system model for one of our sons that my husband and he spent hours painting and assembling. The rest of us helped some, but it was awesome seeing my husband mix the paint and make sure each detail was correct until they completed the project that now graces our son's dresser. What a treasured memory that is to me each time I see that model!

Our daughter loves puzzles, so this past year we bought her a 200-piece puzzle that she, my husband, and I put together while our sons, who aren't puzzle lovers, played nearby. She was so enthusiastic about finishing the whole thing. It was the biggest puzzle she'd put together in her five years.

On quiet days like these, my husband usually pulls out his guitar and plays beautiful hymns while some of us sing along and others pull out their own instruments. I could listen to my husband play his guitar for hours, and sometimes on Christmas I am blessed with that privilege. These memories cannot be bought!

Some might think it's tragic to be far from extended family on such an important holiday, but we see it as a gift to spend that time quietly together. With nowhere to go and no pressures from the outside world, we relish in the simplicity of the day. I understand that it won't be this way forever. One day, our children will be grown and out of the home, and perhaps they'll want to spend Christmas in their own family haven. If that's the case, I'll be even more thankful for these memories. On those Christmases, I will sit by my husband's side as we reminisce about the good, old days when quiet Christmases at home were not really quiet at all, but filled with fun activities and meaningful time together.

— Dana E. Williams —

81

Christmas in July

Christmas, children, is not a date. It is a state of mind.
~Mary Ellen Chase

Christmas spirit fills my home as the central air-conditioning unit kicks in. Bing Crosby sings about snow in the kitchen, despite the outside temperature of 95 degrees and the oppressive humidity. Rows of sugary Christmas trees line the counter, topped with green frosting and loaded with sprinkles. A potpourri of orange rinds, cinnamon sticks and cloves simmers on the stove, their scent bringing to life memories of Christmases past. The red-and-green-plaid paper hugs every gift tightly, each secured with a beautiful ribbon and piled up in front of the living room window.

Tears fill my eyes as I realize how misplaced this Christmas spirit might seem. It's July eighth. It's miserably hot here in Wisconsin. There is no snow, just the brown-tinged grass in desperate need of rain. It's not Christmas — at least not to the rest of the world.

But it's Christmas to me.

My mom had been diagnosed with Stage 4 ovarian cancer just two days before Christmas. That Christmas had been bittersweet, with the reality of the diagnosis settling in while we went about celebrating and keeping the traditions alive, trying desperately to make new memories for Mom and all of us. The joyous celebration was shadowed by this "new normal." It was hard to grasp that this would likely be her last Christmas on earth.

But while I couldn't do anything to change what this cancer did to her body, I could do my best to embrace what one more Christmas would do for her soul. One more Christmas — our Christmas in July.

Having seen Mom getting weaker and sicker, I realized that our family needed a celebration. I talked with my husband about it first. Ryan is a nurse, so he also realized that Mom's time was drawing near. He let me get passionate about getting out all the décor, planning that late July would be the perfect time to have everyone over, turn on the Christmas music, crank the AC way down and have a family Christmas like no other.

Mom had always been over-the-top when it came to Christmas. When my family grunts about my tree going up early or groans over the sheer volume of decorations that magically transform our home in early November, I tell them I was genetically predisposed. Mom always made Christmas a big deal and taught us from a young age that Christmas is Jesus and family.

When I mentioned my idea to Mom in the middle of June, her eyes sparkled. I could tell this was what we needed — not just Mom, but me, too. I craved to plan this out with Mom, to let it be our last "secret" and watch her get excited about something. At the time, I thought this might be a beautiful gift for her and my sisters. Looking back, I realize that it was the best gift I could have given myself.

First things first, we needed gifts. Mom had twelve grandkids and a brand-new great-grandbaby. We discussed what would be a perfect keepsake for them, and I played the busy elf shopping online. I asked Mom if she felt she could read a Christmas storybook, and we would record it to have it for years to come. She beamed at this idea. She asked if I'd mind making my decorated sugar cookies and our Christmas dinner tradition — hot beef sandwiches. I smiled and agreed. I enlisted the help of one of my sisters, and we continued the planning and executing. We told everyone to plan for a cookout the last Saturday of July!

On July first, Mom called and said she wasn't feeling well; her pain was suddenly worse. My sister and I went to her apartment with two of the recordable books that had just arrived from UPS. While we waited for the hospice nurse to arrive, Mom recorded the two stories. The pain meds made her a bit loopy, but she read, and we laughed and cried. I so desperately focused on being present in that moment. I took in the sweet sound of her voice and the feel of her warm hands as we turned each page. I tasted the tears as they fell despite the laughter that filled the room. And I smelled that horrible odor of cancer. I knew that Mom wouldn't be here at the end of July. We had to get this Christmas moved up.

The hospice nurse arrived, and Mom was admitted to acute hospice at the hospital. As they were admitting Mom, she looked at me and said, "Well, I have to fight to make it until Christmas." The nurses looked at us like she was crazy, and Mom winked at me, confirming we still held this secret between us.

Christmas would have to happen immediately, but what about the tree? We couldn't put up a Christmas tree in a hospital in July. I mentioned this to our pastor one day when he was visiting Mom, and within an hour he had delivered a beautiful wooden tree covered in soft white lights, small enough to stand in a corner in Mom's room. I made sure the hospital staff knew what was going on, and they were more supportive than we could have imagined.

And there we were, more than twenty of us enjoying Christmas! I brought along Santa hats, we wore Christmas shirts, and a Kenny Rogers Christmas album was playing softly. One of the nurses took a perfect photo of all of us. The kids enjoyed Christmas cookies, and we all opened a very special gift from Mom. I had chosen an ornament for my sisters and me that read, "Just make it Merry." Mom's name was Mary. This was the last earthly gift given to me from my mom, and it couldn't be more perfect.

I looked around the room. It was oozing the spirit of Christmas. If only I could have bottled up that feeling, those sounds, the laughter and the tears. I saw her teenage and adult grandchildren struggling so hard with goodbye, and then I captured the unknowingness of the little ones who had yet to realize what goodbye even meant. There was a mournful undertone in the room, but the joy was bigger. The contentment on Mom's face was bigger than any sadness. I realized

I was truly cemented in the moment. I felt the magic of Christmas spirit — right there in July.

Mom passed away on July eighteenth, ten days after our celebration.

— Tricia Koeller —

Chapter 9

Four-Legged Festivities

82

A Bull Terrier at Christmas

Dogs do speak, but only to those
who know how to listen.
~Orhan Pamuk

In my childhood home, the holiday season wasn't complete without a Bull Terrier guarding the Christmas tree. As soon as the tree went up and presents began to appear under it, Bushwhack took up sentry duty and wouldn't budge. Her white and pink body, round like a barrel, rested beneath the branches, while her piggy eyes watched family members going about their daily lives. Bushwhack slept there day and night, only leaving briefly for dinner, walks, or outside ablutions. After such necessities, she returned immediately to her chosen spot, settling herself down with a sigh.

"Come away, Bushwhack!" one of us would say, reaching out a hand to try and coax her from the tree. In response, she snarled at the offending hand, wrinkled her nose, and bared her teeth. She didn't bite anyone—she loved her family—but it was a warning: Do not come any closer to this tree!

What made a dog protect the Christmas tree with such fierce determination?

One year, we discovered the reason.

As Christmas Day drew near, my mother added more packages to the growing pile beneath the tree. They arrived from friends and relatives, and none of us knew what surprises lay behind the merry wrappings. Bushwhack's enormous nose sniffed and sniffed the latest additions, and with a steely look of determination, she glared at Mother and bared her teeth. Mother scurried away.

My father, brother Lachlan and I also learned to keep far away from the tree and our dog. Bushwhack's attitude alarmed each of us. "I'll add the rest of the presents while she's on a walk with you," my mother said to me. "It will be much safer that way."

When Christmas morning rolled around, there was a dilemma: How could we pass the gifts to one another?

"A bone is required," said Father.

"Yes," agreed Mother. "I bought one from the butcher's the other day as a treat for Bushwhack." She plucked it from the refrigerator and called the dog: "Bushwhack. Come!"

The plump Bull Terrier peered out from beneath the tree. Her nose quivered, but she refused to move. Instead, she closed her eyes and pretended to sleep.

Mother marched over and waved the bone near Bushwhack's face. The canine snout quivered with more intensity until she snorted with delight. Bushwhack forgot about her self-appointed sentry duty and moved away from the Christmas tree. Eyes on the bone in Mother's hand, Bushwhack trotted outside. The back door slammed shut. She whined, but everyone ignored her cries.

The family managed to unwrap the presents without a Bull Terrier baring her teeth throughout the entire process. Among the many gifts were several food items: a tin of shortbread, several candy bars, and a large box of chocolates. We wondered if these goodies were the motivation behind Bushwhack's protectiveness. Concealed behind Christmas paper, only a dog with sensitive nostrils would realise where potential snacks lurked.

The box of chocolates belonged to Lachlan. He placed it on his bed, ready to sample after our return from church. We each readied ourselves for the morning service and allowed Bushwhack to come back inside. Dirt encrusted her nose, evidence she'd buried her bone. She wagged her tail and pattered over to the tree, now depleted of gifts.

She gave a few disinterested sniffs, turned around, and wandered into the kitchen where the aroma of roasting turkey filled the air.

The Christmas tree's spell had been broken, and Bushwhack no longer felt the need to be its watchdog. Our theory was confirmed: The packages of food were indeed the incentives for Bushwhack's ferocious growls.

After church, we arrived home, but no dog greeted us at the door. She wasn't anywhere near the Christmas tree; nor did she hover inside the kitchen with the overwhelming scent of roast dinner. Where was Bushwhack? We searched the house.

"She's in my bedroom!" shouted Lachlan. The family gathered in his doorway and peered inside the dim and untidy bedroom. It took our eyes several seconds to adjust to the gloom. At first, we couldn't see any sign of our pet.

"Bushwhack ate my chocolates," said Lachlan. "The whole box!"

Remnants of cardboard and aluminum foil lay scattered on the floor and trailed all the way to Lachlan's bed. There, underneath the bed, a roly-poly Bull Terrier slept on her back with all four paws in the air.

She opened her eyes and, realising her whole family had gathered about, wagged her tail.

"Should we call a vet?" asked Father. "Isn't chocolate poisonous to dogs? And what about the foil wrappers she's ingested? They can't be great for her stomach."

Bushwhack must have possessed a digestive system made from steel. She showed no signs of distress. Instead, she flopped over from her upside-down position and inched out from beneath the bed. For a minute or two, she raced around the room like a possessed cannonball. She paused for a second, and then spun herself in frantic circles before coming to rest at our feet, pink tongue lolling.

The following Christmas, and a few more after that, Bushwhack kept to a predictable routine. But we learned to outsmart her. If she ever snarled and bared her teeth, we'd whisk offending packages away from the tree and keep them somewhere high and hidden until Christmas morning.

Our beloved Bull Terrier grew old as the years passed, and one

January, not long after another Christmas, the time came to say goodbye. We stroked her ears, kissed her nose, and shed many tears. Our home wouldn't be the same without Bushwhack.

Three days later, the local vet rang and said, "A baby Bull Terrier has been found wandering the streets. She's got mange and she needs a loving home." The vet paused, "Oh, and she's the spitting image of Bushwhack. I think it's meant to be."

Our hearts melted at the sight of the puppy. She looked so pink and piglet-like that we named her Porkchop.

Next Christmas, the tree went up, and colorful presents began to appear. Porkchop sniffed and sniffed, and sat down. Mother drew near, and the young dog growled and bared her teeth. It made us smile. Christmas wasn't Christmas without a Bull Terrier guarding the tree.

— Sally Dixon —

83

Cat Warning System

Tree decorating with cats. O Christmas tree,
O Christmas tree, your ornaments are history!
~Courtney VanSickle

Quimby was picked up as an emaciated stray and eventually made his way into the shelter where we found him one hot July afternoon. By Christmas, he had fully assimilated into domestic life. As the sole pet in our home, the recipient of all snuggles, cuddles, and chin-scratches, I'm sure he thought life couldn't get any better.

Then the Christmas tree came.

Per our usual tradition, I popped in our DVD of *Christmas Vacation* to get in the spirit. And as Clark Griswold wrestled in the wilderness to get the family tree, I hauled our own heavy boxed tree up from the basement.

As soon as the basement door opened, Quimby rocketed off the couch to investigate. The basement was strictly off limits to him, and on the rare occasion he managed to sneak in, he was immediately shooed back upstairs.

But this time, he dug in and refused to go away. I tried simply closing the basement door as I worked downstairs, but the curiosity was just too much for him to bear. He pressed his face against the bottom of the door and began yowling pitifully to me in the basement.

Well, I'm a big softie, so I thought that maybe if he watched what I was doing, he would calm down a bit.

That turned out to be an incorrect assumption.

I pulled box after box of Christmas décor out from our storage closet under the stairs. Tail flicking, Quimby's excitement grew with each one.

He started by pawing the newspaper wrapping off the big wreath we used for the front door. Delighted to find a wiry evergreen shrub underneath, he latched onto one of the shiny, plastic presents glued onto the wreath and proceeded to start dragging the wreath back upstairs.

"Drop it!" I snapped at him from the bottom step. His bright green eyes dilated as if he'd just taken a whiff of catnip. "Drop. It." I repeated. And he did — right after he yanked the sparkly present off the wreath, and shot off to go play with his prize.

Okay, I thought, *one plastic present isn't so bad in the grand scheme of things.*

The respite lasted long enough for me to haul the rest of the boxes upstairs before Quimby came back for more.

I managed to get all three sections of the Christmas tree up and centered in the tree stand. I was able to fan out and rearrange the branches. I had just started stringing the lights when Quimby skidded under the tree, using the satin tree skirt as a slide. I would soon learn our hardwood floors were the perfect sledding venue. Quimby would get a running start, leap onto the tree skirt, and skid as far as the skirt would take him.

We had brought the outdoors to him in the form of a wonderfully colorful tree with lots of shiny baubles, and he couldn't get enough of it.

Then he started taking ornaments off the tree. My husband and I would turn our heads or step away just long enough to come back and see the tree shaking, immediately followed by the unmistakable cadence of four little feet running down the hallway.

Following him, we'd invariably find him huddled in the middle of a guest bed. He would be curled up as tightly as possible, eyes huge, and his little nose tucked into his paws as he watched us enter the room. One of us would hold his shoulders while the other gently moved his paws away from his belly to discover what he'd taken. He loved snatching one ornament in particular: a silver pinecone covered with glitter. Quimby would steal it every time we put it back on the tree.

We had made peace with the fact that Quimby loved to slide under the tree, and aside from that one silver pinecone, he didn't seem to be taking any other ornaments. But then, he started chewing on the tree. He would get a mouthful of fake pine and chomp away. Short of taking down the tree, we had to figure out a way to keep this cat out!

Quimby didn't realize it, but he was about to help us create a new Christmas tradition.

We knew he would scale or squeeze through any gate we put up around the tree, so we had to come up with a more creative solution.

My husband laughed and said, "I think I've figured out something that might work." A half-hour later, he returned from the local drugstore and held up a large pack of silver bells. He opened them and threaded them along the bottom branches of the tree.

"Watch this," he whispered.

Nonchalantly, we walked away from the tree, pretending to ignore Quimby. Then, we watched him from the corner of our eyes as he quietly inched closer to the tree, before latching onto a low-hanging branch for an evening chew.

Then a handful of bells chimed.

Quimby froze. He tried again — only to be met by a mass tinkling of bells.

"Get out of that tree!" we both said in unison to him. It worked. He shot off.

He tried several times over the night to go back to the tree, but each time the bells rang, we scolded him to get out of the tree. Each time, he would take off like a rocket down the hallway. Thirty minutes would pass, and he'd try again — only to be foiled by ringing bells.

We've celebrated three Christmases with him since then, and each year it's become a tradition to add more bells in various sizes. The entire bottom third of our tree is now nothing but a twinkling mass of silver bells.

Every year, as we sift through all the newspaper-wrapped ornaments and prepare them for hanging, we giggle when we come upon one of the sets of bells. And as each one is unwrapped, Quimby flops under the tree and huffs loudly in defeat, watching us thread the bells through the bottom branches.

True to tradition, Quimby still regularly tests the cat warning system and freezes immediately once the bells ring.

And every holiday season, we still grin when we hear a bell ring. It might be true that somewhere an angel just got her wings, but in our house every time a bell rings, the cat is back in the tree.

— Kristi Adams —

84

Our Amazing Christmas Gift

*It is amazing how much love and laughter they bring
into our lives and even how much closer we become
with each other because of them.*
~John Grogan, Marley & Me

I t was a bitterly cold Yuletide drive from Regina to Saskatoon, my birthplace, but it was truly beautiful, with its stands of snow-covered trees and arched bridges along the South Saskatchewan River. We'd loaded up our trusty Jeep on December 21st with suitcases, survival gear, boxes of wrapped presents, and our ten-year-old Shih Tzu named Keiko. We'd adopted him six years earlier, and he seemed to love road trips as much as we did.

We enjoyed sumptuous dinners and quality time with family for a couple of leisurely days in Saskatoon. Then we headed to Ivan's brother's farm outside Yorkton, which was Ivan's first home, to celebrate Christmas with his parents, brother and sister-in-law, and nephew. Smoky, their five-year-old Siberian Husky, was there, too, lying on a mat recovering from emergency surgery after being hit by a truck.

We opened gifts and were having a relaxing Christmas Eve dinner when it happened. We were all so preoccupied with the delicious food, conversation and each other's company that we didn't notice — until we finished eating, pushed back our chairs and stood up. It was then that we saw the neat little piles of kibble under the table where our feet had been. Keiko had placed them there — deliberately making many trips from his supper dish nearby, carefully taking one or two at a time in his lips and depositing them at our feet — back and forth, back and forth. There was also a small pile beside the stainless-steel feeding dish — undoubtedly for Smoky.

Gentle and affectionate Keiko had shared the most special thing he had — the only thing he had — the food in his dish. Our little rescue dog was saying thank you. We were awestruck by this rare display of generosity.

— Kathie Leier —

85

A Late-Evening Snack

A dog can't think that much about what he is doing;
he just does what feels right.
~Barbara Kingsolver, Animal Dreams

My oldest brother, Dwayne, was a welder. His claim to fame as a welder came from creating an extremely large pie pan. Our community held a Pecan Festival every year. They asked my brother to weld together a pan large enough for their pie to win a spot in the *Guinness World Records* for the largest pecan pie. They won the title and, to my knowledge, it still holds.

Years before welding the pie pan, Dwayne welded a very large smoker. Once finished, he volunteered to smoke the Thanksgiving turkey. "This is going to become a new family tradition," he said. For weeks before the special day, he talked about the perfect temperature, the exact time needed, his use of pecan wood, and his special technique for basting the fowl. We didn't exactly avoid him, but we knew if we were in the same room with him for any length of time, we would have to listen to his "turkey talk."

"I'm smoking the family turkey. I'll cook your turkey, too," he told all his friends. So his buddies brought their turkeys to our house in ice chests. At least six birds were scheduled for smoking. The cooker would barely hold them.

By five o'clock the morning before Thanksgiving, Dwayne had all the birds washed, basted, and cooking on a low heat. "I'll eat out here," he said. "Just put my food on a plate and bring it to the back door." He spent most of the day sitting under the shade tree in his lawn chair, a drink in one hand and his basting brush in the other.

The rest of us prepared everything else. Mom, my sister, and I made pies, cakes, and salads. All we would need to do on Thanksgiving would be to prepare vegetables, reheat the turkey, and make the dinner rolls.

By evening, everyone in the family was bone-tired. We decided to go out to eat. "Come eat with us," Dad said to Dwayne.

"I'll go if you can wait a little bit. These birds are perfectly done. Will you guys help me put them on the table to cool? Then I'll take a shower, and we can go eat. When I get back, you can help me load them into ice chests for the guys to pick up in the morning."

So we brought in the perfectly smoked turkeys. Then we went to a local restaurant where we enjoyed a leisurely meal until we realized that we still had turkeys to pack into ice chests before we could go to sleep.

"Look!" exclaimed Mom as we pulled into the driveway. "Larry made it home!"

Sure enough, my younger brother's pickup was parked in front of us. We hadn't known if he'd make it in for Thanksgiving. It had been at least a year since any of us had seen him.

The five of us rushed into the house, Mom leading the way. "Larry, Larry!" she called.

As she walked through the hallway, headed to the kitchen, an enormous Great Dane loped toward her. She stopped, and the rest of us crashed into her, the dog, and each other.

Larry appeared at the top of the staircase. "Hi, guys. I see you've met Sadie. She travels with me to all my jobs. She's a wonderful companion."

"She's certainly big," said Mom as she slid past the dog and continued on toward the kitchen. "I bet she eats a ton."

"She doesn't eat too much. We often share a meal."

The rest of us petted Sadie as we waited for Larry to join us.

"Ohhhh, nooo!!"

Everyone ran toward the kitchen, Sadie included.

My mother stood by the kitchen table, eyes and mouth wide open. Her face was pale. Her finger pointed to the middle of the kitchen floor.

Our little group formed a semi-circle behind her. Sadie sat to the far right, observing everything. Turkey carcasses were strewn around the floor. One lone bird, totally untouched, lay in the center of the table. None of the other birds had survived.

Sadie licked her lips, and then looked at Larry with soulful eyes as if to say, "I just needed a little snack."

I'm not sure what Dwayne said to his friends as he delivered thawed turkeys to their house early the next morning for them to cook, but we never heard a bad word from him about Sadie or his brother, Larry. The rest of us chose not to bring up the subject, especially in front of Dwayne, but not a Thanksgiving goes by when we don't think about Sadie and her late-evening snack.

— Rita Durrett —

Foiled Again

Never try to out stubborn a cat.
~Robert A. Heinlein

Early December is always exciting. Christmas spirit fills every corner of our house in the form of cookies, music and, most importantly, decorations. In our family, we have certain traditions when we decorate, including fastening the Christmas tree to the wall. This strange family tradition came about due to our cats.

Biscuit, Muffin, and Angus love Christmas just as much as we do. Unfortunately, that involves climbing the branches of the Christmas tree. These are fat cats, and they do a lot of damage. So, after they knocked over one tree too many, we fought back.

We started with a rope that was tied to hooks on the wall, but the "three mouseketeers" took down the tree without a hitch. We needed to be more aggressive. We placed a spray bottle next to the tree so we could spray any cat that crossed enemy lines. But we couldn't stand guard 24/7, so that didn't work either.

The next year, we added a baby gate around the tree, but they found their way around that. The following year, we brought in the big guns (or so we thought): We bought mats that were specially designed with spikes to keep cats out of certain areas. They still found their way to the tree.

Last year, we added even more armament by purchasing mats that emit a high-pitched sound when stepped upon. We believed we had finally solved the problem, but that didn't work either. The mats were very effective, but instead of keeping out the cats, the mats kept *us* out. Almost every day, someone would walk over to admire the tree and step on the mats, forgetting they were there. The deafening noise sent whoever stepped on them racing across the room.

Although our protection mechanisms continue to get more elaborate, the cats still find a way to outsmart us every year. Our attempts to protect the tree from the cats have created my favorite Christmas memories. Our family tradition isn't coming up with barricades; it's sitting around with my family and laughing about yet another plan that failed.

— Alexis Sherwin —

87

Attitude of Gratitude

*In order to really enjoy a dog, one doesn't merely try to
train him to be semi-human. The point of it is to open
oneself to the possibility of becoming partly a dog.*
~Edward Hoagland

G racie, a Boston Terrier, loved Christmas. She was always
thrilled to receive a new toy, one that she could easily
destroy in under three minutes. Gracie may have been ten
years old, with gray fur on her face, but she seems stuck in
perpetual puppydom.

She would lurk quietly at the edges of holiday activity while people
opened their gifts. When I would call out to her that she had a gift,
too, she would race over and then skid to a stop at my feet while I
slowly removed the wrapping from her present. After I handed Gracie
her new toy, she would disappear under the dining table to spend a
few moments slobbering on it before she emerged to strut around the
room, showing her new toy to everyone. She was so proud.

First, she would sashay in front of the fifteen family members
and friends. She would hold the plaything proudly in her mouth for
all to see as she marched around with her head held high. She was so
adorable that everyone acknowledged how wonderful her new toy was.
But Gracie was not finished with show-and-tell. Now that the group
presentation had been completed it was time for the individual sharing.
Gracie would take her toy and briefly lay it in the lap of every person
in the room. After each person acknowledged her and her priceless

gift, she moved to the next. No one could be left out. Even the new baby in the family got the slobbery offering plopped down in the infant carrier. After each person shared in Gracie's delight, she would retreat under the dining table, where she would destroy her new toy.

Gracie set such a good example for her human family. She sure knew how to appreciate Christmas and show her appreciation for her gifts.

— Mason K. Brown —

88

Pawing the Tree

Dogs leave paw prints on our hearts.
~Author Unknown

The cookies baking in the oven filled the air with ginger, cinnamon, and nutmeg, but it was the sound of the rustling branches that were my focus. I knew without looking that my silver Boxer had found his way under the Christmas tree again. With a child's innocent determination, he searched desperately under the branches. His docked tail was wiggling in the air as the front half of his body was bent low. When he turned his regal head to look at me expectantly, there was nothing to do but laugh.

I guided him out from under the tree. A gift for him had been placed under the tree on Christmas morning for nearly eleven years, but this year he was impatient. He knew that "Christmas tree" meant "Christmas treat." No sooner had I turned my back when I heard that telltale sign again; this time, he had the tree rocking side-to-side with his efforts.

As night came on, he seemed to have resigned himself to the fact that there was no smelly present under the tree for him. "Good night, Maverick," I whispered. He lifted his head and looked at me before repositioning it comfortably in a deliberate effort to not look at the tree.

I was in bed only seconds when there was a noise so loud that it shook the floor. I sprang out of bed and slid into the living room, prepared for battle. I flicked on the light to find the tree swaying furiously from side-to-side. It was leaning precariously and there was a large hole halfway up the tree where the branches had been parted. The bottom strands of garland and lights were hanging off the tree and stretched across the floor. In the middle of the rubble, Maverick was standing still as if I wouldn't see him unless he moved.

I burst into laughter as I realized that he had tried to search the higher branches of the tree. Unfortunately, a seventy-pound dog cannot stand on the polyvinyl chloride branches of an artificial tree. As a result, his fawn-coloured head was turning now between the carnage and me, and the floppy ears animating his movement only added to the hilarity of the situation. Both the tree and the dog survived the rest of the holiday season, and it was with marked anticipation that he received an odourous gift purposely placed at the front of the tree on Christmas morning.

Christmases come and go now without him. Instead of placing a gift for him under the tree, we hang a heart-shaped ornament decorated with a fawn Boxer image. Last Christmas, as I hung the heart-shaped ornament, I looked down at the base of the tree where a tiny Boxer pup snored softly.

— Shari Marshall —

89

Solved

After scolding one's cat, one looks into its face and is
seized by the ugly suspicion that it understood every
word. And has filed it for reference.
~Charlotte Gray

"Where on earth have they gone to?" my mother asked as she eyed the half-empty Christmas tree.

"I haven't the foggiest," I said, "but there's definitely less than yesterday."

And the day before that... and the day before that...

Decorations had been disappearing for a while. Most of the lower branches were now bare. No matter where we looked in the house, though, we couldn't find a trace of them.

It was as if they had vanished into thin air.

As we pulled on our coats, we pondered the mystery. It was the day before Christmas Eve. We had some last-minute groceries to collect, so we were about to head out to the local store.

"Who do you think the culprit is?" my mother asked, heading outside. "Faye or Cassy?"

Both of our little felines had shown a keen interest in the tree, it was true. They did every year. Twinkly lights and the fabric "cat-safe" decorations fascinated them. But while Faye was a gentle observer, content to look and not touch, Cassy had to be monitored. Her paws constantly twitched toward the branches like a mischievous toddler's.

So, naturally, she was the prime suspect. But after being told once to leave the tree alone, she hadn't reoffended.

Nevertheless, we had checked the cat beds and their other usual hideouts to be sure. Alas, no decorations.

The entire situation was a mystery.

I shrugged. "Maybe it's neither of them. Maybe it's Dad playing a prank."

Even to myself, I sounded doubtful. It just wasn't his style. But aside from the cats, there was no one else in the house.

"Or perhaps we have a ghost." My mother smiled. "Maybe two or three — the ghosts of Christmas Past, Present, and Yet to Come. And they'll show themselves tomorrow night to tell us the true meaning of Christmas, as well as to return our missing decorations."

"Bah, humbug!" I said, doing my best Scrooge impersonation.

As my mother was climbing into the car and I was locking the front door, I happened, by chance, to turn and look through the bay window in which our Christmas tree stood.

And there, right in front of me, was Cassy.

Mouthing a decoration.

"You little scamp," I muttered.

As I watched, our little tortoiseshell ever-so-stealthily lifted the decoration from the branch, cradling it in her teeth, and then turned and carefully slotted it down the narrow gap between the radiator and the wall, just below the windowsill. Then she let it go.

Moving to the window, I tapped my nails faintly on the glass. Quiet as the noise was, Cassy snapped to attention, her face the perfect picture of: *Oh, busted!*

"What are you doing, Little Miss?"

She sat perfectly still for one frozen second… and then bolted.

"Mum!" I called out. "I think I've solved the case."

Sure enough, when we went back inside, there they were: the missing decorations. All nine were lying in a heap down the back of the radiator. We couldn't help but laugh.

— Nemma Wollenfang —

90

Misty's Thanksgiving

I think dogs are the most amazing creatures;
they give unconditional love. For me,
they are the role model for being alive.
~Gilda Radner

My husband and I purchased our first home about six years ago. We had fallen in love immediately with a bank-owned, three-floor log cabin in a lake community that was part of the Pine Barrens. I recall standing on the porch of our dream house alone with my husband after the Realtor left. We promised the universe that day that if we got the house, we'd rescue one dog that needed it most. It would move in with us the same day we moved in and become part of the family.

We didn't want a puppy; we wanted an unwanted dog, a large one. Those are the ones that usually get left behind in the shelters, anyway, but I wanted a large dog. It would be a companion for the kids and me because my husband worked far away during the day. The dog would watch over us.

I reached out to a rescue group, and we started the paperwork. They approved us and were very excited to have adopters like us. Three days before moving day, we got the call. They had rescued a twelve-year-old German Shepherd on Death Row. She had heartworm, suffered from malnutrition and had lost most of her chest hair. According to them, she certainly wasn't what most adopters considered pretty. She wouldn't need much — just a home to live out her days. We fell in love with Misty before we even met her.

Moving day came, and just as the last truck was unloaded, the rescue arrived. Friends watched eagerly, excited to meet Misty. She was more beautiful than I could have imagined. She moved with a senior grace, her cloudy eyes taking in her new home and family. She was underweight at eighty pounds, but she was aware of where every inch of her was. She was led over to where my infant daughter was stretched out, cooing on a blanket. We held Misty while she sniffed the baby's head and then gingerly lay next to her without touching her blanket.

That evening, my husband set up Misty's new dog bed in the living room. The baby was asleep in her crib, and I passed out on the mattress on the floor. I felt a large body moving next to me, but was too tired to wake up. I snuggled into the dog's warmth, her breath soft against my neck.

I have never seen my husband more emotional than that night. Misty had curled into bed next to me, cuddled up against my body. I could hear my husband's breath hitch as he looked at that poor girl — so full of grace, warmth and love — who appreciated her new family as if we'd always been hers.

My husband covered us with an extra blanket and then lay beside her on the hard floor, petting and comforting her all through her first night with us.

Misty was given the best of everything — home-cooked meals, a seat on the sofa, and all the love this family could muster. She enjoyed the companionship of her doggy brother and sister as much as she adored her human brother and sister.

By Thanksgiving, we were well situated and preparing for our first holiday in our new home. We invited friends and family.

A day before Thanksgiving, I had begun cooking a series of three turkeys so we'd have enough food for everyone. I left the first one cooling on the back of the stove as I stepped out for a short break to have coffee with the neighbor.

Misty, who'd never taken a thing from the counter, must have found that turkey too much of a temptation. I couldn't even be mad at her when it was my own fault for leaving temptation within reach.

When I returned, there were only a few bones remaining, scattered about the kitchen. She slunk under the table, acting as if she was about to be beaten, quivering, shaking and whimpering.

My heart broke; she was terrified by her own behavior. Someone in her past had abused this sweet, gentle girl so horribly that she had wet herself in fear. I spent over an hour gently coaxing her from under the table, comforting her. I will never forget how she finally emerged and buried her big head against my chest, sighing and whimpering. I held her tightly, stroking her coarse fur and kissing her, promising her no one would ever hurt her again.

She recovered and was given all the turkey and apple pie she could eat that Thanksgiving. Every guest greeted her with love and told her what a wonderful girl she was. It was as if, in hearing the story of the turkey, every friend and family member pitched in to give her the lifetime of love she'd missed in just that one day.

Unfortunately, Misty's time with us was short. She passed in my arms the following fall.

To this day, the kids still miss her. We built her a memory garden, and we visit her there. She touched us in her short time with more than a lifetime of love, and we will always be thankful for that.

— Nicole Ann Rook McAlister —

Chapter
10
Special
Memories

91

An Unforgettable Christmas Card

When you forgive, you in no way change the
past — but you sure do change the future.
~Bernard Meltzer

We were planning to leave the warm temperatures of the South, where we had lived for the past twenty-six years, to spend the holidays with our family and friends in Wisconsin. Prior to packing all the gifts and luggage for our long trip, I sat down and wrote out Christmas cards. I wrote one for my aunt and uncle, one for each sibling, one for my in-laws and one for my high-school best friend — all people I had not seen in a while but would be spending Christmas with in just a few days.

After finishing my cards, I noticed one more card in the box. As I picked it up and began writing, it seemed awkward but natural at the same time. For the first time in forty years, I was writing a Christmas card to my dad.

It had been forty years since my dad walked out on my family. I was just a few months old — too young to remember the events surrounding his departure — but the sting and emptiness lingered on for all the years that followed.

On my desk, next to my stack of Christmas cards, was a piece of paper on which I had written, just the day before, an address that might or might not have been my dad's. With one Christmas card left in the box, it seemed right to write a Christmas card that said: "Dear Dad, Merry Christmas!"

After writing a short note explaining who I was, and enclosing our family Christmas picture and my phone number, I sealed the envelope, stamped it and put it in the outgoing mail. I sent that Christmas card with no hope that it would be received with an open heart or even received at all. My only expectation had already been met the moment I mailed the card — to finally be able to send a Christmas card to someone who could possibly be my dad.

A few days later, on Christmas Day, we were sitting at the kitchen table at my in-laws' house in Wisconsin, laughing and enjoying each other's company, when a call came in on my cell phone. It was a number from another state that I did not recognize. I let it go to voicemail. I excused myself from the table and stepped outside to listen to the message that had been left.

"Laurie, this is your dad. We received your Christmas card and would love to talk to you."

For a moment, I felt frozen. I'm not sure if it was the freezing temperatures outside, especially since I had stepped out without a jacket, or if my heart just skipped a beat out of shock. You see, when I wrote that Christmas card and mailed it, I didn't really think things through. What if the card did indeed reach my dad, and he was actually glad to receive it?

That Christmas was unforgettable. I will never forget how cold it was as I stood outside hearing my dad's voice for the first time in forty years. And I will never forget the first conversation I had with my dad when I called him back. For the first time in forty years, I was able to say, "Merry Christmas, Dad." And, for the first time in forty years, I actually heard my dad say, "Merry Christmas" and "I love you."

Six weeks after that special Christmas phone call, I flew to Florida to meet my dad face to face. We were able to spend seven more Christmases together before he died.

— Laurie Adams —

92

Christmas Canter

*The way you spend Christmas is far more important
than how much.*
~Henry David Thoreau

On Christmas Day 2004, I beheld the offering of a precious
gift. It's a memory I will cherish for the rest of my life. It
didn't happen in a stable, but in Clearwater, a village in the
interior of British Columbia. And if I hadn't said "yes" when
I would have preferred to say "no," I would have missed it!

That November, the snow fell deep and cold in Clearwater where
two of our adult children — a daughter and a son — lived with their
spouses. Our older daughter asked if we might join them for Christmas,
weather permitting. From our home in a suburb of Vancouver, we
looked forward to Christmas in Clearwater.

Although a new layer of snow fell in mid-December, we rolled
along freshly cleared highways when we set out at dawn on December
24th. As a bonus, our younger daughter, home from university, travelled
with us. We shared a wonderful Christmas Eve in Clearwater and got
up to date on all the family news, including the wellbeing of the horses
that my older daughter and her sister-in-law had under their care.

On Christmas morning, before I had finished my first cup of
coffee, my daughters and daughter-in-law proposed a horseback ride.
I looked out the window at the snow piled in heaps, and then at the
fire and couch. *What were they thinking?* But seeing their faces, I knew
I couldn't back out.

"It'll be fun," they said. "We'll ride around the hospital, and we will only be out for an hour."

An hour. Right. I knew it would take an hour just to get ready. First, the horses had to be brought in from the field, and then they needed to be brushed and have their feet checked. We needed to outfit them with saddles and blankets. In sub-zero temperatures, bridles and stirrup leathers would be stiff with cold and even harder to buckle and strap with be-gloved fingers. Then, after the ride, another hour would pass during which the whole process would be repeated in reverse. So much for, "We will only be out for an hour." But after opening the presents, taking photos and laughing at the funnier choices, what else does one do while the turkey cooks?

I decided that a chilly ride was preferable to staying in and peeling potatoes, and we had braved a six-hour drive into the snowbound interior to be with some of our kids for Christmas. My husband, not a rider at all, said he would be happy to keep the couch warm for me.

I bundled up in my ancient ski jacket, along with sweaters and long red underwear under corduroy jeans and nylon pants. I borrowed gloves and boots and two pairs of thick socks. I looked like a cross between a skier who had slalomed through a time warp and a multi-hued abominable snowman — with a Santa hat. I wish I could say that I wore a big smile too, but because I was being the good-sport mom, my expression was more like a let's-just-get-this-over-with grimace.

As predicted, the saddling and bridling took an hour. The horses, although loose in the field, came to the gate. They, at least, were eager for whatever their owners had in mind.

We were a mostly merry group of six riders on six frisky horses when my daughter-in-law led our procession up the hill to the hospital under the pale winter sun. I rode an eager mare who was about my age in horse years. However, she had no notion of acting her age. She insisted that if we couldn't at least canter, she would cover the ground frog-hopping, head-tossing, and capering about on the ice and snow-covered verge of the road. I had to remind myself that I loved riding; in fact, I loved this horse. I loved my family, and joining the ride pleased my girls — and my son, too, who was mounted on a sensible Appaloosa and had joined the cavalcade.

My nose ran, and my eyes burned. My fingers ached from yanking a stubborn girth strap, and my toes tingled. I knew I should have worn a third pair of socks. My Santa hat kept slipping off the back of my head. Dropping the reins to pull it down with both hands was not an option.

After twenty minutes, we turned into the driveway to the hospital, a one-story, wood-frame building. Christmas lights strung around the front porch glowed in welcome.

We trotted around to the back, passing windows filled with interested faces: nurses, care workers, visitors and patients who pointed and smiled. We waved and laughed, and this time I truly smiled. We pulled up near the shovelled back terrace.

Nurses and workers had bundled their charges into whatever blankets and outerwear they had grabbed first, loaded them onto wheelchairs and gurneys, and trundled them out the door the better to see the equine delegation of Christmas cheer.

We dismounted and led the horses closer for nose pats and head rubs. I hadn't realized that "going around the hospital" meant visiting the elderly in the extended-care unit. I looked into those brightened eyes and watched smiles spread on furrowed faces. A man in a wheelchair was laughing as he reached out to pet the lowered head of the horse that stood before his chair. I again forced a smile — instead of tears.

This would have been a lovely tradition to continue, but relentless snow and treacherous roads kept us home the next year. The following year, 2006, we again celebrated Christmas in Clearwater with a winter ride, but the horses had been moved to another farm, too far away for us to visit the hospital again. After that, other things changed in our lives and those of our children. And with the arrival of grandchildren over the next few years, traditions evolved and changed, too.

But I will never forget that old man whose Christmas was brightened by the lowered head of a gentle horse. That alone was worth every bit of shivering.

— Rosemary L. Rigsby —

More Precious than Gold

Grandmothers hold their grandchildren
in a special place in their heart.
~Catherine Pulsifer

I foolishly thought that she couldn't die on a beautiful summer day. After all, she had battled cancer for all of her seventies. But suddenly, without warning on an idyllic June morning, she was gone.

The summer weeks that followed were a blur, with everyday life totally eclipsed by the realization that my beloved grandmother had died. No more hearing her voice, her profound wisdom, her wit, and her kindness. Gone was the adorable way she flipped her wrist while poaching an egg, her secret signature clam chowder, and the patience she poured into her perfectly moist raisin cake.

As my familiar hometown trees began to turn beautiful shades of New England umber and gold, I faced the first holiday season without her. December at her home on Douglas Drive had been better than the North Pole, Fifth Avenue, and Walt Disney World all rolled into one.

Since her passing, I found it increasingly difficult to return to my grandparents' home — so much so that when my grandfather asked me to come over one autumn afternoon, I didn't want to go. He said he had something to give me, and I could hear in his voice that his request was non-negotiable.

Within moments of my arrival, he went into the dining room and slowly took four extremely familiar, rolled-up pieces of green fabric from a drawer. He held them out to me. "She wanted you to have it," he said. And I knew exactly what it was. My hands trembled as I fought back one more gallon of tears. I wanted these rolled-up pieces of fabric to stay in her buffet because receiving them was just another painful reminder that she was gone. I realized the honor I was receiving, though. My grandfather had just handed me my grandmother's beloved silver.

My grandparents were exceptionally frugal and my grandmother took great care of the things she had collected in her buffet for her finest occasions: the family Thanksgiving and Christmas dinners. Her silver was not the least bit expensive, and its age showed. But its sentimental value was priceless. Giving the silver to me meant that she trusted me to preserve and maintain her family traditions.

Using her silver on that first Thanksgiving was both comforting and nostalgic. I carefully unrolled the green fabric marked "FORKS" and saw the patterned silver peeking out of the perfectly sewn holders. As I set the first fork at the head of the table, memories of past holidays flooded my thoughts. *Last Thanksgiving, she was here, and it was her table.* While my grandmother would no longer have a place setting, she would forever have a place at every table I would set with her silver. I had discovered a new way to love my grandmother who was no longer here.

This Thanksgiving will mark twenty years since the first Thanksgiving without her. And once again I will joyfully and lovingly continue our family tradition of turkey, cranberry sauce, and a crystal dish of black olives on the table adorned with her silver. When it was my grandmother's Thanksgiving, the same ten family members sat around the table each year. But since I moved to Georgia, with very little family close by, my life has intersected with many new people who have moved to this area and can't go home for Thanksgiving. I decided that family becomes whoever eats with you.

My grandmother's silver has welcomed people from fourteen states, Ecuador, China, the Philippines, and Belgium. I don't think my grandmother ever dreamed that her silver would heal the sorrow in her granddaughter's heart and be held by so many strangers.

We learn to love the people who are no longer here by letting the love that they gave us transform and grow in new and fascinating ways. That love, and its manifestation in something as simple as a modest set of silverware, is more precious than gold.

— Dana Lamb-Schaubroeck —

Christmas Above the Arctic Circle

We were born to unite with our fellow men, and to join
in community with the human race.
~Cicero

My husband, twin daughters, and I stood on the porch of a little, wooden church 150 miles north of the Arctic Circle, waiting for the villagers to come for their first Christmas Eve candlelight service. We could see movement down the hill, but no one seemed to be coming our way. A little girl had broken her leg in a snowmobile accident, and many of her Iñupiat relatives were waiting for the helicopter to arrive and take her to the hospital in Fairbanks, Alaska.

My husband Dave was an Air Force Chaplain representing the Presbyterian Church that Christmas of 1996. We were stationed at Eielson Air Force Base, about thirty miles southeast of Fairbanks. Dave connected with the Presbytery of Yukon and had preached in that small village of Anaktuvuk Pass. The Presbyterian church was without a pastor, and members of the Presbytery approached him about leading a Christmas Eve service.

I was reluctant. I did not want him to go alone, away from us at Christmas. But the idea of flying to a village that far north in the dead of winter scared me as well. I didn't think our ten-year-olds would go for it either. But they said enthusiastically, "Let's do it," so we did.

The minute our boots hit the snow-packed ground, I fell in love with the place. I always considered Fairbanks to be "real Alaska," with its three hours of daylight in the winter and temperatures hovering around minus 40 degrees. Anaktuvuk Pass, surrounded by the Brooks Range with snow from August to June, truly represented life in Alaska.

Flying or dogsledding was the only way in and out of the village. The building at the landing strip also served as the post office. The people mainly lived off the land and what they could catch during whaling season. One whale could feed the village for months, not to mention the many uses for blubber, skin, and bones.

We stayed in the school, which had running water and an Olympic-size swimming pool thanks to oil-pipeline money. Many of the villagers had lived in sod huts just twenty years before our visit. Many still used outhouses and honeypots. The family and consumer science room had a kitchen we could use to heat up food if we needed, and the library had a television with a VCR so we could watch movies.

We didn't spend much time in our "living quarters" as the town was meeting in the gymnasium for their annual Christmas Eve gift exchange. We did not know about the exchange, but we needn't have worried. Some of the church members gave gifts to our daughters so they would have something to open.

During the evening, I watched how loving the people were to each other. The villagers had a bond that came from living and working together in a harsh environment just to survive. That bond extended to us. As I sat admiring a little baby, her mother thrust her into my arms and went to help someone. Being from the suburbs of Chicago, I was surprised she trusted a perfect stranger to watch her child. Dave pointed out that we were in a very small village where everyone knew each other. Really, where could I take the baby? Good point.

Everyone was polite, even to Santa, who had started getting his merry on earlier in the day. The children were all respectful, and adults were not afraid to scold any child, whether it was their own or not. And everyone treated the elders as if they were a precious commodity, which of course they were. People listened to them, saw to their needs and generally gathered around them to hear whatever wisdom they imparted. I thought about how our non-indigenous culture does not treasure our elders enough.

After the meal of caribou stew, it was time to get ready for the church service, at least for us. The chapel stood at the top of a hill overlooking the village. Inside it was one room heated with a woodburning stove. I can't put into words the feeling I had while we set up the chairs, got the programs ready, and waited for the congregation to show up.

I remember standing on that porch and commenting to Dave that the only thing that would make the evening more perfect was if the Northern Lights came out. Dodo, a church member, heard me and said it was too warm that night.

The church service itself was magical. Dave spoke through a translator for those who were not comfortable with English. And when it came time to sing "Silent Night," it was the most beautiful rendition I had ever heard.

To top it off, as we walked outside after cleaning up, the Northern Lights were dancing across the vast sky — a perfect ending to a marvelous adventure.

— Victoria Terrinoni —

A Special Delivery

However motherhood comes to you, it's a miracle.
~Valerie Harper

I had just arrived in the labor-and-delivery suite to work the evening shift on Christmas Eve. With an anxious look on her face, the charge nurse Annie guided me toward the conference room. "Thank God, you're here," she said, "but you need to sit down."

"Is there a problem?" I asked.

I could hear the wails of a labor patient in the background when she answered. "We admitted a patient in active labor nearly an hour ago. She told us Dr. Benson is her doctor, but when we called to advise him of her admission, he said she is not his patient." Annie shuffled her feet, twisted her hands, and continued. "It's her sixth baby, and she's progressing rapidly."

"But if he isn't her doctor, then who is?"

"All I know is that she gave us his name, and when his receptionist checked the files, she verified that Dr. Benson had treated Mrs. Lange during previous pregnancies, but he had not seen her during this one. You're the head nurse. What shall we do?"

"I'll talk with him," I replied.

Quickly, I stashed my cold-weather gear, reviewed the patient's record, and headed for the phone. When he answered my call, I could tell he was in no mood to repeat what he had said previously — she was not his patient, and he was not coming to the hospital.

"But she's in active labor, sir, and I don't know what else to do

Special Memories | 295

except deliver her myself."

"I have delivered her babies in the past, but I haven't seen her in more than a year," he retorted. "She has some nerve to give my name!"

"Doctor, please listen. There's not much time." A desperate thought prompted me to say, "You know, her name is Mary."

"So? I'll bet you're going to tell me her husband's name is Joseph."

"You got it — and that's not all — he's a carpenter!"

There was silence on his end of the line. I thought he had hung up. Then I heard him grumble, "Oh, all right. I'll be there."

Within five minutes of his arrival, Dr. Benson delivered the baby — a boy. When I went with him to the waiting room to tell the father, Joseph said, "I'll pay you for your services as soon as I can get back to work."

"No need for that; this one's on me."

"But I want to pay, sir. I didn't know Mary was pregnant until she was four or five months along. By then, my busiest time of year with carpentry work was coming to an end, and she didn't want me to worry about the bills. That's why she didn't go to see you. We just didn't have the money."

Dr. Benson sat down beside Joseph and touched him on the shoulder. "Hear me out, son. I've done a lot of things in my life I'm not proud of, but when I thought about it, there was one thing for sure. I wasn't going to refuse to help a woman named Mary, in labor on Christmas Eve, with a husband named Joseph, who is a carpenter. I could never have lived with myself."

Joseph smiled and shook the doctor's hand. "Thank you. I'm grateful for your kindness."

Mary and Joseph named their baby Emmanuel Benson Lange.

— Mildred L. Farrior —

A Christmas Like No Other

*Christmas is not a time or a season but a state of
mind. To cherish peace and good will, to be plenteous
in mercy, is to have the real spirit of Christmas.*
~Calvin Coolidge

We were newlyweds looking forward to our first Christmas.
The required "First Christmas" ornament had been purchased and hung front and center on our Christmas tree.
Our personalized stockings decorated the fireplace, and
we were enjoying quiet winter evenings in our cozy home.

My grandparents arrived from Florida a week before Christmas.
They had been making fewer trips to Ohio because of my grandmother's
health. We hadn't seen them since they'd made the trip in July for our
wedding.

Three days before Christmas, our phone rang well before dawn.
My parents had called an ambulance to take my grandmother to the
hospital. We lived just across the street, and they didn't want us to
worry if we saw flashing lights. After I hung up, I went straight to the
window and waited for the ambulance to stop at the curb outside my
childhood home. I watched from my second-story bedroom as EMTs
maneuvered the stretcher down the icy steps, carefully guided it into
the back of the vehicle, and closed the doors. As they drove away in
the silence of that snowy morning, I prayed for my grandmother.

At the hospital, they discovered my grandmother had a twelve-inch blood clot in her leg. The doctors removed it, requiring several days in the hospital. The family unanimously decided to postpone our Christmas celebration without even discussing it. It wouldn't be Christmas without Gram. So, we waited, but her incision didn't heal. She spent two weeks in the hospital and was finally released after they instructed my mother in wound care. And still we waited. The once lush Douglas fir, standing in the living room, turned brown and lost its needles. It was surely a fire hazard, but no one gave it a thought. Christmas was still on hold until Gram felt up to it.

Finally, on January twenty-second, we celebrated Christmas. The house was still decorated, the gifts still under the tree, and the scent of delicious foods filled the air. With snow on the ground and carols playing on the stereo, we joyfully began the festivities. There was much laughter, especially after such a long delay. Now, the gift givers were as surprised as the receivers, having forgotten what they had bought and wrapped so many weeks earlier.

That Christmas in January was our first Christmas as husband and wife, but also our last with my beloved Gram, who died just a few months later. We were all so glad we'd waited. It was a Christmas like no other.

— Sheryl Maxey —

Full House

Christmas is a time when you get homesick —
even when you're home.
~Carol Nelson

It's been said you can't go home again
And maybe this is true;
But Christmas finds me on a trip
There is something I must do.

Memories flood my thoughts
As I travel down the road…
Back home to Alabama
And my childhood abode.

I think of all the holidays
Spent in my childhood town.
A roller coaster of emotions
Has my head all spinning 'round.

I remember how my momma
Would put a wreath upon the door,
And we'd bake gingerbread cookies,
Eat them all, and make some more.

The family would all arrive
So early on Christmas Day —
All my cousins and I
Just couldn't wait to play.

Grammy would bring her famous nog
The kids weren't allowed to drink.
One time I snuck a sip or two
And spit it in the sink!

I laugh as I recall the time
When my crazy Uncle Lou
Enjoyed too much of Grammy's nog
And started playing his kazoo!

And the year there was a blizzard —
Now that was something rare!
But in my home, we were nice and warm
And we didn't have a care.

More memories start to fill my mind
As the miles are passing by.
Sometimes I get a little choked up
And I'm trying not to cry.

Then another moment comes to me
Of a Christmas from the past.
It seems like only yesterday —
But the years go by so fast.

The year that I was ten years old
Is one I never will forget…
Dad surprised me with a puppy.
It was, by far, my favorite pet!

I used to love to get up early
Just my little sister and me —
To see what was in my stocking
And all the presents 'round the tree.

And every Christmas morning,
Each memory I can recall —
Started with a kiss from Dad to Mom
Under the mistletoe in the hall.

Now I'm facing all those moments
As distant visions from the past
Because all I have left are memories
And I want to make them last.

That home, it now sits vacant
Just furniture and boxes remain.
A chapter in my life has ended
And things will never be the same.

Mom and Dad are gone now
The year's been really tough.
And now the task is left
To sort through all the stuff.

I pull up and see my sister
Standing at the old front door.
"I can't believe it," she says to me.
"It's just not our home anymore."

A strong embrace I give her
Then we turn to walk inside…
We both look at each other
And for a while, we just cry.

Then we have to face our task
As hard as it will be
To sort through every corner
And face every memory.

We start in the attic
Where former lives are sent to hide
And with every trunk we open
We marvel at what is inside.

We laugh at some old costumes
Which were worn on Halloween;
And baby dolls and Barbies
And dress-up clothes fit for a queen.

"Look," my sister says to me —
"Here's a trunk that's meant for you.
It's full of your old high-school stuff
And even a prom dress or two!"

"And here are some of your old toys!"
I can't believe all we have found
Mom has kept almost everything...
The childhood memories abound.

"Oh, my goodness," says my sister.
"I used to love this little guy!"
She holds up a ragged Kermit the Frog
And I laugh until I cry.

When we finish with the attic
We decide to take a break
And head downtown to the bakery,
For a coffee and some cake.

We talk about the past —
How we grew up with such love
From two wonderful, giving parents
Now in heaven up above.

Back at the house we finish up
And work all through the night.
Exhausted, we finally both collapse
With the dawn of morning's light.

"It's Christmas," my sister says to me,
And I acknowledge, "This is true."
I glance around as if to say,
"Is there something we should do?"

A loud knock upon the door
Suddenly disrupts our reverie;
I look at Sis and then exclaim,
"Now I wonder who could that be?"

I open up to a surprise
And see a family standing there —
My cousin and his wife…
And food enough to share.

Behind them comes an uncle
With my favorite aunt, as well.
The way I felt that very moment
Words just aren't enough to tell.

"I knew you'd be here," Auntie says,
"Your sister told me so;
Let's have one more Christmas in this house
Before we have to let it go."

Sis and I are stricken speechless
And we're not sure what to do…
I guess you really can go home again
If your family comes to you!

So I dust off the big, old table
And find the china to unpack.
We sit down as if it's yesterday
And the clock we've just turned back.

We laugh a lot and cry a little
And eat until we're full.
The stories we share are priceless
Food for a sorrowful soul.

It was a Christmas that began
With a difficult job to do —
Saying goodbye to a life that's gone
Preparing for something new.

But it turned into a holiday
Of love and peace and cheer…
And leaves me feeling better
Than I really had all year.

When Sis and I finally say goodbye,
Feeling closer than we have in years
We hug each other tight
And don't fight back the tears.

The house stands ready for a family
To claim it for their own —
Fill the halls with love and laughter
And the warmth that makes a home.

I smile as I drive away
With the highway ahead of me...
I'll start my life, as I know it now,
With my heart full of memories.

—Jennifer "JennyMac" McCarthy—

The Accident

*Thankfulness is the beginning of gratitude. Gratitude
is the completion of thankfulness. Thankfulness may
consist merely of words. Gratitude is shown in acts.*
~Henri-Frédéric Amiel

As a parent, my worst fear had always been household accidents, and I took the necessary precautions to prevent them. Turning the handle of the pan on the stove inward, making sure outlets were covered, and keeping knives out of reach were just a few of the things I did to keep my children safe. However, I could not have prepared for what happened the morning of December 22, 1994.

I got three kids off to school and was settling in with my two youngest for a quiet morning and a cup of coffee. I didn't know my quiet morning would change in an instant. As I turned to place the kettle back on the stove after pouring the steaming hot water in my coffee mug, my two-year-old son came up behind me, reached up and grabbed the handle of my mug, spilling the boiling water onto him. My worst fear had suddenly become a reality.

As my son stood screaming, my first instinct was to get off his shirt. What I did not realize was the boiling water had fused the polyester shirt fibers to his skin. A piece of advice I can give parents who find themselves in this situation is to leave clothing intact. It will act as a bandage until help arrives.

It was only a matter of minutes before the ambulance came.

Paramedics wrapped my son's body in sterile sheets saturated with cold sterile water. They rushed us to the nearest hospital, but I was horrified at what happened next. When the doctor finally walked into the trauma room, forty-five minutes after we arrived, I watched as he touched my son's burns with his ungloved hands.

At this point, I grabbed my child, still mostly wrapped in the sterile blankets, and asked to leave the hospital. The doctor insisted it was just a mild burn (similar to a sunburn), and he would put some ointment on it, wrap it and send us home. I knew I needed a second opinion.

I called a friend whose son had suffered a serious burn and asked her to drive us to Shriners Hospital for Children in Boston, about fifty miles away. She had told me about this hospital many times, probably so that I would know where to go if one of my children ever needed burn care.

When we arrived at Shriners Hospital, my son was examined immediately. He had second- and third-degree burns covering 20 percent of his little body. We would not be going home. A very caring and soft-spoken nurse came into the room and asked me exactly how this had happened. As I spoke, I was ashamed and embarrassed at not protecting my son from such an accident, but she explained to me the definition of the word "accident": an unplanned and unfortunate event that results in damage, injury, or upset of some kind. She made me understand that this was not my fault, and that any parent whose two-year-old hadn't had an accident had only been lucky.

Even though I now understand why they call them accidents, I will never forget the guilt that I went through. My husband and four other children needed to celebrate Christmas without us. Fortunately, my son made a complete recovery, and we left the hospital at the end of January. But I will never forget that Christmas — not because of the terrible accident, but because of what it gave to my family. The following year, as Christmas drew closer, my children started asking if other moms had to stay with their children at the hospital. That is when our tradition began.

My children took their own presents from under the tree, and we brought them to the hospital so the families would know that we were thinking about them. From that year on, my family and I have traveled to Boston on Christmas Eve with gift baskets overflowing with toys, books, games, toiletries and more.

One year, however, proved to me just how special our visits and gifts are to these families. When we arrived at the hospital, a nurse met us on the eighth floor of the acute ward. They had now come to expect us every year.

She asked if we had time to meet another family that visits on Christmas Eve to bring dinner to all the families staying at the hospital. The nurse introduced me to a woman who was serving turkey and fixings to patients and their families.

She dropped her serving spoon, walked around to the front of the table and took my hand in hers. The woman said, "I have been hoping to meet you for the past seven years. That's when my son was also burned during the holidays. You delivered one of your baskets to my family when we were going through a most difficult time. When my son needed to be cheered up, I reached into the basket and pulled out something that would make him smile. When I needed to write a letter or brush my teeth, I reached into the basket, and what I needed was there. It was like you knew what we needed the most, and it's the reason we now come back every year and give our time to these families."

Not only had I instilled the gift of giving in my own family, but I had passed it along to strangers.

— Iona Dupill —

99

Open Last

Our hearts grow tender with childhood memories and
love of kindred, and we are better throughout the year
for having, in spirit, become a child again
at Christmas-time.
~Laura Ingalls Wilder

I was the only grandchild, so I was my grandparents' worker elf: dabbing fake snow on their windows; sticking holiday cards in the doorframes; choreographing the placement of holiday bears Papa had won in claw machines; applying red and green frosting to the sugar cookies Grandma baked; and throwing tinsel on the tree.

I wasn't allowed to help wrap the presents though. I'd leave their house, show up the next day, and find that a mound of wrapped gifts had magically appeared under the Christmas tree.

My favorites were the ones labeled "Open Last" in permanent marker. When my grandparents weren't around, I'd rub my fingers along the smooth paper and shake them ever so carefully, even if they were for my parents, not me. My first Nintendo system was one of those "Open Last" gifts.

My grandparents continued this tradition even into my adulthood. But at some point while growing up, the holiday magic diminished. College, work, and the hullabaloo of holiday shopping kept me from being the worker elf who helped my grandparents decorate their home. As my grandparents' health deteriorated, there were fewer decorations and an artificial tree replaced the real one.

My grandma passed away three years ago, and my grandfather followed her this year. So, this Christmas will be the first without either of them.

In October, I received a call from my aunt. She had spent weeks remodeling my grandparents' house, and she asked me to drop by. When I arrived, she handed me a giant, yellow Tonka truck. She was cleaning an alcove in the garage when she spotted the truck. Insects had eaten much of the cardboard box it was in, but the metal truck was in perfect condition. It was a Mighty Loader from the 1980s, with a large bucket and hard, plastic wheels.

We decided it must be a Christmas gift that my grandparents forgot to give me — a present buried in thirty years of dust. My name was written on the box in Papa's handwriting. I bit the inside of my cheek and held back tears. It pained me to think they had purchased this gift, but stashed it away and then forgot to give it to me. I wished they could have seen the joy I would have felt to receive it as a boy.

I felt that joy now, mixed in with my sadness. And then I felt something else sneaking back into my heart. It was that feeling my grandparents brought to my childhood — that Christmas magic.

That Tonka truck was their final "Open Last" gift to me, a present from them when I needed it the most. Some gifts are worth the wait.

— Cory Rasmussen —

100

Lessons in Living

When you arise in the morning, think of what a
precious privilege it is to be alive — to breathe, to
think, to enjoy, to love.
~Marcus Aurelius

When I was twelve, my family couldn't agree on the right Christmas tree, so we compromised by getting two wrong trees in a row — neither of which would stand up. After that, choosing the tree became a father-daughter adventure, and I cherished our annual tradition because it was the only day I got to spend entirely alone with my dad. Those December days together — walking, talking, laughing — were precious.

One year, we immediately saw what was, for us, the perfect tree. We looked at each other knowingly, but then we shook our heads, "Nope, not that one." We didn't want our excursion to end so soon.

After I went away to college, the tree we chose would be tied on top of the car for the remainder of the day while we would catch up at some little pub. At one such place, way out in the middle of nowhere, my father and I took on the locals in a pool tournament and won. After a few hours at this place, one of the men — who was still wearing a fluorescent orange snowmobile suit — said to me, "Honey, you're cuter than a speckled puppy in a little red wagon. But I still like your dad better!" And I laughed. I knew what he meant.

Dad's easygoing manner, his zest for life — it was refreshing for everyone he met, not just for me.

The day my father was diagnosed with Stage 4 lung cancer was the worst day of my life. My brother and I looked at each other, stunned, as the doctor patted Dad on the shoulder. But what I remember most is later that night when my dad offered to ride along with me as I ran a quick errand. In the car, he said, "What a great day!"

I searched his eyes as mine filled with tears, wondering if the cancer had traveled to his brain. Didn't he get it? Didn't he hear the doctors?

He looked at me, realizing that it had been a most dreadful day for me. And he replied, "Oh, well. There was that." That, of course, being his death sentence.

But what he had meant, in my dad's most beautiful way of looking at the world, was, "Yes, it was a beautiful day." He had seen two of his kids, played with three of his grandchildren, and had dinner at a favorite restaurant with people he loved. He had lived. And, yes, for him, it was a great day. Even while faced with death, he was teaching me how to love life.

After my dad died, a friend gave me a tree to plant in his memory. After my town was hit with a severe ice storm, the tree looked like it wouldn't survive. But today it is strong and alive and full of promise. It makes me smile.

My favorite tradition died along with my dad. But the love of life, the admiration of trees and the realization that life is short and we had better make it good, those are lessons I got from our days alone together during all those Decembers.

— Julie Ottaway Schmit —

All Those Years

Creating memories is a priceless gift. Memories will
last a lifetime; things only a short period of time.
~Alyice Edrich

Aunt Dizzer traveled to our home in Brookhaven, Mississippi every Christmas for nearly sixty years. She was my mom's older sister and her real name was Louisa, but as a child my mother couldn't pronounce that so she called her Dizzer. It stuck.

She was as special as her name. She lived in Nashville, Tennessee, and worked as a dietitian for Tennessee State University for thirty years. Her early marriage at the age of sixteen ended in divorce, and she never remarried or had children. But circumstances that many would describe as sad or unfortunate never changed Aunt Dizzer's love for my siblings and me.

Christmas at our home would not have been the same without Aunt Dizzer. She made the trip by Greyhound bus, traveling with her camera, a suitcase and one or two apple boxes filled with surprises Santa had asked her to deliver. Those boxes would always contain a homemade pound cake, a rum-soaked fruitcake, and some nuts, apples and oranges. The experience of watching her cut the strings and unpack the boxes thrilled us to no end!

Later, my siblings and I would gather around her and share all our news — school, family, church, whatever came to mind, while we cracked pecans for pies and cakes for our Christmas dinner. Aunt Dizzer always seemed interested in what we had to say and never appeared anxious for us to finish our conversations. Often, she would laugh out loud at our tales and say, "Y'all are enough to make a dog laugh."

Until I was five years old, my mom gave me a doll for Christmas every year I enjoyed combing her hair, dressing her, and feeding her. When I was six years old, Aunt Dizzer brought me my first African-American doll. She was the most beautiful doll I had ever seen. She had black curly hair like mine and would walk if I held her hand. She wore a pretty blue dress and wasn't Barbie thin. I was elated to have a doll that looked like me.

Aunt Dizzer usually arrived the day before Christmas Eve and stayed for a week. When it was time for her to leave, my entire family would pile into the car to take her to the bus station. She always sat by a window, and we would wave until the bus was out of sight. Then we'd go home and each write a letter to mail—thanking her for her visit, her gifts, and her love.

Aunt Dizzer is now ninety-six and lives in Georgia. She has late-stage Alzheimer's. The disease has robbed her of her memories, but not of her sweet spirit. In a recent phone visit, I said, "I love you and said a prayer for you today. Would you like a pound cake to share and enjoy like the ones you made so often for us?" Her response didn't make sense, but I didn't care. I was just happy to hear her voice. I listened patiently as she spoke—the same way she listened to me all those years.

—Betty White Coleman—

Meet Our Contributors

Kristi Adams is a travel writer on a mission to explore as many European Christmas markets as she can. She lives in Germany with her husband, who is serving on active duty, and their cat Tiki. Kristi is a proud nine-time contributor to the *Chicken Soup for the Soul* series. Learn more at www.kristiadamsmedia.com.

Laurie Adams has been sharing her life experiences through Christian devotional writing since 2006. She and her husband of thirty-four years are Assemblies of God pastors. Laurie lives in Arkansas with her husband and they have four children and eight grandchildren.

Briana Almengor writes privately to order the chaos in her head. She writes publicly to offer anything but a formulaic view of life, yet one you just might resonate with. On a wooded lot in Maryland, together with her husband, she is attempting to raise twin boys and a girl to human decency. God be with her.

Kate E. Anderson has lived in twenty-five cities, including Ann Arbor, MI where this story happened. A columnist for *The Herald Journal*, she shares her North Logan, UT home with an amazing husband, one daughter, four sons, and a shamelessly obese Beagle.

Allison Andrews is an Emmy award-winning producer who left a career in television news to help other people tell their stories and find more time to tell her own. She has a teenage daughter and is preparing to visit fifty places she's never been the year she turns fifty!

Valerie Archual is a blog writer and a children's book author. Aside from writing, Valerie is also an avid reader and loves a good story! She enjoys running, hiking, and the great outdoors. Her favorite hobby by far is spending time with her family and creating memories, which, of course, are the best stories of all!

JoAnne Bennett has raised her three daughters alongside her husband of forty-three years. Her two young grandchildren bring so much pure joy into her life. Although her life journey has been difficult at times, she loves focusing on her passion — writing. JoAnne's work has been published in a number of publications over the years.

Francine L. Billingslea is a retired "Glam-ma" who has found a passion for writing in her later years. She is proud to have over sixty-three publications including several in the *Chicken Soup for the Soul* series. She loves writing, traveling, shopping, and spending quality time with her loved ones.

Loreen Martin Broderick, proud mom, grandmother, and Wisconsin native, is busy pursuing an MA degree in Psychology at Tennessee Technological University. A recipient of the 2003 Beulah Davis Outstanding Writer Award and a winner of the 2015 Chattanooga Writers' Guild contest, this is her second *Chicken Soup for the Soul* story published.

Steffanie Brooks-Aguilar received her master's degree in Clinical Psychology from Vanguard University in 2006. She is a Healing and Relationship Coach in San Juan Capistrano, CA. Steffanie has published a book on parent-child reunification for therapists and another book coming out in early 2019 about healing childhood wounds.

Mason K. Brown moves between her homes in Seaside and Forest Grove, OR. An author, speaker and storyteller, she writes primarily inspirational nonfiction and humor with a smattering of fiction tossed in. She is widely published in anthologies and devotionals. Learn more at www.masonkbrown.com.

Jill Burns lives in the mountains of West Virginia with her wonderful family. She's a retired piano teacher and performer. She enjoys writing, music, gardening, nature, and spending time with her grandchildren.

After getting a bachelor's and a master's degree in advertising, **Traci Clayton** got a job in (surprise!) advertising. She currently works as a copywriter in Austin, TX. She listens to Christmas music on repeat — but ONLY after Thanksgiving. It's a very strict policy.

Betty White Coleman received degrees from Jackson State University and Virginia College. She is retired from the State of Mississippi and currently does contract work as a Career Readiness Counselor. Reading and writing are two of her favorite activities.

Darin Cook is a freelance writer who draws material for his nonfiction work from all of life's experiences, whether travelling the globe, journeying into his past, exploring the mundane aspects of life, or analyzing the intricacies of fatherhood.

Laurie Decker received a Bachelor of Arts degree and two teaching credentials. She has been a California special education teacher since 2007. Laurie is artistic and she enjoys crafting in her spare time. She has traveled the world on mission trips to help trafficked and orphaned children. She longs to be an author.

Rita Warren DeFoe is a native North Carolinian currently living in Virginia with her husband. She is a cancer survivor who spends her time writing, crafting, and loving life! At the present time, she's working on two children's books and a nonfiction book about her personal cancer journey and the juggernaut of treatment.

With a background in fine art and psychology, **Sergio Del Bianco** is an artist and writer interested in the intersection of art, psychology and the humanities. He resides in Europe with his spouse and growing family of rescue animals. E-mail him at sergiodelbianco@yahoo.com or through Twitter @DelBianco97.

Sally Dixon is an author, freelance writer, and textile artist from South Australia. She specializes in writing for children but also enjoys writing creative nonfiction. She is the author of an international craft book called *Pipsqueaks: Itsy-Bitsy Felt Creations to Stitch & Love*.

Rhonda Dragomir and her family live in Wilmore, KY. A graduate of Asbury University, she is also a pastor's wife and Bible teacher. Rhonda is an award-winning writer, with published works in *Chicken Soup for the Soul* anthologies and *Spark* magazine. E-mail her at Rhonda@dragomirgroup.com.

Iona Dupill is a writer/editor for the government. She has five grown children and one granddaughter. She plans to continue creative writing and wants to someday publish her own book.

Rita Durrett lives in Elk City, OK. She is the mother of two sons and grandmother of six boys and one girl. When Rita isn't playing with grandchildren, she is writing, traveling, or crafting. She is also a reluctant blogger. Learn more at www.RitaDurrett.com.

Kathy Eliscu is a retired RN, mom, and grandma whose Maine column "Lightly Roasted" has earned her two National Society of Newspaper Columnists awards for Humor. She's been widely published in Maine and beyond, and is the author of the humor novel *Not Even Dark Chocolate Can Fix This Mess*. She loves God, family, and good pizza.

M. Ellison resides in Northern California with her wonderful husband. She's a CSU, Chico graduate with a B.A. in Theatre Arts. She recently published her first book, *Rachel and the Mighty Arm that Built Egypt*.

Mildred L. Farrior is a retired registered nurse who lives on the beautiful Crystal Coast of North Carolina in the same town where she was raised. She earned a Bachelor of Science degree in Nursing at East Carolina University. She enjoys beachcombing, writing poetry, dressmaking, and working as a licensed manicurist.

Margaret Jan Feike writes and lives in central Ohio with the two youngest of her four children. She recently completed a memoir dealing with how her young family coped during the first year after her husband's sudden death.

Author **Edith Hope Fine** leads three lives: regular, reading, and writing. A former teacher, her eighteen books include *Under the Lemon Moon*, *Cryptomania!* and *Nitty-Gritty Grammar*. A longtime SCBWI member (scbwi.org), Edith grows veggies in the front yard, swims, reads, bakes, and has fun with friends, family, and her four grandkids.

D. Dina Friedman is the author of two young adult novels, *Escaping Into the Night* and *Playing Dad's Song*. Her first book of poetry, *Wolf in the Suitcase*, will be published by Finishing Line Press in 2019. Dina has an MFA from Lesley University and teaches at UMass Amherst. Learn more at www.ddinafriedman.com.

Michael Fulton grew up in San Diego County. He married his high school sweetheart and together they raised four children. Michael and his wife have one granddaughter. Michael works as an IT Manager and enjoys coaching youth sports.

Linda Gabris is a full-time writer whose inspirational stories, articles, poetry and columns have appeared in publications across North America and Europe. Linda is an avid outdoors person who enjoys instructing writing workshops and writing about her own adventures. E-mail her at inkserv@telus.net.

Amanda Girolamo is an auditor who spends free time with her energetic sons as their live-in chauffeur to the finest football fields, campsites and trampoline parks. She recently landed a side gig as Cub Scout committee chair, and on occasion she and her husband steal a moment for a date night. She hopes to one day become an author.

Sherry Hall is a former special education teacher and an instructional specialist in Texas. She is the author of several books, including *The Charming Bracelet, Motocross: Crossrut, Motocross: Roosted, Whomp!* and *Tallulah and the Three Cowgirls*. Find her online at www.sherryhallwrites. com.

Jessica Harrington is an environmental activist and middle school teacher living in Tampa, FL. She is the founder of Straw Free Florida as well as an aspiring author. She enjoys traveling, reading, and writing. She plans on writing books to teach people about saving the environment.

Eriqa Hermen got the nickname "Q" while living in Oregon, and it is the name she prefers. She grew up in Sweden, but left in her early twenties to see the world and currently lives in Australia. She enjoys rugby, skydiving, and anything outdoors in her time off.

Rozanne Hill received a Bachelor of Arts in Physics from Texas A&M University in 1983. Widowed in 2003, she lives north of Houston, TX with her daughter and her sister. Rozanne is part owner of a small company and enjoys reading, music, drawing, writing, spending time with family, and journaling about her experiences.

Erika Hoffman is a Duke University alumna who taught public high school for ten years. She raised four children. Now she writes. Some of her books are on Kindle. Soon, she will publish a compilation of her stories that have appeared in *Sasee* of Myrtle Beach and in the ezine "Page & Spine."

Mark A. Howe is a native of Topeka, KS and has been living in northern Indiana since 1999, when he met his wife on a dating website. Neither of them thinks that's especially weird. They have two sons, Matthew and Michael, and he is a writer with the *Times-Union* in Warsaw, IN.

David Hull lives in the small upstate New York town of Holley, where he enjoys reading, writing, gardening and spoiling his nieces and nephews. He is a retired teacher.

Cindy Hval is the author of *War Bonds: Love Stories from the Greatest Generation*, which tells the stories of thirty-six couples who met/married during WWII — available online. Cindy's work is featured in ten *Chicken Soup for the Soul* books. Follow her blog or contact her at CindyHval.com or on Twitter @CindyHval.

Jeffree Wyn Itrich has been writing professionally most of her life and has penned numerous books, articles, and web content. She spent the bulk of her working life in medical communications. When she's not writing, she can be found in her sewing room making quilts, in the garden, or in the kitchen concocting new recipes.

Jeanie Jacobson is on the Wordsowers Christian Writers leadership team and has been published in *Focus on the Family* and *Live* magazines, the *Chicken Soup for the Soul* series, and other anthologies. Jeanie loves visiting family, reading, hiking, and dancing. Her book, *Fast Fixes for the Christian Pack-Rat*, can be found online. Learn more at JeanieJacobson.com.

Lori Carpenter Jagow is a freelance counselor, teacher, writer, speaker, and photographer. She received her Bachelor of Science degree from Empire State College and took postgraduate courses in Pastoral Counseling. She and her son enjoy collaborating on creative arts and music projects for film. E-mail her at Loriannjagow@gmail.com.

JL Kennedy is a freelance writer specializing in parenting, family, anti-cancer and health topics. She also does marketing/PR copywriting and would love to write a children's book series. She lives in the Philadelphia area with her husband, sports-loving sons and well-loved dog. E-mail her at jenniferkennedypr@gmail.com.

Tricia Koeller is a registered nurse turned stay-at-home mom to five kids. She loves Christmas, family and reading any book that she can't put down. Her book club, The Chapter Chicks, inspired her to share this first published story.

Alanna Parke Kvale is a widow who lives in Plano, TX. She is also the author of *Widowhood Is Not Funny* as well as several other titles. She enjoys crocheting and spending time with her three grandchildren.

Dana Lamb-Schaubroeck is a Grammy semifinalist, music educator and Billboard charted songwriter. She lives in Fayette County, GA with her husband Mark Schaubroeck and her two children. She manages her successful music-teaching studio in Peachtree City, GA. E-mail her at danaclamb@gmail.com.

Sharon Landeen, a retired elementary teacher, keeps young by volunteering at local schools through Literacy Connects, and by making blankets for Project Linus. She is a graduate of the University of Oregon and enjoys traveling and spending time with her children, grandchildren and great-grandchildren.

Charlotte A. Lanham has been writing her family stories since the late 1980s. She is currently a facilitator in the Lifelong Learning Institute at Washington University in St. Louis where she shares her love of memoirs with other like-minded writers.

Mandy Lawrence is a registered nurse and a Christian author and speaker. She is the author of *Wisdom from Wilbur: How My Dog Has Brought Me Closer to God* and the novel *Replay*. Mandy loves animals, chocolate, and traveling. She and her husband Shane live in Lexington, NC.

Arlene Janet Ledbetter earned her Bachelor of Arts in English from Dalton State College in Georgia. She enjoyed writing adult Sunday school curriculum for many years. Arlene has been published in numerous magazines and in five previous *Chicken Soup for the Soul* books. Learn more at www.arleneledbetter.net..

Andi Lehman holds a degree in communications from The University of Memphis, and freelances in diverse markets. She enjoys writing devotionals and true stories about ordinary people doing extraordinary things. A popular wildlife speaker, Andi continues to work on a series of nature books for children.

Kathie Leier, her husband Ivan, and Keiko, their beloved senior Shih Tzu, moved from Regina, SK in 2016 to retire to the beauty and solitude of Riding Mountain National Park, MB. In November 2017, after being a most loving companion for ten years, Keiko went to doggie heaven at the age of fourteen. He is dearly missed.

Donna Lorrig is a homeschooling mother of seven who studied Art at Middle Tennessee State University and Politics at Pikes Peak Community College. This is her fourth story featured in the *Chicken Soup for the Soul* series. She enjoys sharing encouraging and uplifting stories. She is also working on a picture book project designed to inspire children.

Shari Marshall started blogging in 2015. She credits her writing to a supportive husband, two hilarious sons, and her Boxers. "Pawing the Tree" was inspired by a mischievous Boxer who stole her heart and made her fall in love with the breed. Shari's writing has appeared in *ParentsCanada*, *Mamalode* and *The Quarterly*.

Sara Matson and her family live in Minnesota, where Christmases are cold but cozy. She's especially looking forward to this Christmas, when she plans to unveil her story to her family during the annual game of Yankee Swap! Visit her website at www.saramatson.com.

Sheryl Maxey graduated from The Ohio State University with a degree in special education. She spent twenty-six years homeschooling her seven sons. She enjoys quilting, genealogy, and the beach. She has been writing a weekly devotion on her website since 2011. She and her husband currently reside in Florida.

Nicole Ann Rook McAlister studied journalism and has pursued a self-study of world religion. She and her husband live with their seven-year-old daughter, nineteen-year-old son, and a plethora of fur, feather and finned babies in a log cabin in the Pine Barrens. When she isn't writing, she is painting, crafting, canning, gardening or reading.

Jennifer "JennyMac" McCarthy says, "poetry is my heart beating in words." She loves her hobby, though her time is spent homeschooling her three sons, taking care of the home, and serving as swim practice chauffeur. A graduate from Stetson University (B.A.) and USF-Tampa (M.A.), she worked in the school system before becoming a home educator.

Patricia Merewether is a painter who has exhibited her work at the Saginaw Art Museum, Shiawassee Arts Center, and galleries. She lives in a rural area of Michigan with her husband of fifty-one years and two rescued Havanese pups. She enjoys creating art, crocheting/knitting, plants and animal rescue. E-mail her at Patsarts@comcast.net.

Catherine (Cat) Moise lives in rural Ontario where she is in awe of the trees and the secrets they whisper. Working with and raising children inspired her regular contributions to a parenting column. Her work has been published in *Today's Grandparent*. She is a grandmother to five amazing children.

Dawn Murrell is a mom of two boys and a girl named Liberty, Freedom and Justice. She lives in Kentucky, where she is a social worker helping people with disabilities. She is hoping to produce a children's movie about a princess with a disability.

Alice Muschany writes about everyday life with a touch of humor. Her grandchildren make wonderful subjects. Her essays have appeared in numerous anthologies, magazines and newspapers. When she's not busy writing, you can find her hiking, swimming or taking pictures. E-mail her at aliceandroland@gmail.com.

C.L. Nehmer lives with her husband and three teenagers in Wisconsin, where Lake Michigan always provides inspiration. She loves baking, walking her hound dogs and writing poetry. Colleen's work has been published in *Southern Poetry Review* and *Pedestal Magazine*. E-mail her at colleen.nehmer@hotmail.com.

Connie Nice is a wife, mother, and grandmother from Washington State. Writing for thirty-plus years, she loves creating children's stories, blog articles and has one adult novel "in the works." She shares her passion for history, nature, travel, family, and faith through the written word. Follow her at connienice.com.

Ela Oakland lives in a place where there are lots of trees so she can chop down a Christmas tree any time she wants.

Maureen FitzGerald O'Brien has written for travel magazines, daily newspapers and business publications. A career in marketing/PR has now segued into writing her "own" stories again. She lives with her husband in North Carolina, and has three children and six grandchildren. She is a graduate of St. Joseph's College, NYC.

Jenny Pavlovic, Ph.D., is the author of *8 State Hurricane Kate: The Journey and Legacy of a Katrina Cattle Dog*, *The Not Without My Dog Resource & Record Book*, and many stories. She lives in Wisconsin with her dogs Chase and Cayenne and her cat Junipurr. She loves to walk dogs, swim, kayak, and garden. Learn more at www.8statekate.net.

Jon Peirce holds a B.A. and a Ph.D. in English and a master's in industrial relations. A retired English professor and labor relations officer, he's a playwright and acts in community theatre. Jon enjoys cooking, tennis, dancing, and bridge. His publications include an essay collection and an industrial relations textbook.

Mary C. M. Phillips is a caffeinated wife, working mom, and writer. Her work has been published in numerous national bestselling anthologies. She blogs at CaffeineEpiphanies.com. Follow her on Twitter @ MaryCMPhil.

Kira Popescu lives in New Jersey. She has a dog named Lily and a cat named Dr. Zeus. She enjoys reading, writing and volunteering.

AJ Sandra Principe started her career with degrees in piano performance. After experiencing severe grief and losses in her own life, she became a certified life skills coach with degrees in Thanatology and Bereavement Education.

Connie Kaseweter Pullen lives in rural Sandy, OR near her five children and several grandchildren. She earned her B.A. at the University of Portland in 2006, with a double major in Psychology and Sociology. Connie has been caring for her now-ninety-eight-year-old mother for ten years. E-mail her at MyGrandmaPullen@aol.com.

Debby Kate Stahl Ramsey is the mother of three and "Nona" to one adorable grandson. Since her kidney transplant she wants to encourage others going through their own transplant journeys. Say "yes" to organ donation and live life to the fullest.

Cory Rasmussen is an English teacher in Huntington Beach, CA. He spends his winter break listening to holiday music, writing, and dressing his dog Zelda in ugly Christmas sweaters. He dedicates this story to the memory of his grandparents and all the magic they created.

Shirley Redcay received her B.A. in education and M.S. in counseling from Florida State University. During her career she taught and counseled on every level, pre-K to community college. She enjoys family and mission trips to teach English in Ukraine. The American School

Counselor Association honored her as Writer of the Year in 1999.

Grace Rice graduated from Abilene Christian University in 1986 with an Associate of Science degree. She has two grown sons and a teen-aged daughter. Grace has spent time living and traveling abroad and is currently settled in the Dallas-Fort Worth area. She enjoys reading, yoga, cooking classes and teaching a weekly ladies' Bible class.

Rosemary L. Rigsby retired three times before writing full-time, and family memories are a source of inspiration for stories, as are travels with her husband. When not writing, travelling, or running behind a grandchild on a strider bike, Rosemary reads, knits, or draws, often while she and her husband watch their favourite TV shows.

Heather Rodin serves as Executive Director for Hope Grows Haiti. An award-winning author, she has a passion for personal stories, many coming from her work with the mission. Heather is mom to six married children and grandma to twelve. She and her husband live near Peterborough, ON.

Linda Sabourin lives in western Arkansas just a few miles from the Oklahoma border. She goes to estate auctions, sells vintage goodies on eBay, and spends most of the rest of her time rescuing cats and kittens and nursing them back to health. You can follow her feline escapades at River Valley Cats on Facebook and Twitter!

John M. Scanlan is a 1983 graduate of the U.S. Naval Academy and served twenty years in the Marine Corps. He is now pursuing a second career as a writer.

Michael J. Schlagle is a retired Disabled Veteran, broadcaster and award-winning magician known as Majik Mike. He is a graduate of Rowan University and has two sons. In his spare time he is the MC of numerous music and arts festivals. Michael enjoys playing guitar, writing, fishing, and mentoring young artists and musicians.

Julie Ottaway Schmit lives and laughs in Clarence Center, NY, where she tries hard (with varying degrees of success!) to carry on fun holiday traditions with her husband and their three children, Annie, Griffin and Tanner.

Jaime Schreiner is a writer and speaker from the Canadian prairies, where she lives with her husband and daughters. Besides previous stories in the *Chicken Soup for the Soul* series, she has been published with *Hallmark*, *Focus on the Family*, *MOPS*, *(In)Courage* and more. Learn more at forhisfridge.wordpress.com.

Joyce Newman Scott worked as a flight attendant while pursuing an acting career. She started college in her mid-fifties and studied screenwriting at the University of Miami and creative writing at Florida International University. She is thrilled to be a frequent contributor to the *Chicken Soup for the Soul* series.

Alexis Sherwin attends University of Massachusetts Amherst, pursuing an education in environmental law. She shares a home with her parents, her younger sister, three cats, and a dog. Her pets were her inspiration for writing her story. Alexis also enjoys traveling, fitness, and spending time with her friends.

Christine Shultz is a wife, mother, and newly minted grandma. She works as a registered nurse and plays at being a self-professed chocolate connoisseur. Christine enjoys running, baking, and writing her nursing blog, "RN Living." She is currently writing a women's fiction book connecting baking and relationships.

Geno Sloan and her husband traveled the Western Hemisphere during his career in industrial construction. She self-published a biography of how they dealt with different cultures in South America and Mexico. For information about her book, e-mail her at gsloan@ndsupernet.com.

Jessica Snell is a writer whose work has appeared in *Christ and Pop Culture*, *Daily Science Fiction*, *The Lent Project*, and more. She blogs about books, faith, and family at jessicasnell.com and you can follow her on Twitter @theJessicaSnell.

Diane Stark is a wife, mother of five, and freelance writer. She is a frequent contributor to the *Chicken Soup for the Soul* series. Diane loves to write about the important things in life: her family and her faith.

Victoria Terrinoni was a military spouse for thirty-one years until her husband's retirement from the U.S. Air Force in 2018. She and her husband have twin daughters, two sons-in-law, and three grandchildren. Victoria loves to read, travel, and spoil the grandchildren.

Candace Thompson received her bachelor's degree from Ashland University in 2006 and currently teaches fourth grade. She enjoys spending time with her husband, two children, and extended family as well as reading, writing, digital scrapbooking, and baking.

Julia M. Toto shares stories of hope, forgiveness, and second chances. She is a published author of inspirational fiction and a previous contributor to the *Chicken Soup for the Soul* series. Learn more at www.juliamtoto.com.

Roz Warren writes for everyone from *The New York Times* to *Funny Times* and has appeared on *Today* and *Morning Edition*. She's the author of *Our Bodies, Our Shelves: A Collection of Library Humor* and *Just Another Day at Your Local Public Library*. E-mail Roz at roswarren@gmail.com or visit www.rosalindwarren.com.

Brian Wettlaufer has for years followed the Wanderlust Fairy into many weird and wonderful adventures and he recounts those stories in his writing. He describes his writer-self as a corkscrew in search of bottled-up stories. Learn more at www.blwwrites.weebly.com or e-mail him at blwcommunications@gmail.com.

Dana E. Williams is a homeschooling mom of four, best friend to her husband Michael, and a freelance writer. She attended college for counseling psychology, but as a result of passionate English teachers, her inner love for words was unveiled. She loves reading, writing, singing with her children, and family time.

Nemma Wollenfang is an MSc Postgraduate and prize-winning short story writer who lives in Northern England. Her fiction has appeared in several venues, including four of Flame Tree's bestselling *Gothic Fantasy* series. She enjoys rambling around ancient ruins and is currently working on several novels.

Whitney Woody works as a developmental editor. When work is done you can find her baking, spending time with her fiancé and their four cats, and counting the days until fall. She was previously published in *Chicken Soup for the Soul: The Joy of Christmas* and is excited to be a part of the team again this year!

Amy Catlin Wozniak lives in Ohio where she shares her life with her soul mate, four children, two grandsons, and a Great Pyrenees named Scarlett O'Hara, who has absolutely no problem living up to her namesake. She enjoys reading, writing, and sharing stories that reflect God's hope.

Meet Amy Newmark

Amy Newmark is the bestselling author, editor-in-chief, and publisher of the *Chicken Soup for the Soul* book series. Since 2008, she has published more than 150 new books, most of them national bestsellers in the U.S. and Canada, more than doubling the number of Chicken Soup for the Soul titles in print today. She is also the author of *Simply Happy*, a crash course in Chicken Soup for the Soul advice and wisdom that is filled with easy-to-implement, practical tips for enjoying a better life.

Amy is credited with revitalizing the Chicken Soup for the Soul brand, which has been a publishing industry phenomenon since the first book came out in 1993. By compiling inspirational and aspirational true stories curated from ordinary people who have had extraordinary experiences, Amy has kept the twenty-five-year-old Chicken Soup for the Soul brand fresh and relevant.

Amy graduated *magna cum laude* from Harvard University where she majored in Portuguese and minored in French. She then embarked on a three-decade career as a Wall Street analyst, a hedge fund manager, and a corporate executive in the technology field. She is a Chartered Financial Analyst.

Her return to literary pursuits was inevitable, as her honors thesis in college involved traveling throughout Brazil's impoverished northeast region, collecting stories from regular people. She is delighted to have come full circle in her writing career — from collecting stories "from the people" in Brazil as a twenty-year-old to, three decades later, collecting stories "from the people" for Chicken Soup for the Soul.

When Amy and her husband Bill, the CEO of Chicken Soup for the Soul, are not working, they are visiting their four grown children and their first grandchild.

Follow Amy on Twitter @amynewmark. Listen to her free podcast, The Chicken Soup for the Soul Podcast, on Apple Podcasts, Google Play, the Podcasts app on iPhone, or by using your favorite podcast app on other devices.

About Toys for Tots

Your purchase of this *Chicken Soup for the Soul* book supports Toys for Tots and helps create Christmas miracles for children who might not receive gifts otherwise! The mission of the U.S. Marine Corps Reserve Toys for Tots Program is to collect new, unwrapped toys during October, November and December each year, and distribute those toys as Christmas gifts to less fortunate children in the community in which the campaign is conducted.

You can contribute to your local Toys for Tots campaign in several ways. You can donate a toy at one of the area toy drop locations, host a Toys for Tots event at your home, office or other venue and collect toys for Toys for Tots, or volunteer at the local warehouse.

Local campaigns are conducted annually in over 800 communities covering all 50 U.S. states, the District of Columbia and Puerto Rico. Local toy collection campaigns begin in October and last until mid to late December. Toy distribution also takes place mid to late December.

Members of the community drop new, unwrapped toys in collection boxes positioned in local businesses. Coordinators pick up these toys and store them in central warehouses where the toys are sorted by age and gender. At Christmas, Coordinators, with the assistance of local social welfare agencies, church groups, and other local community agencies, distribute the toys to the less fortunate children of the community.

Over the years, Marines have established close working relationships with social welfare agencies, churches and other local community agencies which are well qualified to identify the needy children in the community and play important roles in the distribution of the toys. While Toys for Tots Coordinators organize, coordinate and manage the campaign, the ultimate success depends on the support of the local community and the generosity of the people who donate toys.

You can learn more about Toys for Tots by visiting their website at https://www.toysfortots.org.

Thank You

We owe huge thanks to all of our contributors and fans. We were overwhelmed with fabulous holiday stories. There had to be at least 6,000 submissions on this very popular topic, and we had a team that spent months reading all of them. Elaine Kimbler, Susan Heim, and Mary Fisher found so many "10s" that we made two books' worth of holiday cheer. This book will be followed by another one next year with another 101 stories that we all loved from this same batch of submissions.

Susan Heim did the first round of editing, D'ette Corona chose the perfect quotations to put at the beginning of each story, and Amy Newmark edited the stories and shaped the final manuscript.

We finished this book in July, and it was fun having Christmas spirit in the office while we were having a heat wave. As we finished our work, Associate Publisher D'ette Corona continued to be Amy's right-hand woman in creating the final manuscript and working with all our wonderful writers. Barbara LoMonaco and Kristiana Pastir, along with Elaine Kimbler, jumped in at the end to proof, proof, proof. And yes, there will always be typos anyway, so feel free to let us know about them at webmaster@chickensoupforthesoul.com and we will correct them in future printings.

The whole publishing team deserves a hand, including our Senior Director of Marketing Maureen Peltier, our Senior Director of Production Victor Cataldo, and our graphic designer Daniel Zaccari, who turned our manuscript into this beautiful book.

Sharing Happiness, Inspiration, and Hope

Real people sharing real stories, every day, all over the world. In 2007, *USA Today* named *Chicken Soup for the Soul* one of the five most memorable books in the last quarter-century. With over 100 million books sold to date in the U.S. and Canada alone, more than 250 titles in print, and translations into nearly fifty languages, "chicken soup for the soul®" is one of the world's best-known phrases.

Today, twenty-five years after we first began sharing happiness, inspiration and hope through our books, we continue to delight our readers with new titles, but have also evolved beyond the bookstore with super premium pet food, television shows, podcasts, positive journalism from aplus.com, movies and TV shows on the Popcornflix app, and licensed products, all revolving around true stories, as we continue "changing the world one story at a time®." Thanks for reading!

Share with Us

We all have had Chicken Soup for the Soul moments in our lives. If you would like to share your story or poem with millions of people around the world, go to chickensoup.com and click on "Submit Your Story." You may be able to help another reader and become a published author at the same time. Some of our past contributors have launched writing and speaking careers from the publication of their stories in our books!

We only accept story submissions via our website. They are no longer accepted via mail or fax. Visit our website, www.chickensoup. com, and click on Submit Your Story for our writing guidelines and a list of topics we are working on.

To contact us regarding other matters, please send us an e-mail through webmaster@chickensoupforthesoul.com, or fax or write us at:

Chicken Soup for the Soul
P.O. Box 700
Cos Cob, CT 06807-0700
Fax: 203-861-7194

One more note from your friends at Chicken Soup for the Soul: Occasionally, we receive an unsolicited book manuscript from one of our readers, and we would like to respectfully inform you that we do not accept unsolicited manuscripts and we must discard the ones that appear.

The Best Advice I Ever Heard

101 Stories of Epiphanies and Wise Words

Amy Newmark

Paperback: 978-1-61159-984-8
eBook: 978-1-61159-284-9

Hope, Wisdom, and Tips

Chicken Soup for the Soul

Messages from Heaven and Other Miracles

101 Stories of Angels, Answered Prayers, and Love That Doesn't Die

Amy Newmark

Paperback: 978-1-61159-985-5
eBook: 978-1-61159-285-6

to Start Your New Year Right

FROM THE EDITOR-IN-CHIEF OF THE NEW YORK TIMES BESTSELLING SERIES

Chicken Soup for the Soul

Simply Happy

A Crash Course
in Chicken Soup
for the Soul
Advice and
Wisdom

Chicken Soup for the Soul

Chicken Soup for the Soul Miracles Happen

Chicken Soup for the Soul It's Christmas!

Chicken Soup for the Soul My Dog's Life

Chicken Soup for the Soul Think Positive

Chicken Soup for the Soul Food and Love

Amy Newmark

Paperback: 978-1-61159-949-7
eBook: 978-1-61159-254-2

The Tools You Need to Be Happy

Chicken Soup for the Soul

Think, Act & Be Happy

How to Use Chicken Soup for the Soul Stories to Train Your Brain to Be Your Own Therapist

Amy Newmark & Dr. Mike Dow
New York Times Bestselling Author & Therapist

Paperback: 978-1-61159-979-4
eBook: 978-1-61159-279-5

Are Already in Your Brain

Changing your world one story at a time ®
www.chickensoup.com